CAMBRIDGE
Primary Mathematics

Workbook 1

Cherri Moseley & Janet Rees

CAMBRIDGE
UNIVERSITY PRESS

University Printing House, Cambridge CB2 8BS, United Kingdom

One Liberty Plaza, 20th Floor, New York, NY 10006, USA

477 Williamstown Road, Port Melbourne, VIC 3207, Australia

314–321, 3rd Floor, Plot 3, Splendor Forum, Jasola District Centre, New Delhi – 110025, India

103 Penang Road, #05–06/07, Visioncrest Commercial, Singapore 238467

Cambridge University Press is part of the University of Cambridge.

It furthers the University's mission by disseminating knowledge in the pursuit of education, learning and research at the highest international levels of excellence.

www.cambridge.org
Information on this title: www.cambridge.org/9781108746434

© Cambridge University Press 2021

This publication is in copyright. Subject to statutory exception
and to the provisions of relevant collective licensing agreements,
no reproduction of any part may take place without the written
permission of Cambridge University Press.

First published 2014
Second edition 2021

20 19 18 17 16 15 14 13 12 11 10 9 8 7 6

Printed in Malaysia by Vivar Printing

A catalogue record for this publication is available from the British Library

ISBN 978-1-108-74643-4 Paperback with Digital Access (1 Year)

Additional resources for this publication at www.cambridge.org/9781108746434

Cambridge University Press has no responsibility for the persistence or accuracy of URLs for external or third-party internet websites referred to in this publication, and does not guarantee that any content on such websites is, or will remain, accurate or appropriate. Information regarding prices, travel timetables, and other factual information given in this work is correct at the time of first printing but Cambridge University Press does not guarantee the accuracy of such information thereafter.

NOTICE TO TEACHERS IN THE UK
It is illegal to reproduce any part of this work in material form (including photocopying and electronic storage) except under the following circumstances:
(i)   where you are abiding by a licence granted to your school or institution by the Copyright Licensing Agency;
(ii) where no such licence exists, or where you wish to exceed the terms of a licence, and you have gained the written permission of Cambridge University Press;
(iii) where you are allowed to reproduce without permission under the provisions of Chapter 3 of the Copyright, Designs and Patents Act 1988, which covers, for example, the reproduction of short passages within certain types of educational anthology and reproduction for the purposes of setting examination questions.

Contents

How to use this book — 5
Thinking and Working Mathematically — 6

1 Numbers to 10
1.1 Counting sets of objects — 8
1.2 Say, read and write numbers to 10 — 17
1.3 Comparing numbers — 20
1.4 Number words — 24
1.5 Odd and even numbers — 27

2 Geometry
2.1 3D shapes — 30
2.2 2D shapes — 37

3 Fractions
3.1 Fractions — 43

4 Measures
4.1 Length — 49

5 Working with numbers to 10
5.1 Addition as combining — 56
5.2 Subtraction as take away — 63

6 Position
6.1 Position — 70

7 Statistics
7.1 Sets — 79
7.2 Venn diagrams — 89

Contents

8 Time
8.1 Time — 97

9 Numbers to 20
9.1 Counting to 20 — 105
9.2 Counting, comparing, ordering and estimating — 108
9.3 Number patterns — 118

10 Geometry (2)
10.1 3D shapes — 125
10.2 2D shapes — 133

11 Fractions (2)
11.1 Halves — 144

12 Measures (2)
12.1 Mass and capacity — 156
12.2 How do we measure? — 162

13 Working with numbers to 20
13.1 Addition by counting on — 170
13.2 Subtraction by counting back — 176
13.3 Using the number line — 181
13.4 Money — 186

14 Statistics (2)
14.1 Venn diagrams, Carroll diagrams and pictograms — 189
14.2 Lists, tables and block graphs — 196

15 Time (2)
15.1 Time — 208

16 Position, direction and patterns
16.1 Position, direction and patterns — 216

Acknowledgements — 228

How to use this book

This workbook provides questions for you to practise what you have learned in class. There is a unit to match each unit in your **Learner's Book**. Each exercise is divided into three parts:

- **Focus:** these questions help you to master the basics.
- **Practice:** these questions help you to become more confident in using what you have learned.
- **Challenge:** these questions will make you think very hard.

Each exercise is divided into three parts. You might not need to work on all of them. Your teacher will tell you which parts to do.

You will also find these features:

Important words that you will use. ⟶ equal fraction half pair part

Step-by-step examples showing a way to solve a problem. There are often many different ways to solve a problem.

These questions will help you to develop your skills of thinking and working mathematically.

Thinking and Working Mathematically

There are some important skills that you will develop as you learn mathematics.

Specialising is when I test examples to see if they fit a rule or pattern.

Characterising is when I explain how a group of things are the same.

Generalising is when I can explain and use a rule or pattern to find more examples.

Classifying is when I put things into groups and can say what rule I have used.

Thinking and Working Mathematically

Critiquing is when I think about what is good and what could be better in my work or someone else's work.

Improving is when I try to make my maths better.

Conjecturing is when I think of an idea or question linked to my maths.

Convincing is when I explain my thinking to someone else, to help them understand.

1 Numbers to 10

> ## 1.1 Counting sets of objects

Exercise 1.1

count   estimate   how many?   set   total

Focus

1   Count each set of animals. Say the numbers out loud.

Talk to a partner or carer about how you counted each set of animals.

1.1 Counting sets of objects

2 Put 1 object in each space.

   Count them.

   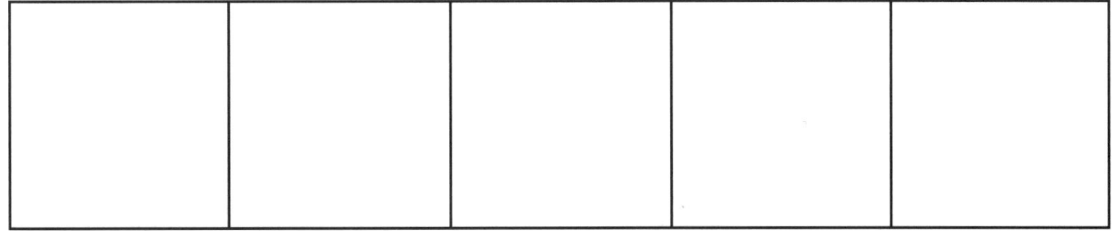

   Put the same objects into different spaces. Count again.

   Did you count to the same number each time?

3 Match each set to the correct number.

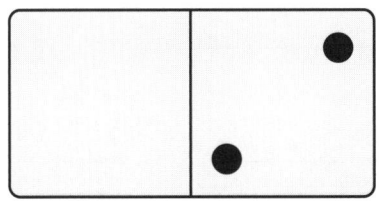

2

3

5

7

9

1 Numbers to 10

 4   How many animals are there?
Estimate then count.

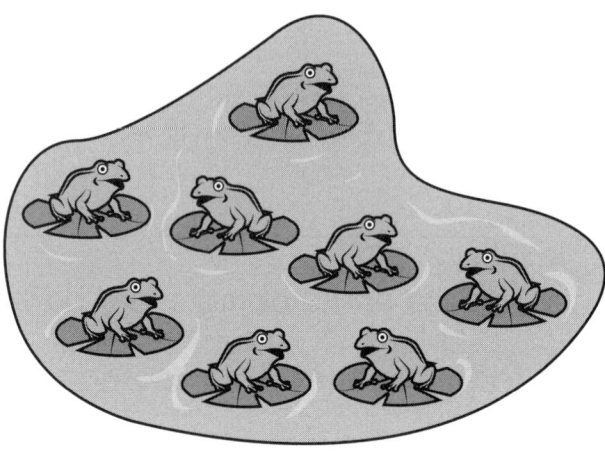

Estimate	Count	Estimate	Count

1.1 Counting sets of objects

Practice

5   Draw the correct number of animals in the last two rows.

11

1 Numbers to 10

6 Put 1 object in each space.

   Count them.

   Put the same objects into different spaces. Count again.

   Did you count to the same number each time?

7 Which domino has 7 spots?

   Draw a ring around the correct domino.

   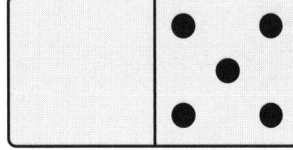   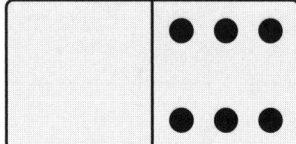   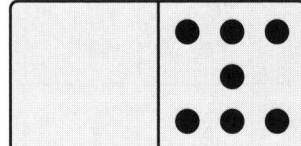

8 How many animals are there?

   Estimate then count.

	Estimate	Count

1.1 Counting sets of objects

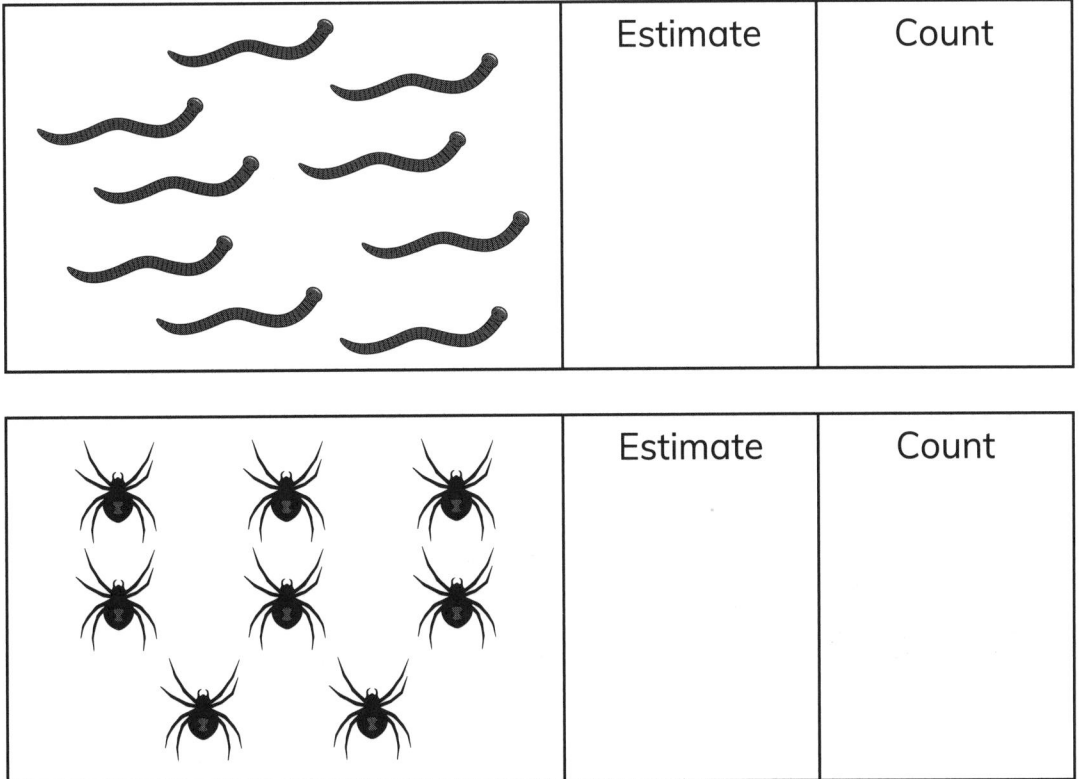

Challenge

 9 Here are the domino patterns for 6, 7, 8 and 9.

Design a domino pattern for 10.

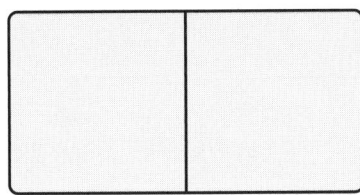

Tip
Keep one part of the domino blank.

1 Numbers to 10

Worked example 1

Look at each of the sets below.

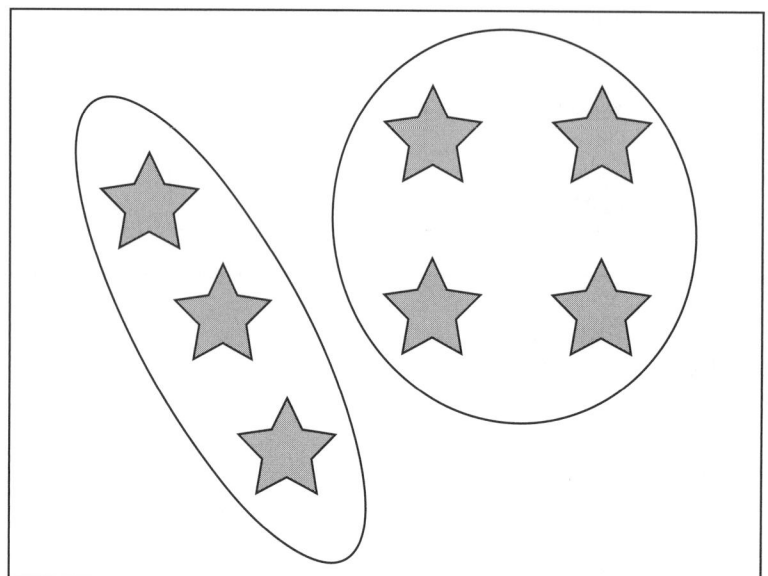

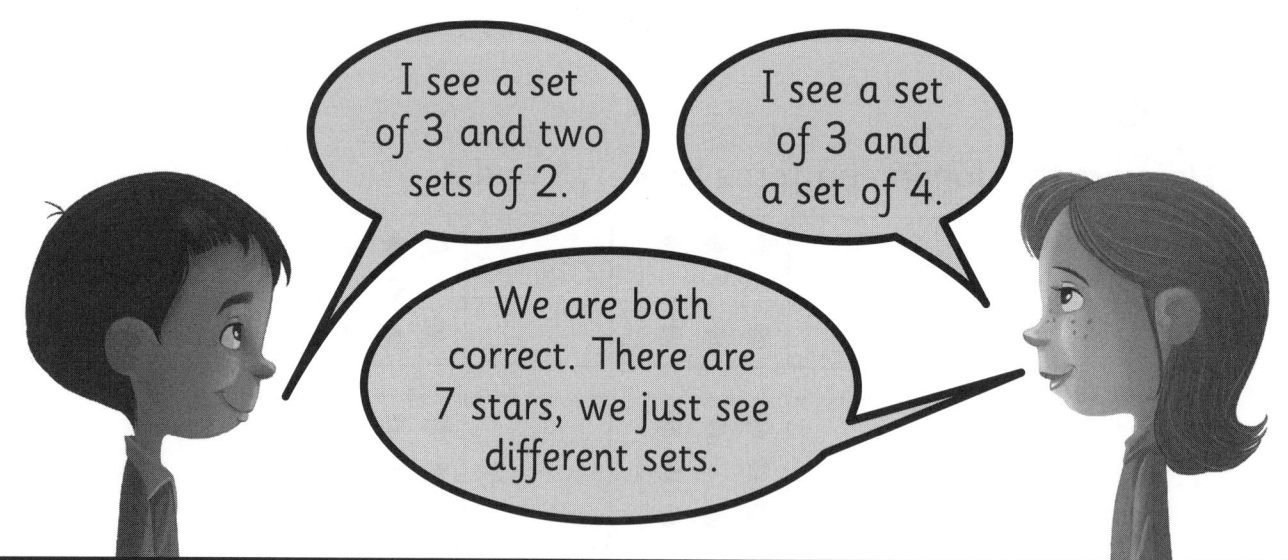

1.1 Counting sets of objects

 10 Look at each of the sets below.

Can you see smaller sets inside each set?

Draw a ring around the smaller sets you notice.

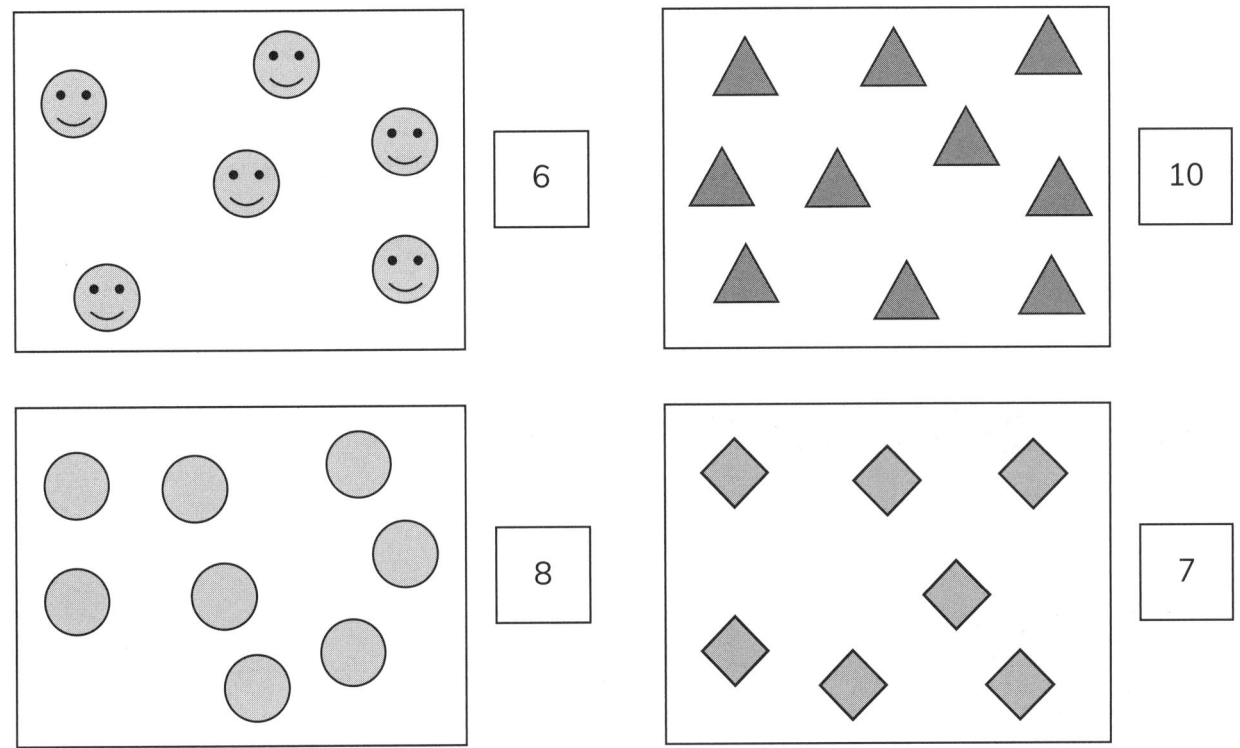

Talk to a partner or carer about what you see. Ask them what they see.

1 Numbers to 10

11 Estimate then count.

Estimate	Estimate	Estimate	Estimate	Estimate	Estimate	Estimate
Count	Count	Count	Count	Count	Count	Count

> 1.2 Say, read and write numbers to 10

Exercise 1.2

> between   order   point   number track

Focus

1   Say each number. Point to it on the number track.

   Start here ⎯⎯⎯⎯⎯⎯⎯⎯⎯⎯⎯⎯⎯⎯→ Finish here

1	2	3	4	5	6	7	8	9	10

2   Colour the squares on this number track.

   Colour the 1, 4, 7 and 10 squares red.

   Colour the 2, 5 and 8 squares green.

   Colour the 3, 6 and 9 squares blue.

1	2	3	4	5	6	7	8	9	10

3   Write the missing numbers.

	2	3	4	5	6	7	8	9	

   Talk to a partner or carer about how you found the missing numbers. Ask them what they would do.

1 Numbers to 10

Practice

4 Count to 10.

Write the missing numbers.

| 1 | | 3 | | 5 | | 7 | | 9 | |

| | 2 | | 4 | | 6 | | 8 | | 10 |

 5 Where is the mistake in this number track?

| 1 | 2 | 3 | 4 | 5 | 6 | 8 | 9 | 10 |

Talk to a partner or carer about how you found the mistake. Ask them what they would do.

6 Write the number that comes after.

| 3 | |

| 5 | |

| 7 | |

| 9 | |

1.2 Say, read and write numbers to 10

Challenge

7 What are the mistakes in this number track? Circle them.

| 1 | 7 | 3 | 5 | 6 | 2 | 8 | 9 | 10 |

8 Write the number that comes before.

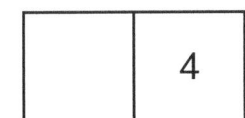

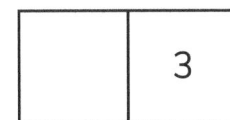

| | 4 | | | 8 |

| | 10 | | | 3 |

9 Write the missing numbers.

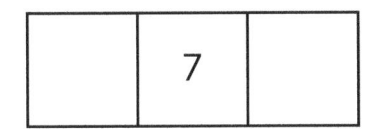

| 2 | | 4 | | 6 | | 8 |

| 7 | | 9 | | | 3 | |

| | 7 | | | | | 10 |

Talk to a partner or carer about how you found the missing numbers. Ask them what they would do.

1 Numbers to 10

> 1.3 Comparing numbers

Exercise 1.3

compare   equal   fewer   less   more   same

Focus

 1 Compare the sets.

Tick ✓ the set that has fewer counters.

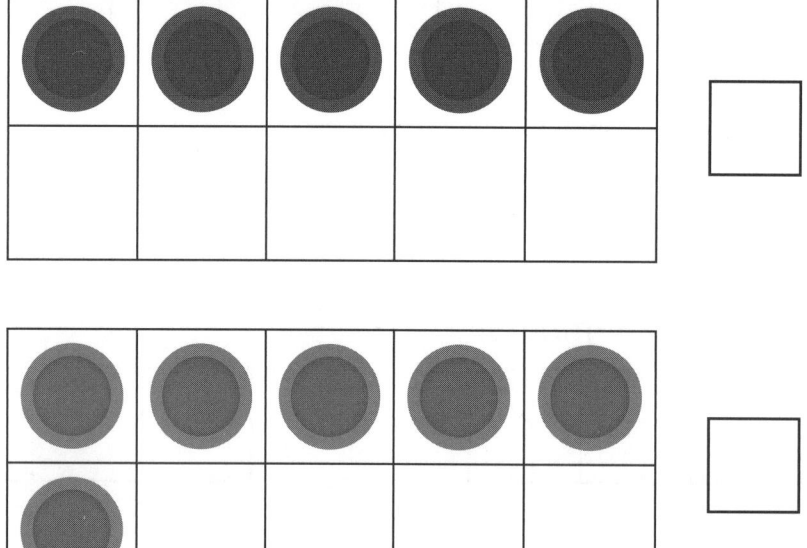

Talk to a partner or carer about how you know.
Ask them what they would do.

2 Compare the dominoes.

Tick ✓ the domino that has more spots.

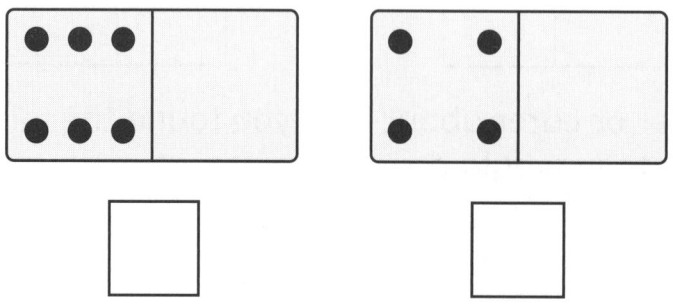

1.3 Comparing numbers

3 Compare the sets.

Tick ✓ the sets that have the same number of objects.

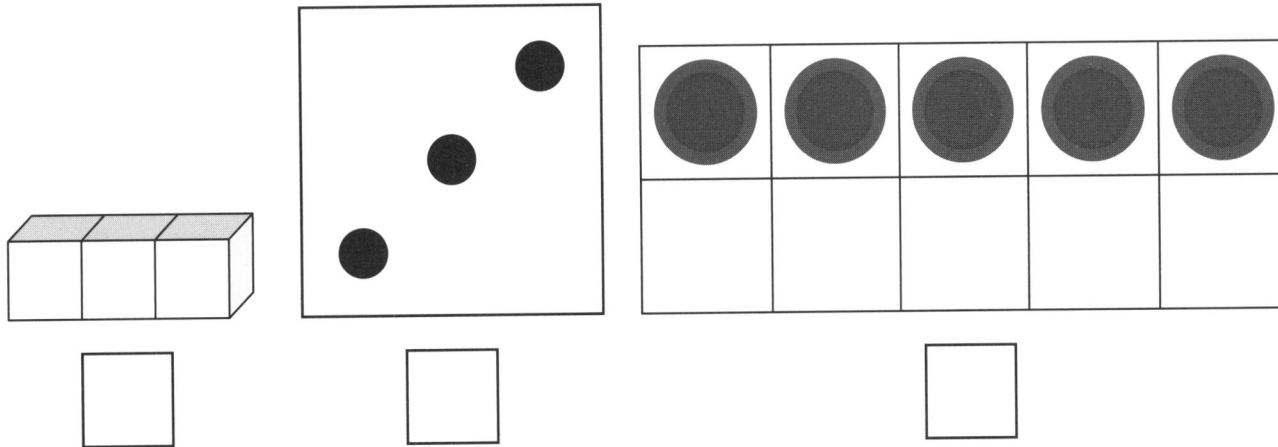

Practice

4 Compare the dominoes.

Draw a ring around the domino that has the most spots.

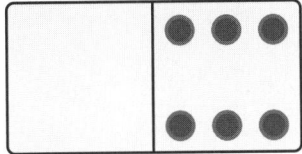 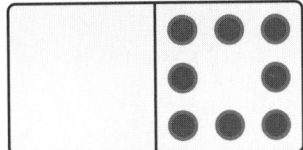 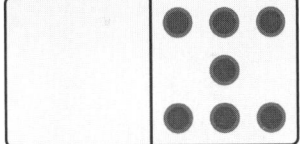

5 Compare the sets.

Draw a ring around the set that has the fewest counters.

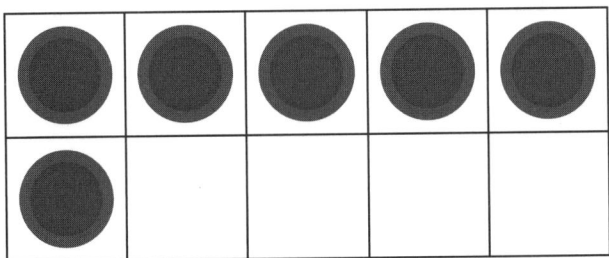 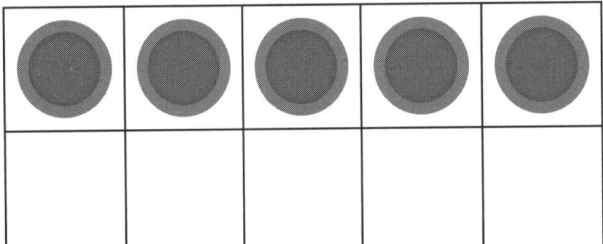

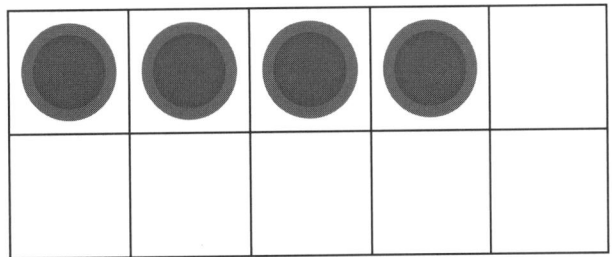

1 Numbers to 10

6 Compare the sets.

Tick ✓ the sets that have an equal number of objects.

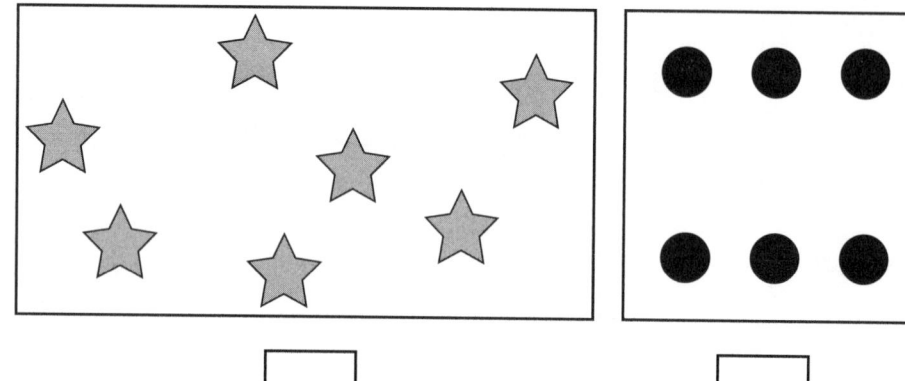

☐ ☐ ☐

7 Compare the sets.

Complete the sentences.

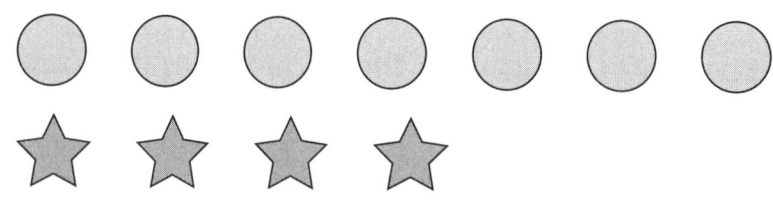

There are _____ ◯

There are _____ ★

There are more _____ than _____ so there

are fewer _____ than _____ .

8 Look at question 7.

How many more circles than stars? ☐

How many fewer stars than circles? ☐

9 Write a number that is greater than 9. ☐

1.3 Comparing numbers

10 Write a number that is fewer than 7. ☐

Talk to a partner or carer about how you answered questions 9 and 10. Ask them what they would do.

Challenge

11 Compare the sets.

Complete the sentences.

5 is more than 4.

_____ is fewer than _____ .

12 Compare the sets.

Complete the sentences.

9 is more than 7 and 8.

_____ is fewer than _____ and _____ .

13 Write a number that is more than 5 and fewer than 9. ☐

Talk to a partner or carer about how you chose your number. Ask them what they would do.

14 Complete the sentences comparing 3 and 5. Use **more**, **fewer**, **less** or **greater**.

3 is _____ than 5.

5 is _____ than 3.

1 Numbers to 10

> 1.4 Number words

Exercise 1.4

> zero: 0   one: 1   two: 2   three: 3   four: 4   five: 5
> six: 6   seven: 7   eight: 8   nine: 9   ten: 10

Focus

1   Draw a ring around the number word that matches the set.

| one | two | three |

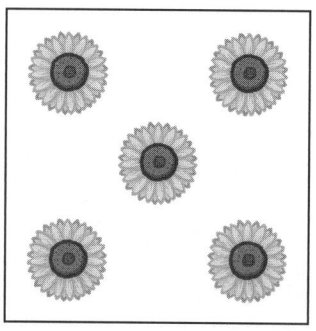

| four | five | six |

| five | six | seven |

| eight | nine | ten |

24

1.4 Number words

2. We write 0, zero if there are no objects.

   Draw a plate with zero biscuits on.

Practice

3. Write the missing number words.

1	2 two	3	4 four	5
6 six	7	8 eight	9	10

4. Look at this picture for 9.

9	••••• ••••
••• ••• •••	nine

   Draw a picture like this for 7.

1 Numbers to 10

5 Complete the number word track.
   Look at page 24 for the number word spellings.

zero	one							eight		

Challenge

6 Write the missing number words.

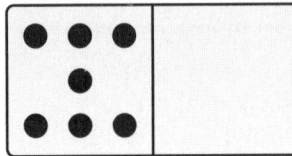 _____   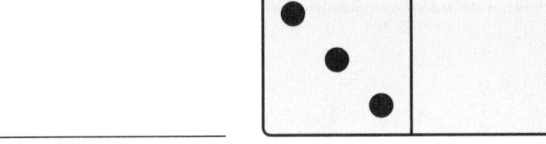 _____

Talk to a partner or carer about how you found the missing words.
Ask them what they would do.

7 Complete the number words.

| s | | v | | n |

| | | | o |

| | | v | e |

| f | | | r |

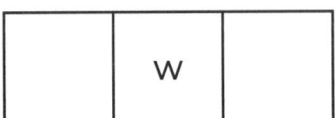

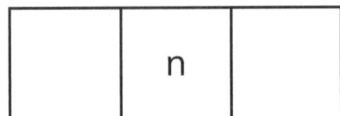

> 1.5 Odd and even numbers

Exercise 1.5

even   odd   pair   pattern

Focus

1 Look at the gloves.

How many gloves are there? ☐

Is that an odd or even number?   **odd / even**

How do you know?

_____

_____

1 Numbers to 10

2 Look at the socks.

How many socks are there? ☐

Is that an odd or even number?

How do you know?   **odd / even**

_____

_____

Practice

3 Odd or even?

Draw a ring around the correct word.

| 4 | | 5 |

odd / even   **odd / even**

| 6 | | 7 |

odd / even   **odd / even**

Talk to a partner or carer about how you know if a number is odd or even. Ask them what they know about odd and even.

4 Draw a ring around the correct word in each sentence.

9 is an **odd / even** number.

10 is an **odd / even** number.

Use some cubes to check.

Were you correct?

1.5 Odd and even numbers

5. Draw an odd number of socks on the ten frame.

   Make it easy to see that there is an odd number of socks.

Challenge

6. How can you describe an odd number?

   _____

   _____

   How can you describe an even number?

   _____

   _____

   Are there any numbers that are odd *and* even?

   Why?

   _____

   _____

7. Zero is an even number but you cannot put 0 cubes into twos.

   Why is 0 an even number?

   _____

   _____

2 Geometry

> 2.1 3D shapes

Exercise 2.1

> 3D   cube   cylinder   edge   face   sphere

Focus

1 Draw a ring around the correct label.

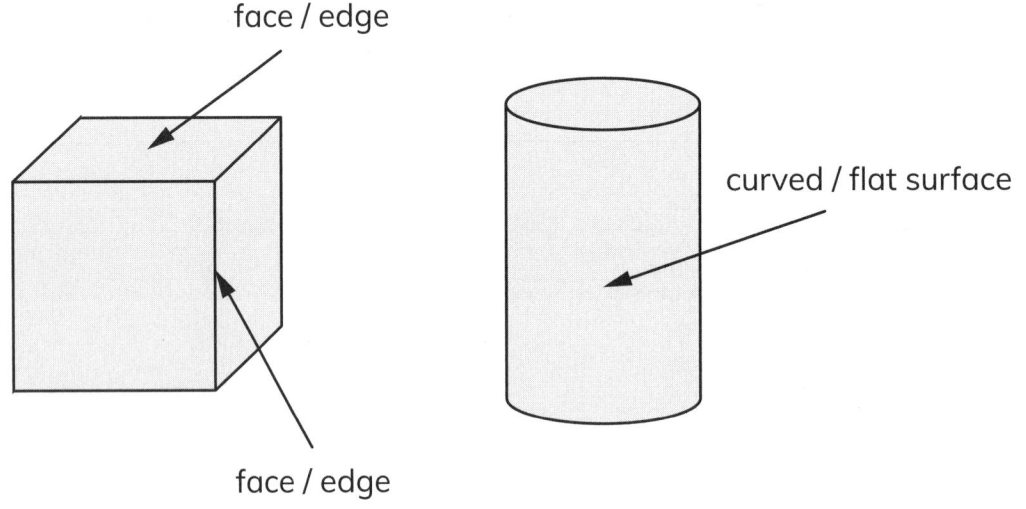

face / edge

curved / flat surface

face / edge

Worked example 1

Will each shape roll?

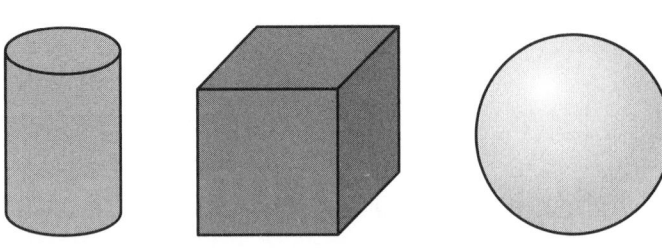

2.1 3D shapes

Continued

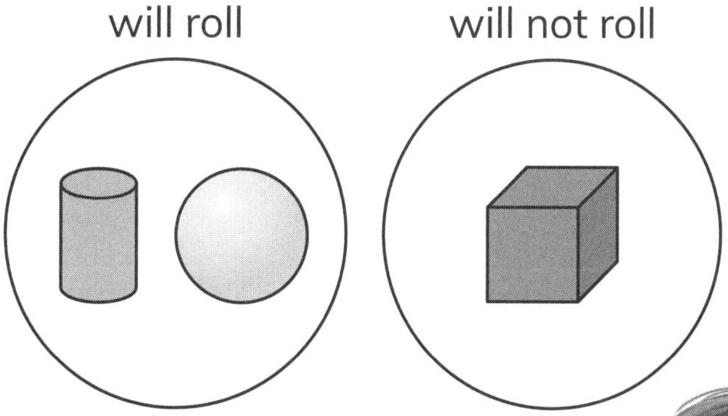

will roll   will not roll

Does it have only flat faces? A flat face won't roll but it will slide.

2 Draw a ring around the shapes that have only flat faces.

Will each object roll? Draw lines to the correct circle.

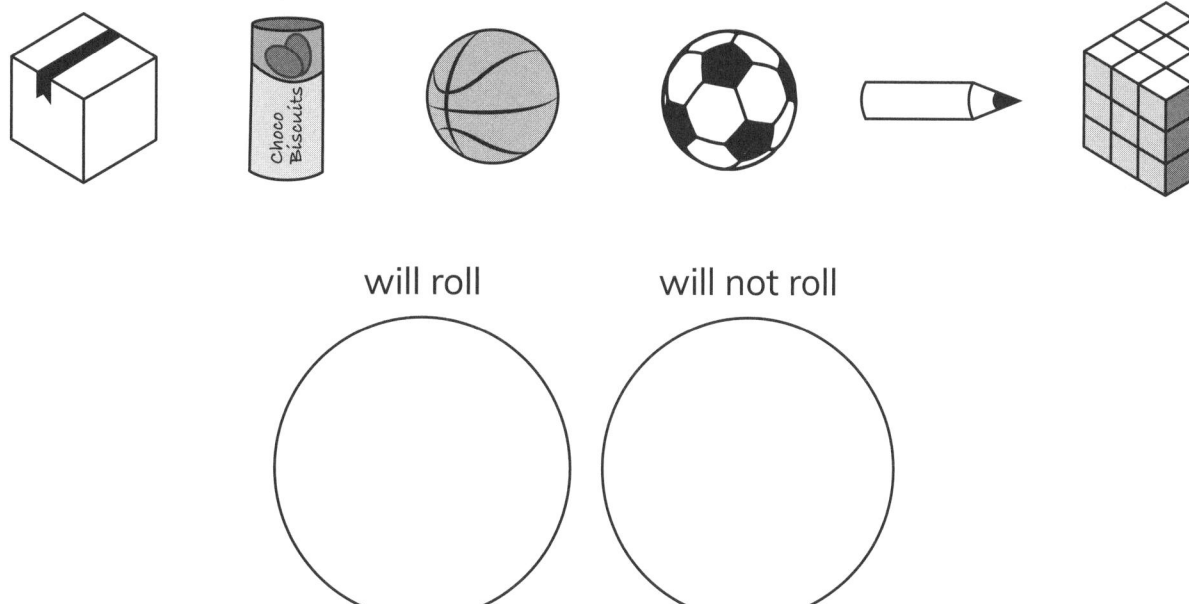

will roll   will not roll

31

2 Geometry

Practice

3   Colour the spheres blue, the cubes yellow and the cylinders green.

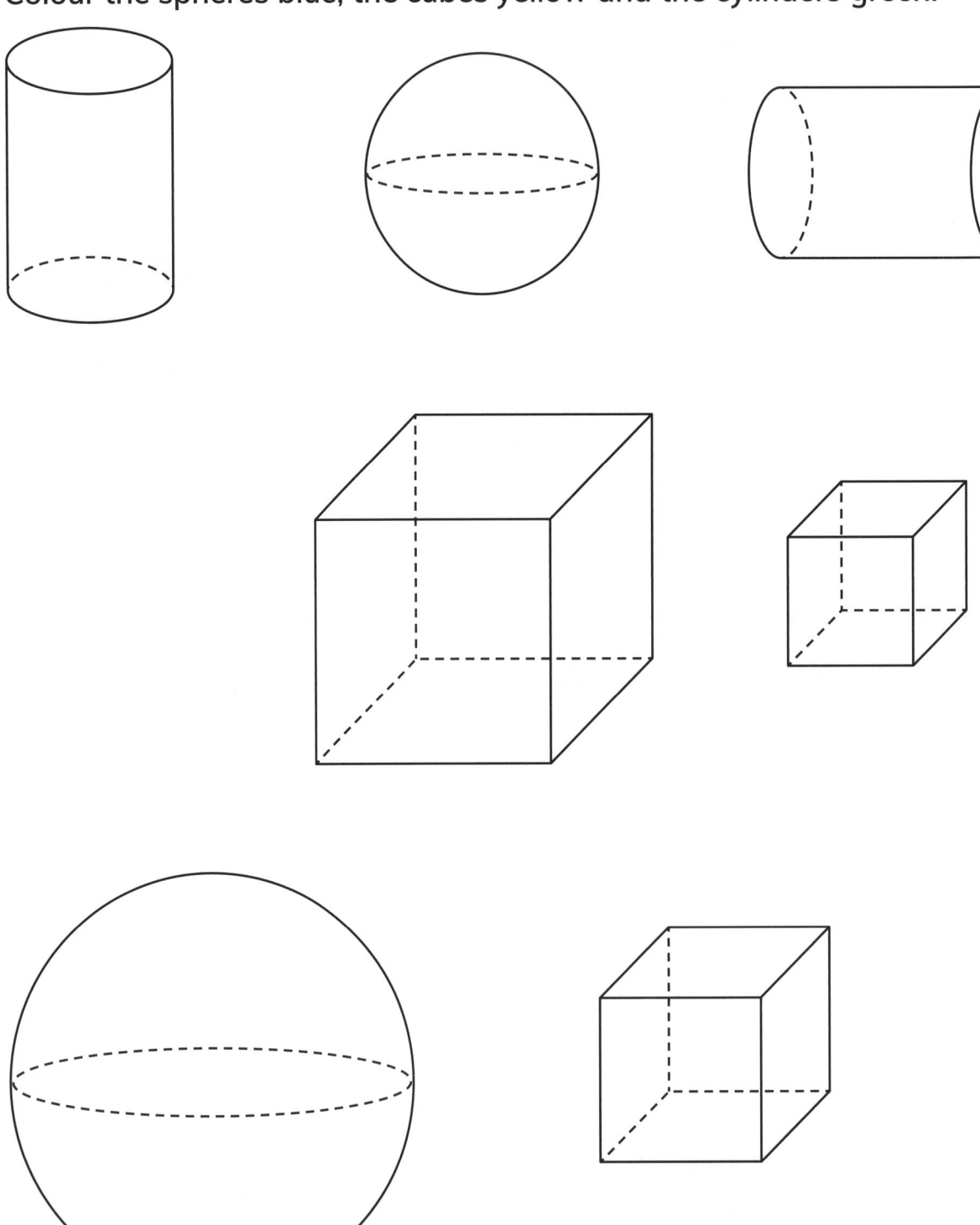

2.1 3D shapes

 4

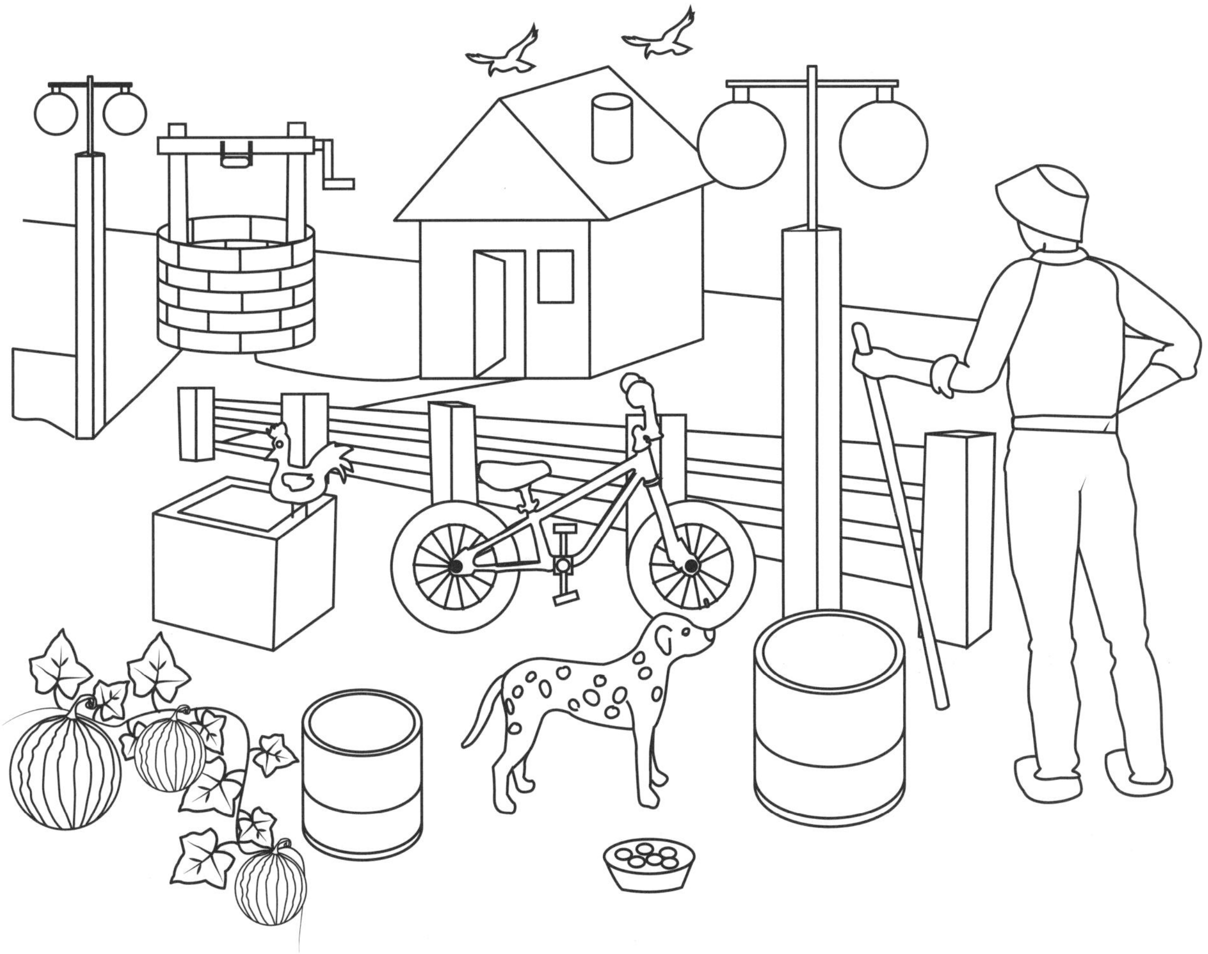

Colour the spheres 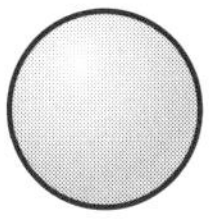 ⬤ yellow.

Colour the cylinders ▯ blue.

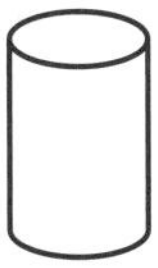

Colour the cubes ◻ green.

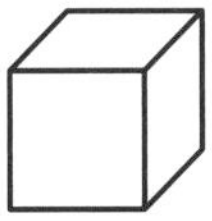

Draw a ring ◯ around the curved edges.

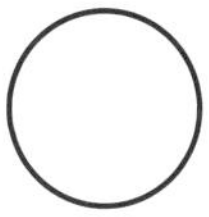

Draw a square ☐ around the flat faces.

2 Geometry

5. Use 3D shapes to build a house.
   Write how many of each shape you used.

   I used ☐ cubes, ☐ spheres and ☐ cylinders.

6. Write the missing words. Choose words from the cloud.

   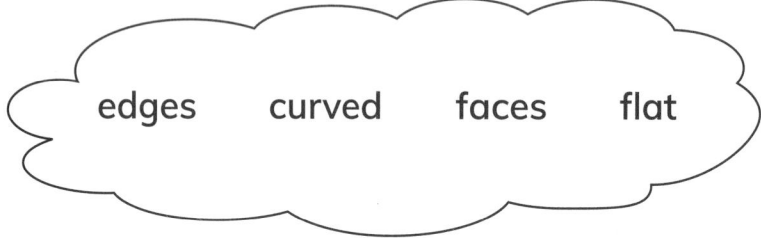

   edges   curved   faces   flat

   A sphere has a _____ surface.

   A cylinder has a curved surface and 2 _____ faces.

   Shapes with only flat _____ do not roll.

   A cube has 12 _____.

2.1 3D shapes

Challenge

 7 Write the name of the shape that each object looks like.

   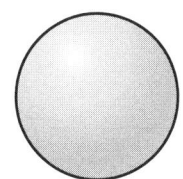   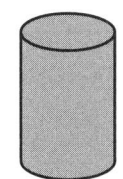

cube   sphere   cylinder

_____   _____   _____

   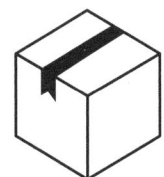   

_____   _____   _____

 8 Draw a ring around the shapes in each row that are **not** the same shape as the one in the box.

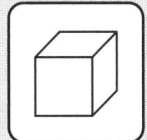   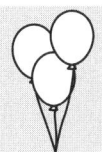   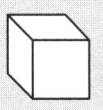   

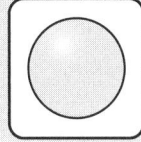         

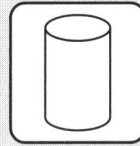      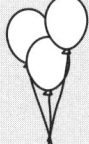   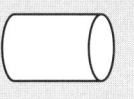

35

2 Geometry

9 Are these sentences true or false? Tick the correct boxes.

	True	False
A cylinder has 4 edges.	☐	☐
A cube has 8 faces.	☐	☐
A sphere has 3 straight edges.	☐	☐
A sphere has no flat faces.	☐	☐
A cylinder has a curved surface.	☐	☐
A cube has 5 flat faces.	☐	☐
A cylinder has 2 flat faces.	☐	☐
All 3D shapes are flat.	☐	☐

> 2.2 2D shapes

Exercise 2.2

Focus

> 2D   circle   curved   rectangle   side
> square   straight   triangle

1   Draw a ring around the shapes that have curved sides.

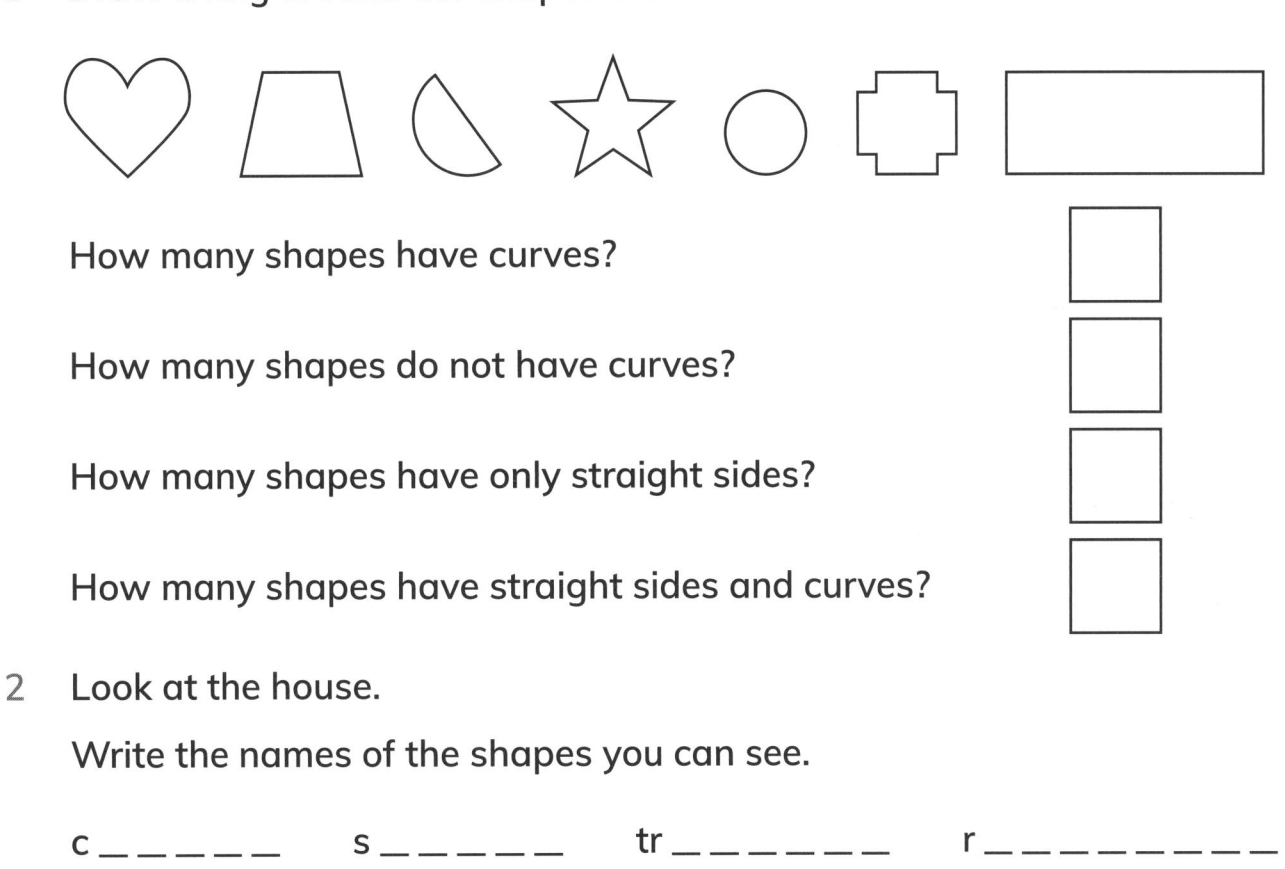

How many shapes have curves?

How many shapes do not have curves?

How many shapes have only straight sides?

How many shapes have straight sides and curves?

2   Look at the house.

Write the names of the shapes you can see.

c _ _ _ _ _   s _ _ _ _ _ _   tr _ _ _ _ _ _ _   r _ _ _ _ _ _ _ _ _

How many triangles?

How many squares?

How many circles?

How many rectangles?

2 Geometry

3   Draw a ring around all the 3D shapes.

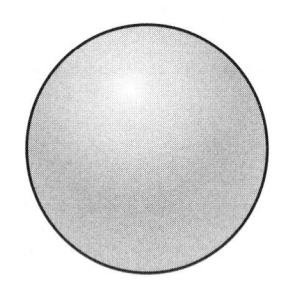

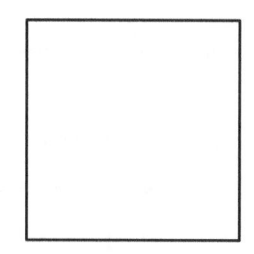

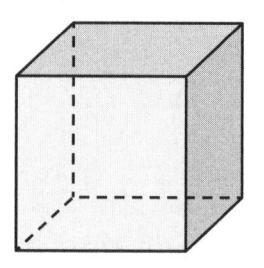

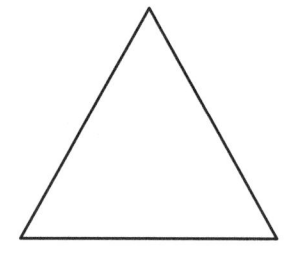

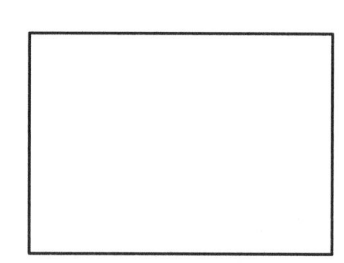

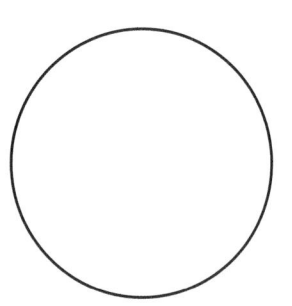

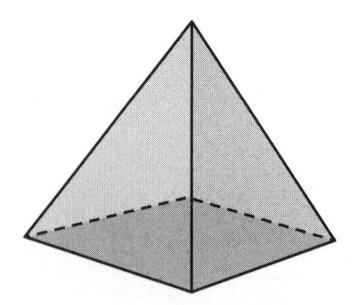

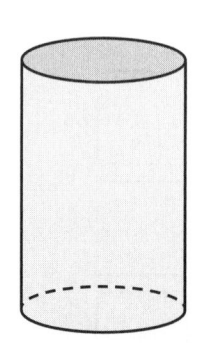

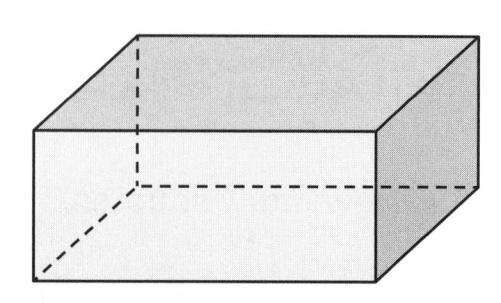

2.2 2D shapes

Practice

4 Follow the ☐ to help the children get home.

Colour the ☐ along the way.

2 Geometry

5 Colour the circles red.
Colour the triangles green.
Colour the squares blue.

How many circles? ☐

How many triangles? ☐

How many squares? ☐

6 Name these shapes.

_____   _____   _____

7 Write the number of sides for each shape.

sphere ☐   triangle ☐

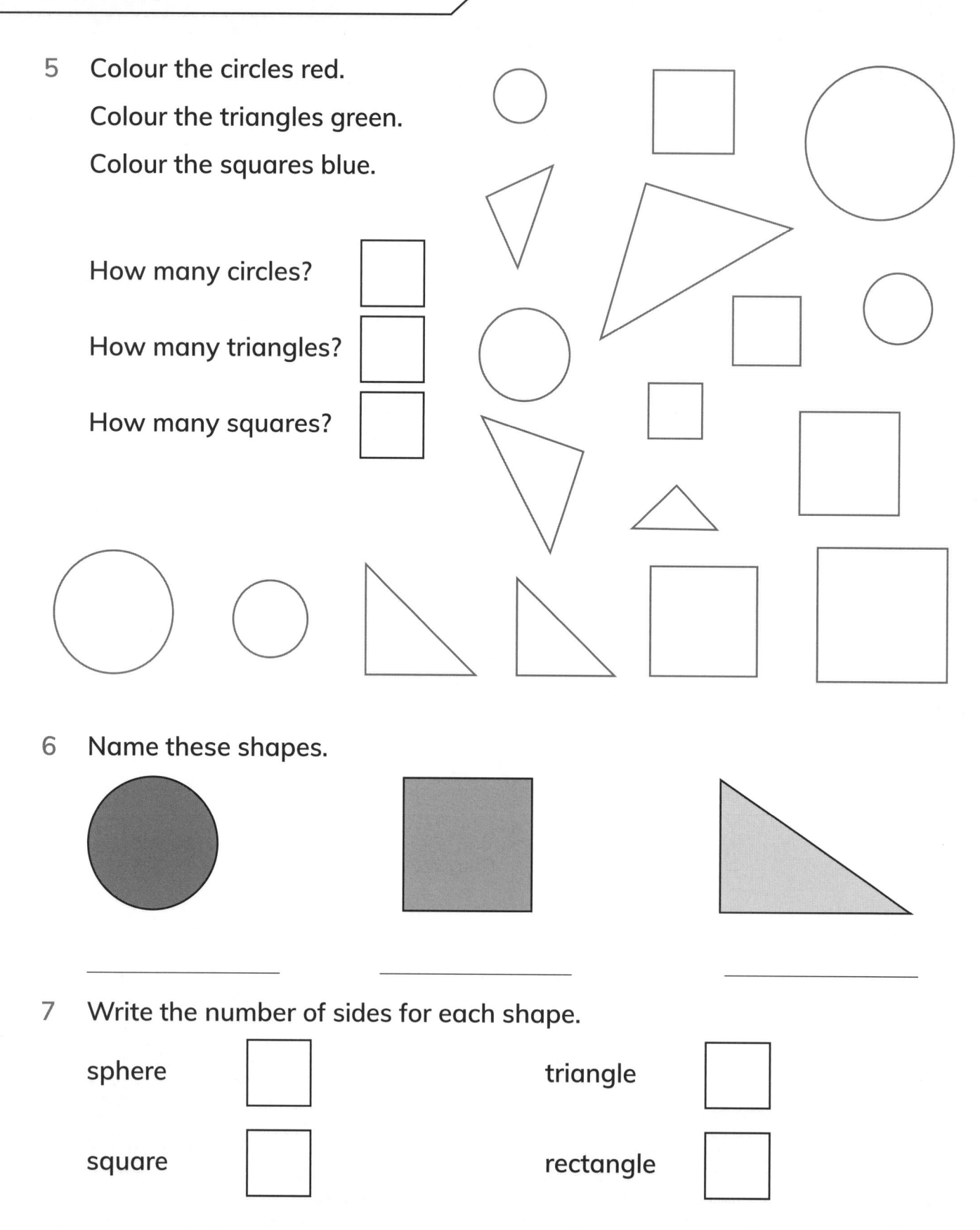

square ☐   rectangle ☐

Challenge

8   What shape am I?

I have 4 straight sides. The sides are all the same length.

I am a _____.

I have 4 straight sides. Two of the sides are longer than the other

two sides. I am a _____.

I have one curved side. I am a _____.

I have three straight sides.

I am a _____.

I have edges and faces. I am a **2D / 3D** shape.

2 Geometry

9 Some shapes fit together with no spaces.

Use 5 squares and make 2 different patterns.

Fit the squares together in your pattern. Sketch your pattern.

3 Fractions

> 3.1 Fractions

Exercise 3.1

fraction   half   part

Focus

1   Colour half of each shape.

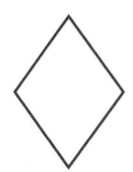

2   This shape has two halves.

   This shape does not have two halves.

   Draw 2 shapes that have two halves.

3 Fractions

Draw 2 shapes that do not have two halves.

3   Draw the other half of this tree.

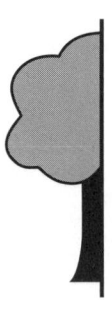

4   This shows one half of a square coloured in.

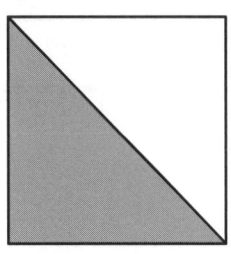

How else could you cut a square in half? Colour in half of each square below using a different way.

Practice

5   Sofia bought 2 pizzas.

   She cut each pizza into 2 pieces.

   Marcus took the biggest piece.

   Draw a ring around the piece Marcus took.

   Now draw a ring around the correct answer.

   Marcus took: **half a pizza / more than half a pizza / less than half a pizza**.

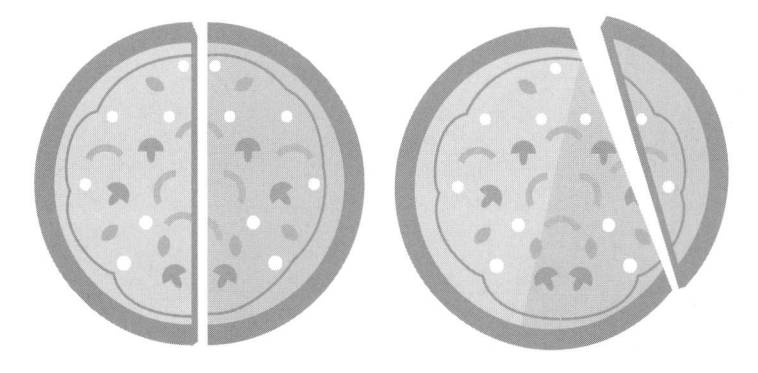

6   Draw a ring around the picture in each row that shows two **equal** parts.

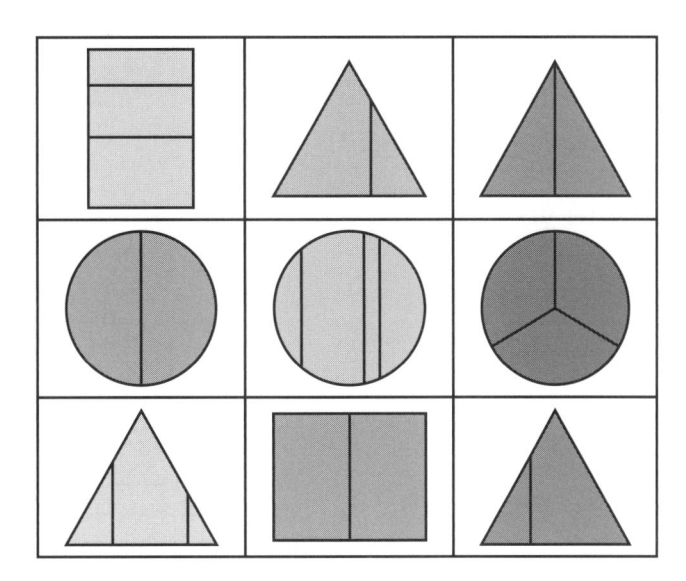

3 Fractions

7 Draw a ring around the part you would choose in each pair.
Explain your choices to a parent or carer.

8 Has each shape been cut in half?

Draw a ring around yes or no.

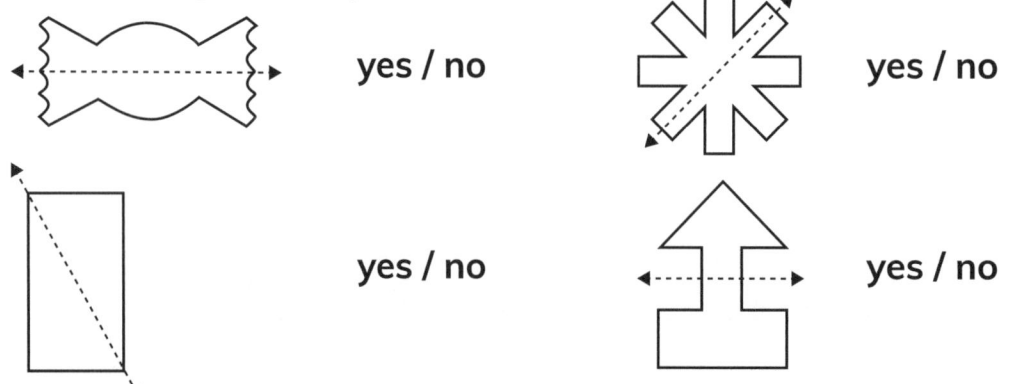

yes / no   yes / no

yes / no   yes / no

46

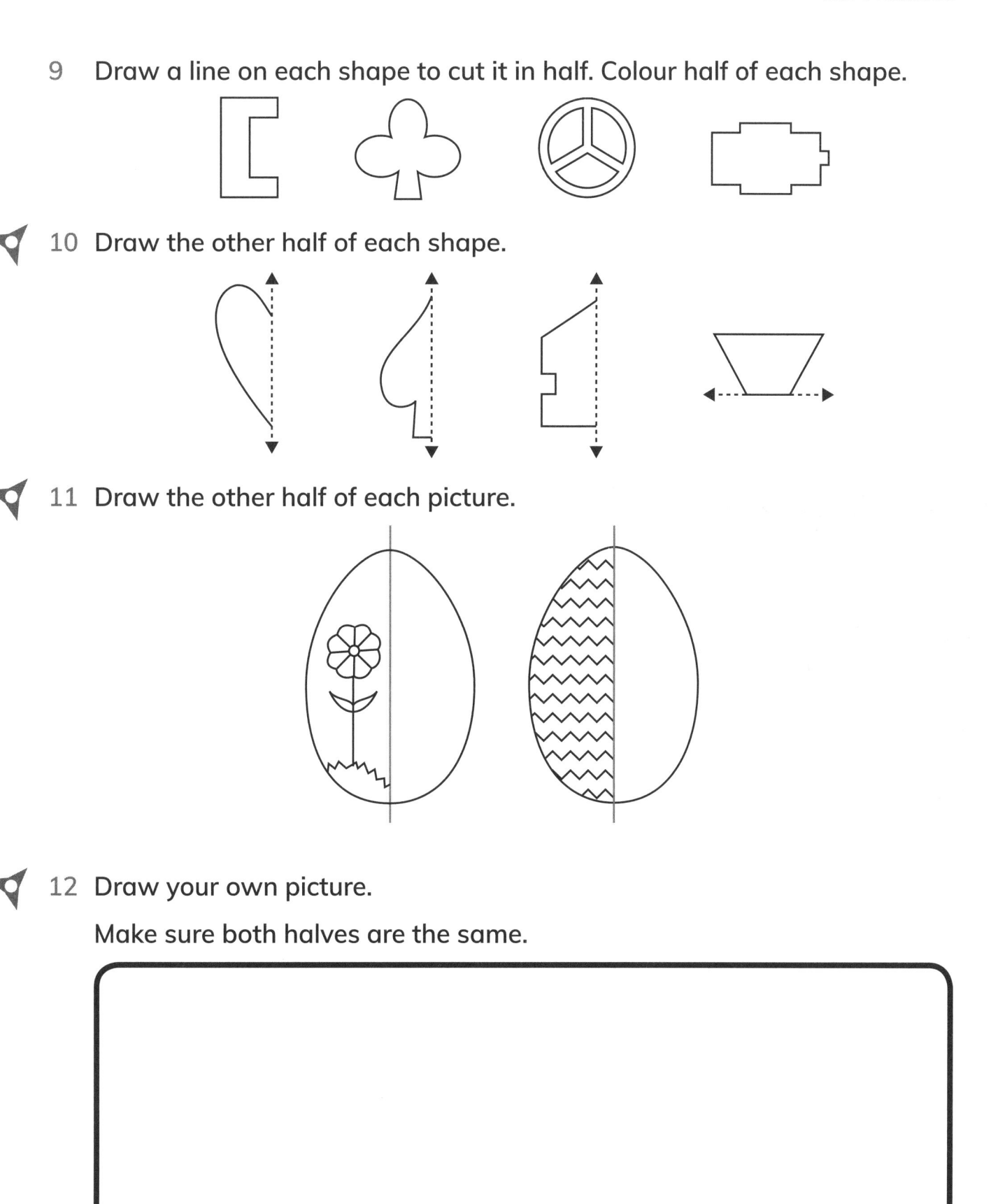

9 Draw a line on each shape to cut it in half. Colour half of each shape.

10 Draw the other half of each shape.

11 Draw the other half of each picture.

12 Draw your own picture.

   Make sure both halves are the same.

3 Fractions

Challenge

13 Draw lines to cut each shape in half in a different way.

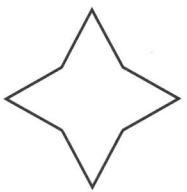

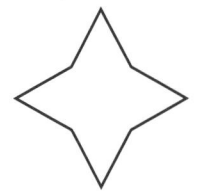

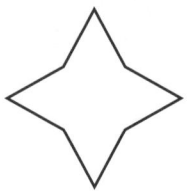

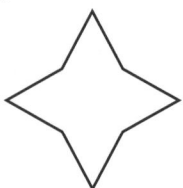

14 Colour half of this shape.

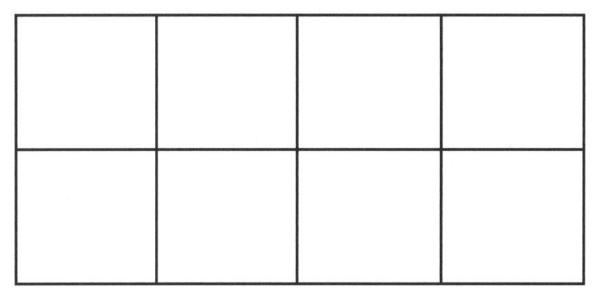

15 How many different ways can you halve a triangle?

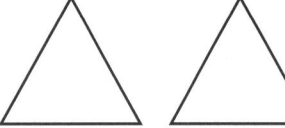

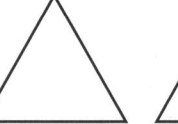

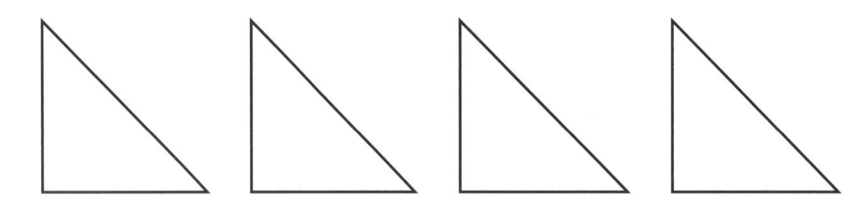

16 How many different ways are there to halve a square?

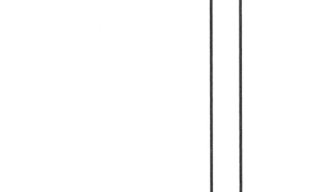

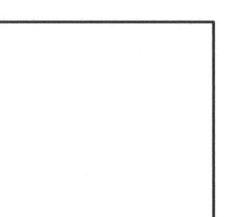

Have you found all the ways?

4 Measures

> ## 4.1 Length

Exercise 4.1

Focus

length long short tall thin wide

Worked example 1

Colour the object that is longer than the pencil.

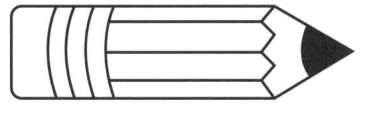

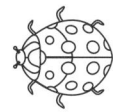

Answer:

The shoe is longer than the pencil.

> The two ends of the shoe are further away from each other than the two ends of the pencil.

4 Measures

1. Colour the thinnest tree.

2. Colour the longer object in each pair.

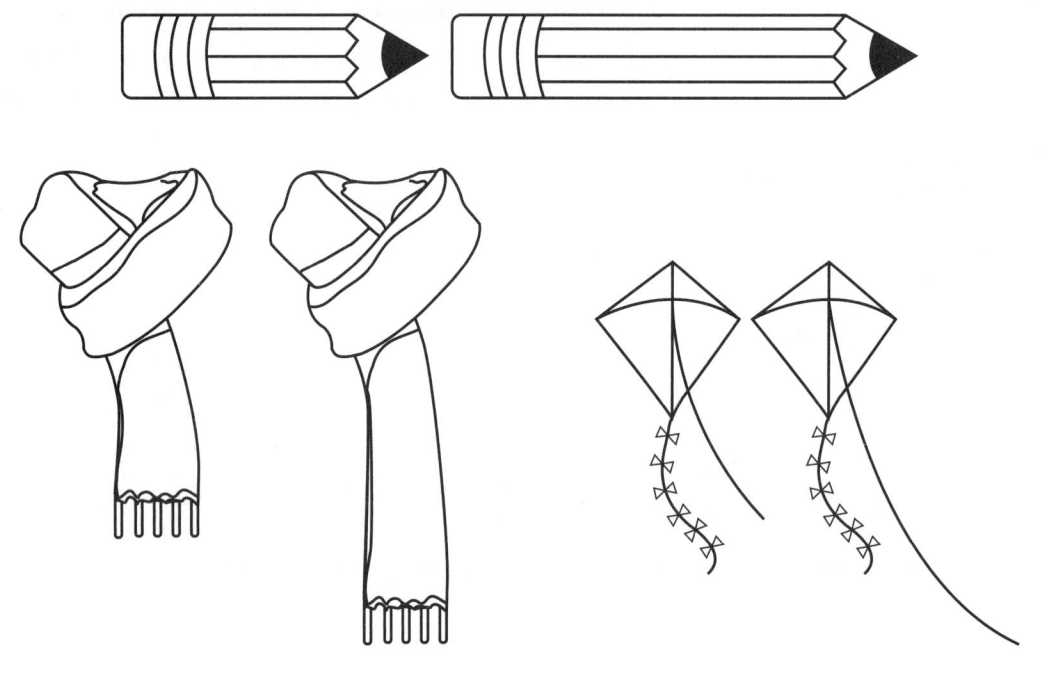

Colour the shorter object in each pair.

4.1 Length

Practice

3   Colour the shorter object in each set blue.

Colour the taller object in each set red.

4

Colour each car a different colour.

The longest car is _____ .

The shortest car is _____ .

4 Measures

5 Compare the length of these cars.

Label them in order 1 to 5.

1 is the longest car.

5 is the shortest car.

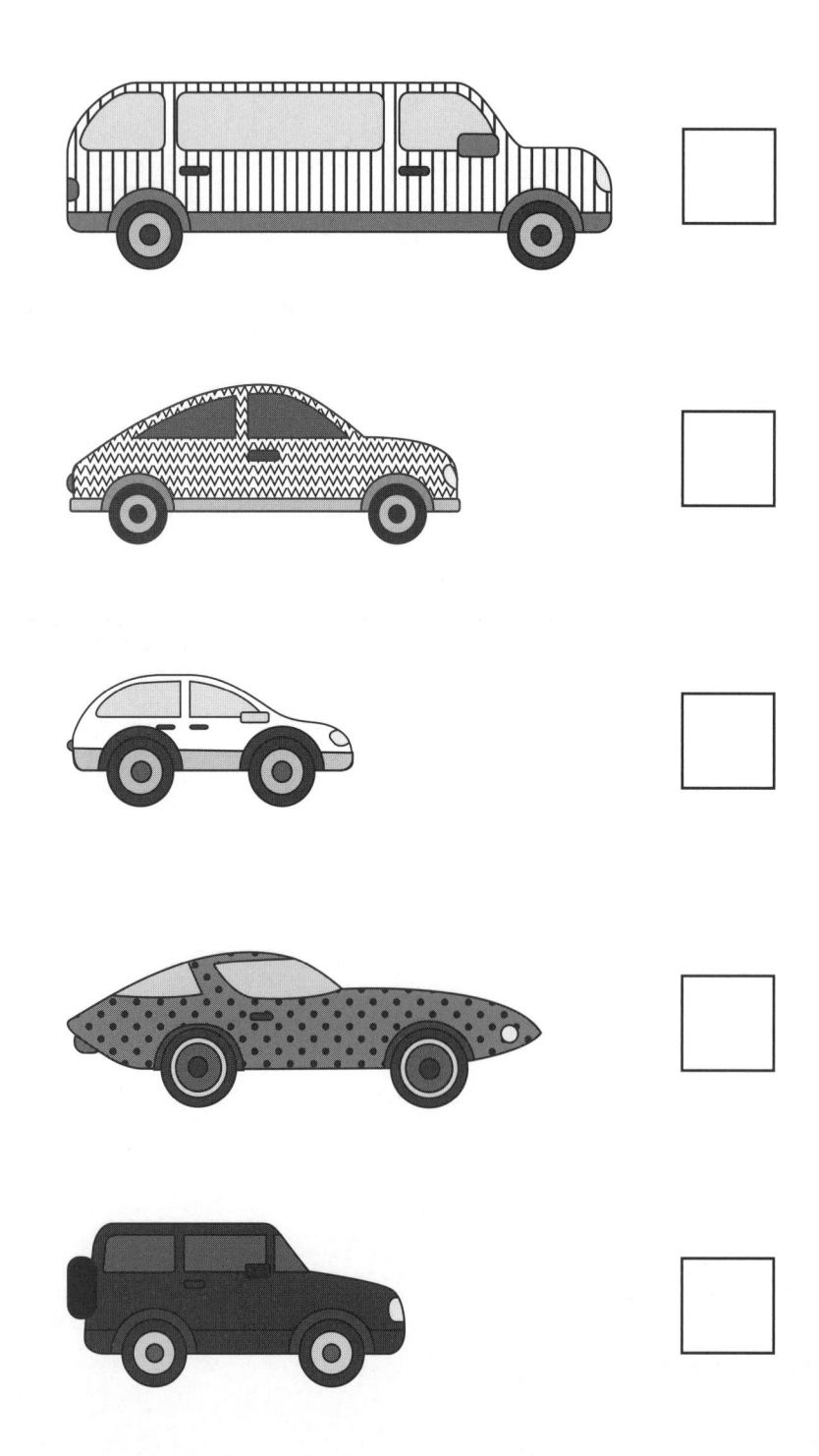

4.1 Length

6   Colour the longest ribbon in each row.

Challenge

7   These caterpillars are made of circles.

    Draw a caterpillar on each empty leaf.

    Make one caterpillar longer than the other.

    How many circles does the longer caterpillar have? ☐

    How many circles does the shorter caterpillar have? ☐

    Make sure the longer caterpillar has more circles than the shorter caterpillar.

4 Measures

8

"We are going on a length hunt."

"Find 3 things that are longer than our pencil."

"Find 3 things that are shorter than our pencil."

Draw 3 things that you find in the correct place in the table.

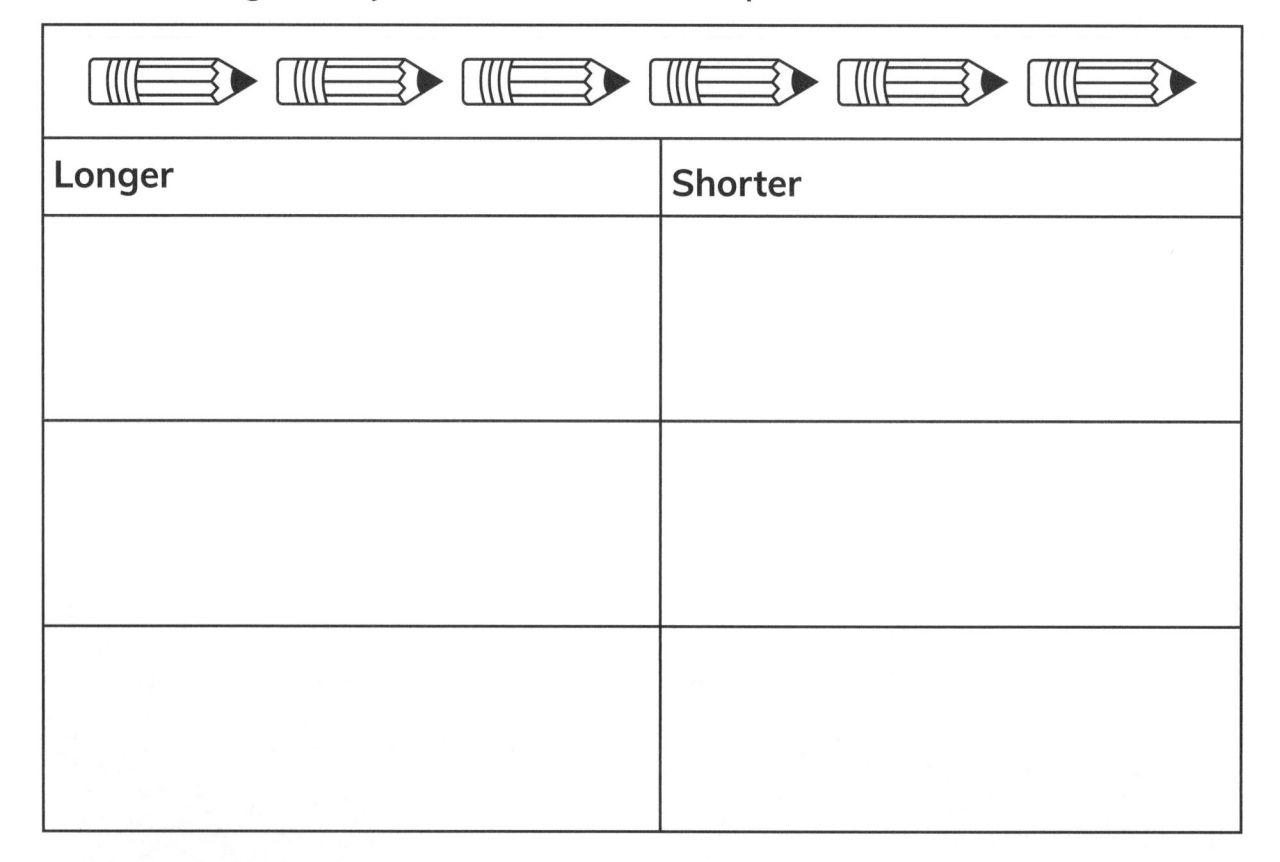

Longer	Shorter

4.1 Length

9 Longer or shorter? Taller or shorter?

These words are used to describe the length of something.

short   □   long   ▭
shorter ▭   longer ▬
shortest ▪   longest ▬▬

We can also draw pictures to show the height of something.

Draw trees to match these words.

tall		short	
taller		shorter	
tallest		shortest	

5 Working with numbers to 10

> 5.1 Addition as combining

Exercise 5.1

Focus

> add   altogether
> number bond   whole

1   Draw 1 more counter in each ten frame.

   How many counters are there now?

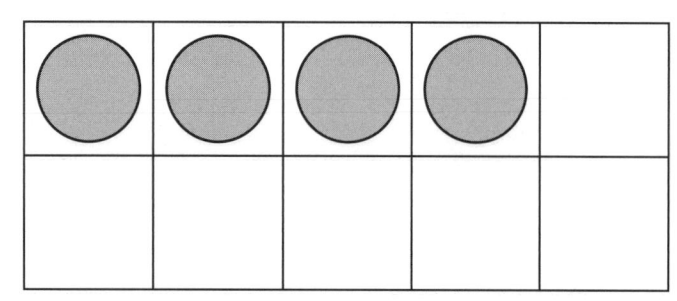

   4 add 1 equals ☐

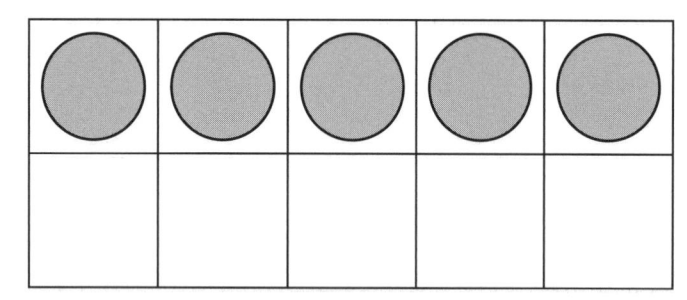

   5 add 1 equals ☐

56

5.1 Addition as combining

2   Draw 2 more counters in each ten frame.

    How many counters are there now?

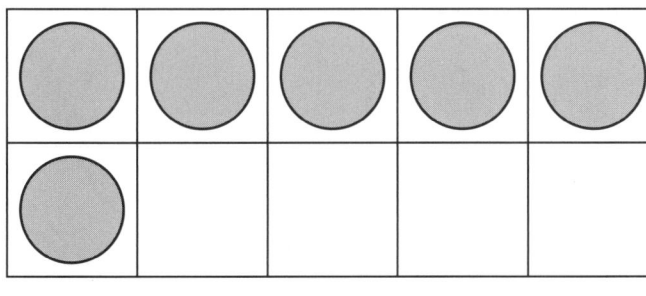

    6 add 2 equals ☐

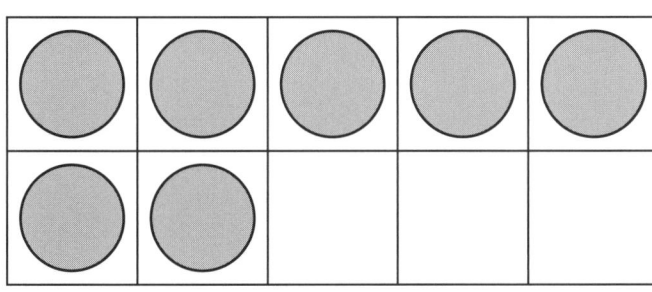

    7 add 2 equals ☐

3   Write the number sentence for this story.

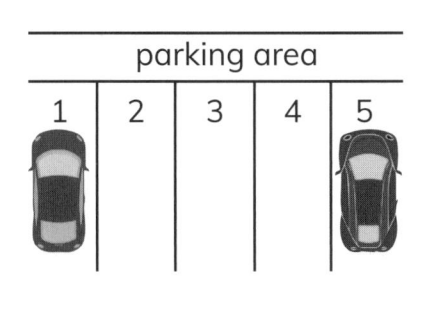

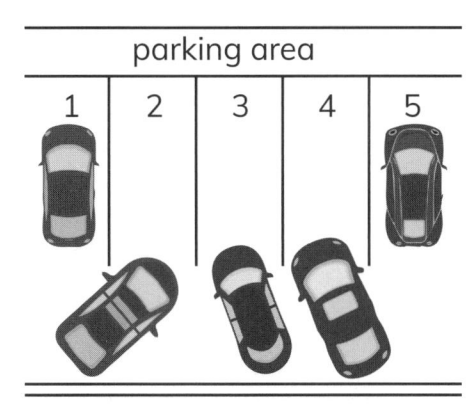

    parking area   parking area   parking area

    First   Then   Now

    2 add 3 equals 5

    ☐ + ☐ = ☐

5 **Working with numbers to 10**

4 Write the number sentence for this story.

First   Then   Now

2 add 4 equals ☐

☐ + ☐ = ☐

5 Use some counting objects on the part-whole diagram to help you find how many there are altogether. Combine the parts to find the whole.

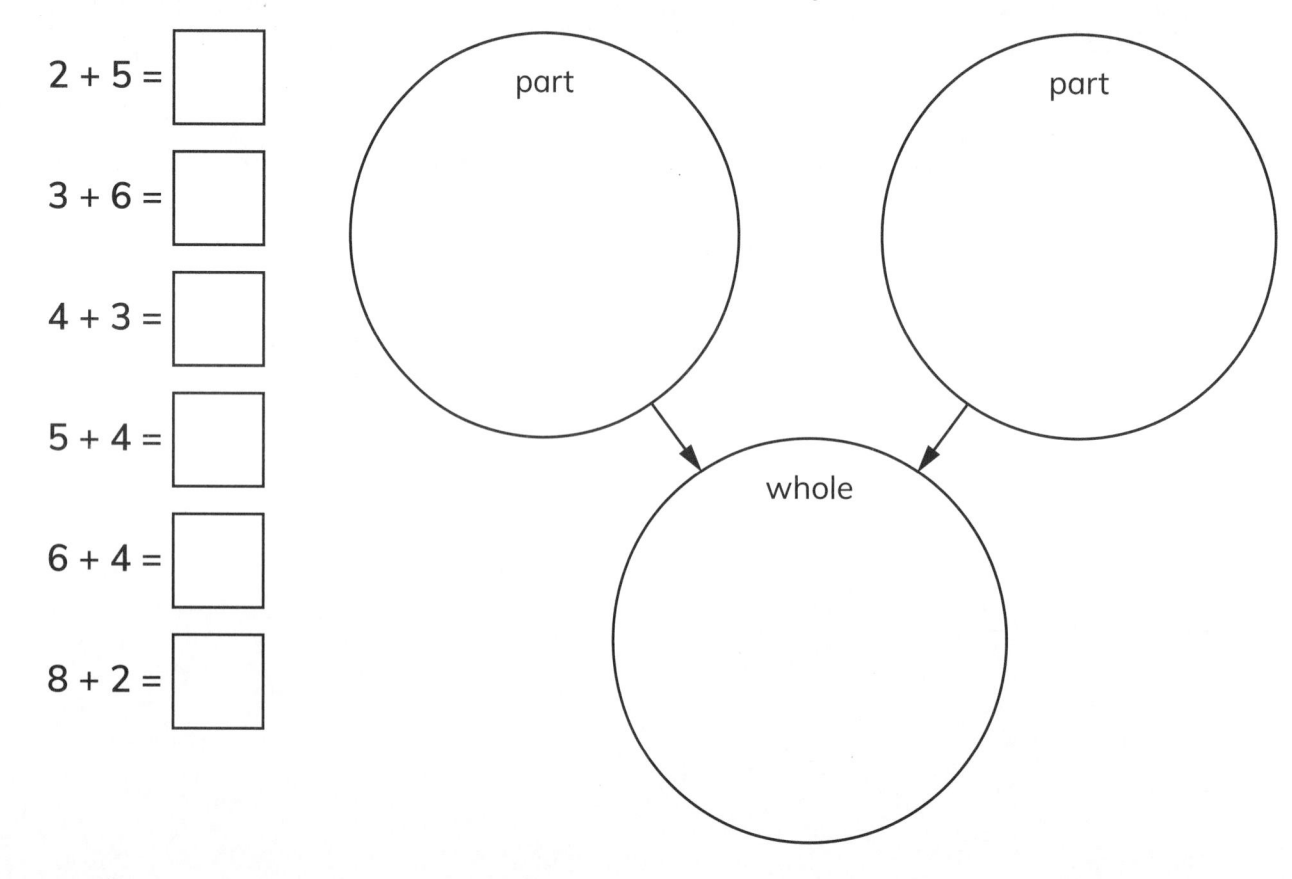

2 + 5 = ☐

3 + 6 = ☐

4 + 3 = ☐

5 + 4 = ☐

6 + 4 = ☐

8 + 2 = ☐

part

part

whole

5.1 Addition as combining

6   Complete the part-whole diagram.

Write a number sentence for each diagram.

Use the large part-whole diagram and counting objects to help you.

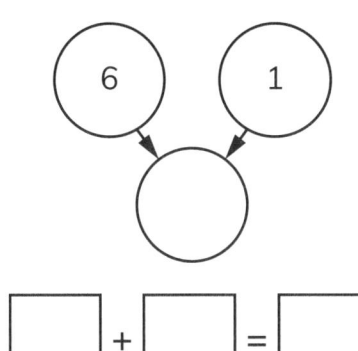

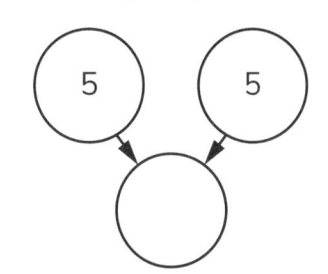

☐ + ☐ = ☐   ☐ + ☐ = ☐

Practice

7   Tell a story to match this number bond for 10.

6 + 4 = 10

Tell your story to a parent or carer.

8   Estimate the number of spots on each domino.

Then write a number sentence for each domino.

Was your estimate close?

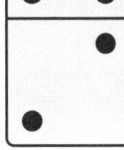

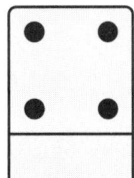

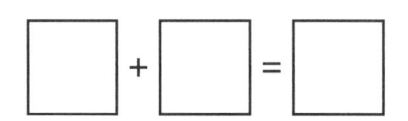

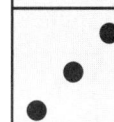

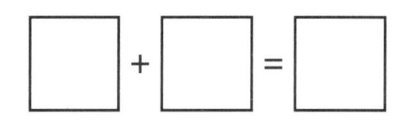

Estimate =

☐ + ☐ = ☐

Estimate =

☐ + ☐ = ☐

Estimate =

☐ + ☐ = ☐

Estimate =

☐ + ☐ = ☐

5 Working with numbers to 10

9 Complete each part-whole diagram.
   Write a matching number sentence.

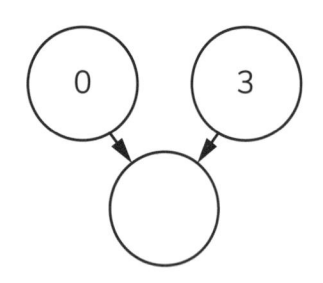

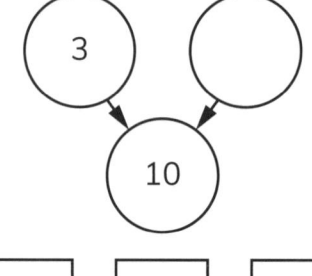

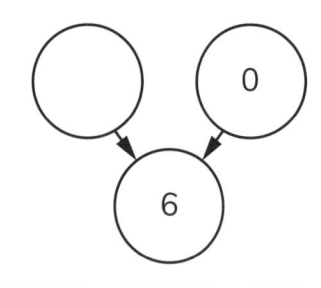

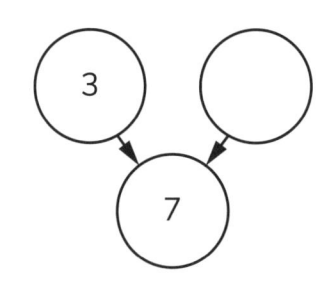

   (0) (3) → ( )
   ☐ + ☐ = ☐

   (3) ( ) → (10)
   ☐ + ☐ = ☐

   ( ) (0) → (6)
   ☐ + ☐ = ☐

   (3) ( ) → (7)
   ☐ + ☐ = ☐

10 Complete the addition walls.

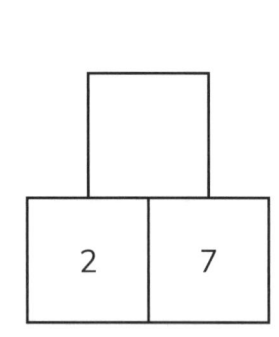

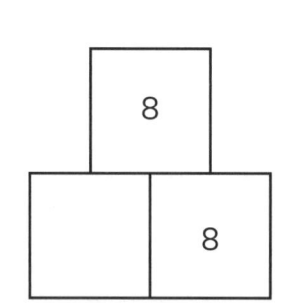

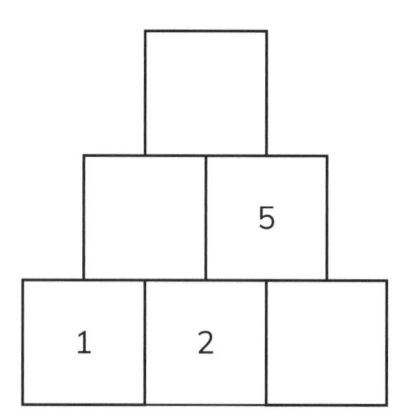

   [ ]
   [2][7]

   [8]
   [ ][8]

   [ ]
   [ ][5]
   [1][2][ ]

5.1 Addition as combining

Challenge

11 Add 1 more.

Look at the numbers in each column.

What do you notice?

Write a sentence to explain.

$0 + 1 = \square$

$1 + 1 = \square \qquad 2 + 1 = \square$

$3 + 1 = \square \qquad 4 + 1 = \square$

$5 + 1 = \square \qquad 6 + 1 = \square$

$7 + 1 = \square \qquad 8 + 1 = \square$

$9 + 1 = \square$

_____

_____

Think about odd and even numbers.

5 Working with numbers to 10

12 Each domino has a total of 10 spots. Every domino is different. Draw the spots. Write a number sentence for each of your dominoes.

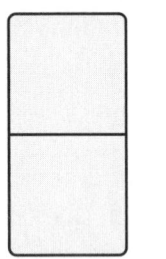

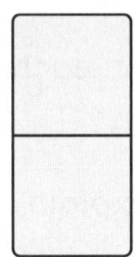

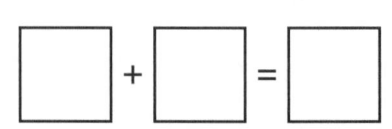

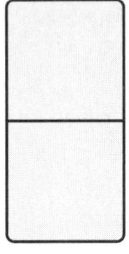

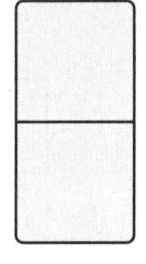

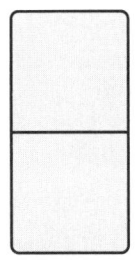

☐ + ☐ = ☐

☐ + ☐ = ☐

☐ + ☐ = ☐

☐ + ☐ = ☐

☐ + ☐ = ☐

13 Which number bond for 10 is shown in the ten frame?

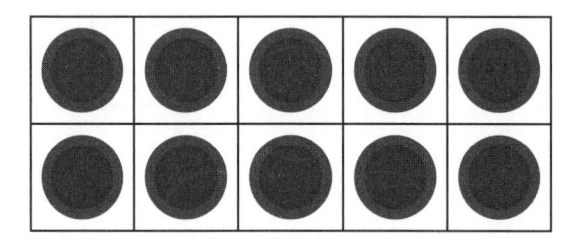

☐ + ☐ = ☐

14 Complete the addition walls.

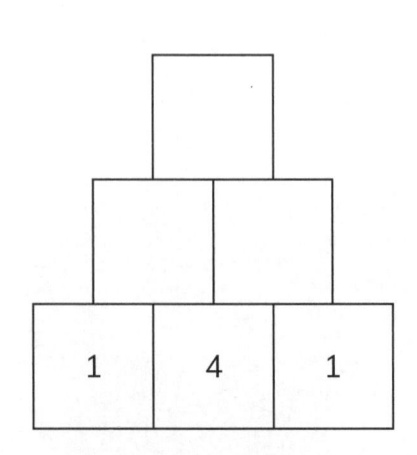

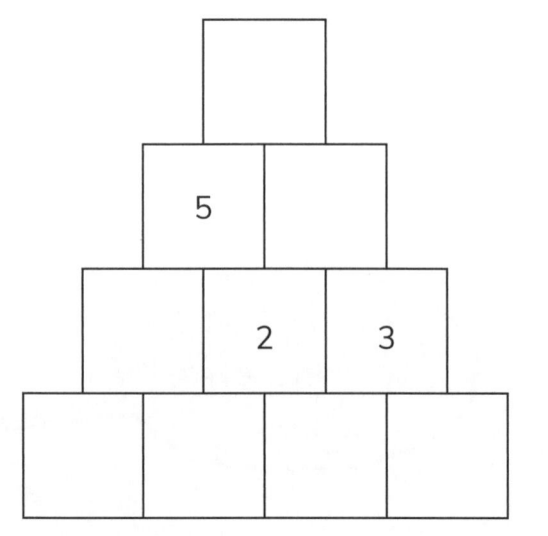

1 4 1

5

2 3

> 5.2 Subtraction as take away

Exercise 5.2

subtract   take away

Focus

1 Use the number track to help you find one fewer.

| 0 | 1 | 2 | 3 | 4 | 5 | 6 | 7 | 8 | 9 | 10 |

| one fewer | 3 |

| one fewer | 5 |

| one fewer | 7 |

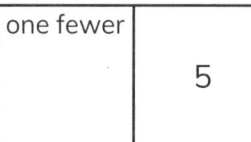

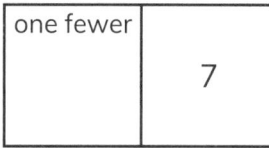

2 Write the number sentence for each story.

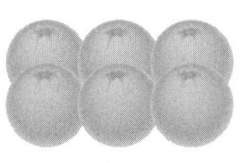

First 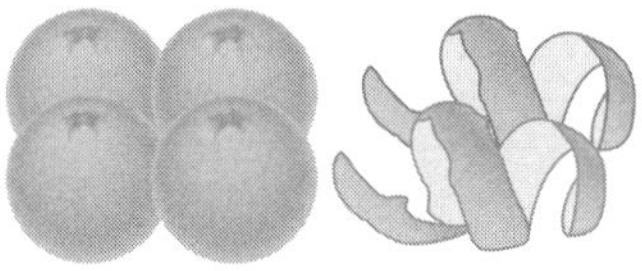   Then 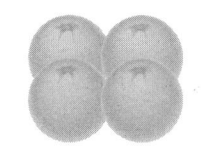   Now

6 take away 2 equals ☐

First    Then    Now

☐ take away ☐ equals ☐

☐ − ☐ = ☐

63

3   Take a part away from the whole. How many are left?

Estimate first, then use the part-whole diagram to help you find the answer.

Use the ten frame to help you find out how many are left.

6 − 3 = | Estimate | Answer   7 − 4 = | Estimate | Answer

4 − 2 = | Estimate | Answer   5 − 4 = | Estimate | Answer

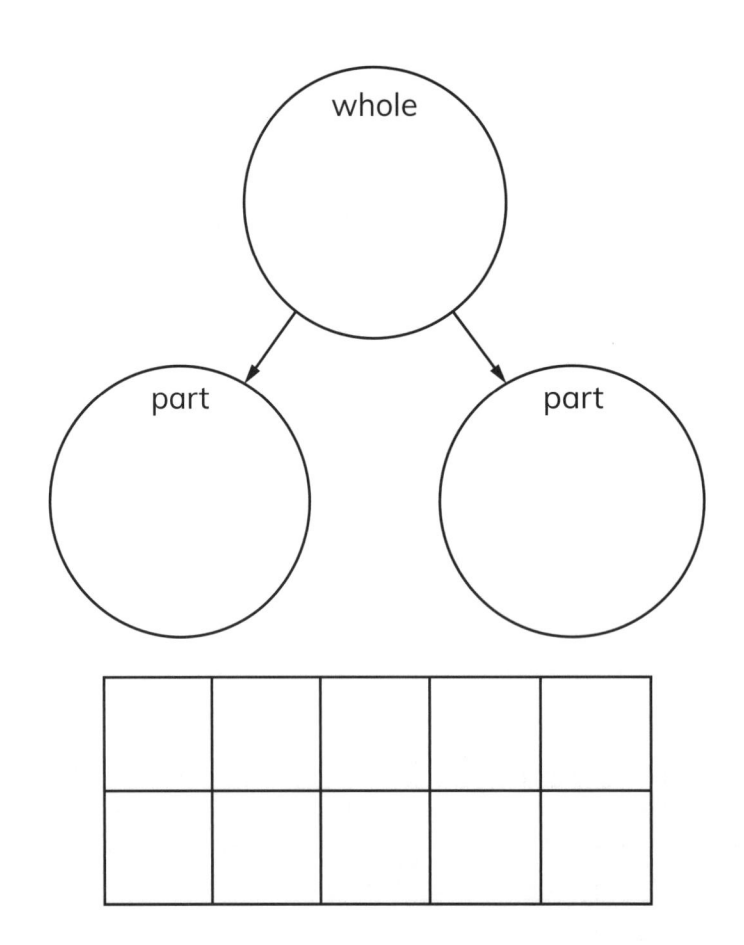

whole

part   part

5.2 Subtraction as take away

4 Complete each part-whole diagram.

   Write a number sentence for each diagram.

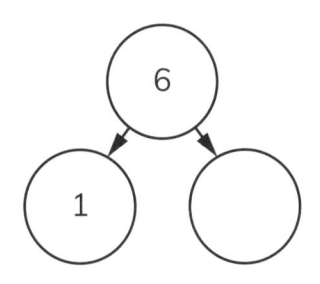

   ☐ – ☐ = ☐   ☐ – ☐ = ☐

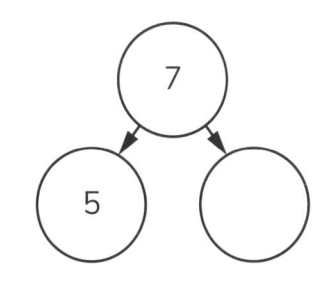

Practice

5 Write the number sentence for this story.

   First   Then   Now

   ☐ take away ☐ equals ☐

   ☐ – ☐ = ☐

65

5 Working with numbers to 10

6 Choose how many monkeys leave.

Write or draw the rest of the story.

Write a number sentence for your story.

First   Then   Now

☐ − ☐ = ☐

7 Complete each part-whole diagram.

Write a number sentence for each diagram.

8
↙ ↘
1   ◯

☐ − ☐ = ☐

8
↙ ↘
2   ◯

☐ − ☐ = ☐

8
↙ ↘
3   ◯

☐ − ☐ = ☐

8
↙ ↘
4   ◯

☐ − ☐ = ☐

Use the part-whole diagram in question 3 and some small objects to help you.

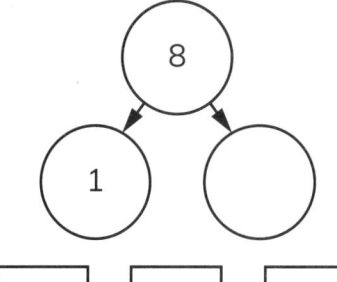

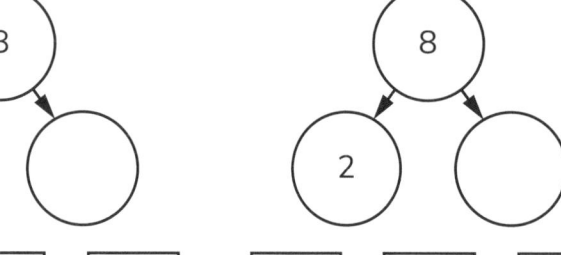

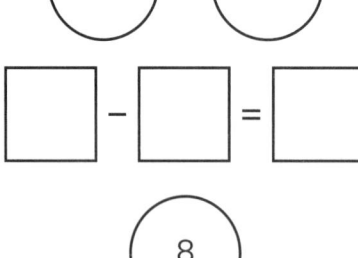

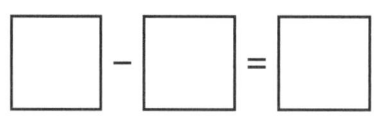

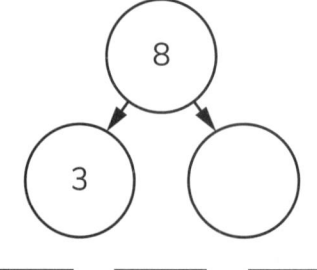

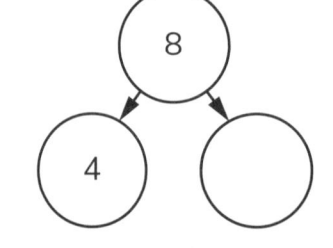

5.2 Subtraction as take away

Write your number sentences in a list.

Continue the list until you have found all the number sentences for 8 − ☐ = ☐.

8 Complete each subtraction wall.

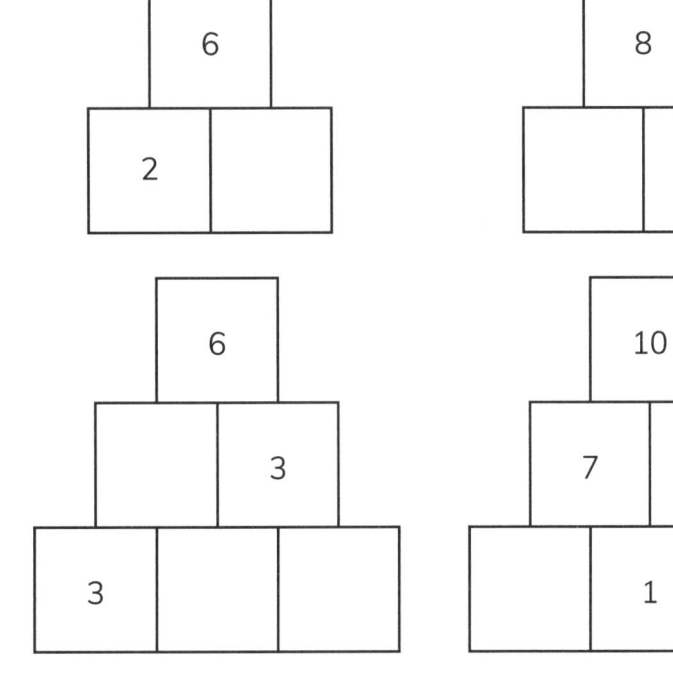

5 Working with numbers to 10

Challenge

9

| 0 | 1 | 2 | 3 | 4 | start 5 | 6 | 7 | 8 | 9 | 10 |

Place a bean on start, 5.

Use a paper clip and pencil to spin the spinner.

Move your bean along the number track, adding 1 or taking away 1.

You are aiming to reach 0 or 10.

How many spins did it take to get there?

Play with someone at home.

Take turns to spin the spinner and move your bean.

Who reached 0 or 10 first?

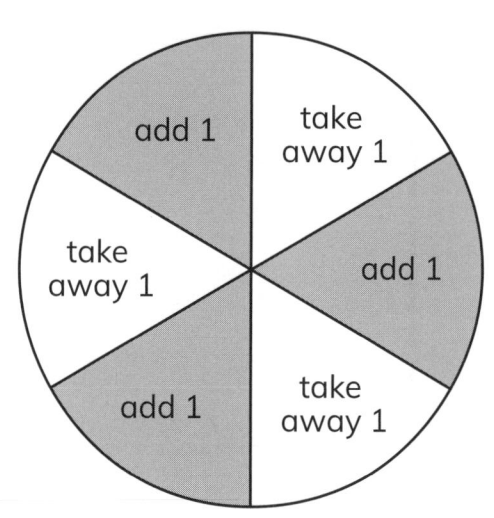

10 Complete each part-whole diagram.

Write a matching number sentence to show whether you added or subtracted to find the missing number.

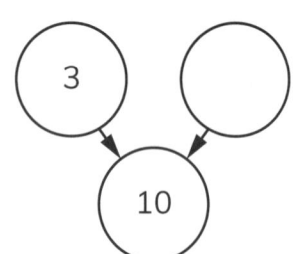

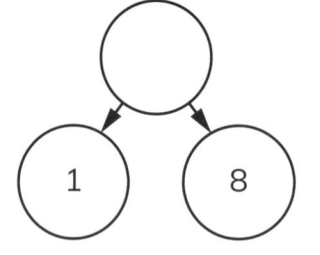

3 → 10 ←

☐ ○ ☐ = ☐

1 ← → 8

☐ ○ ☐ = ☐

Tip

Write + or – in each circle.

5.2 Subtraction as take away

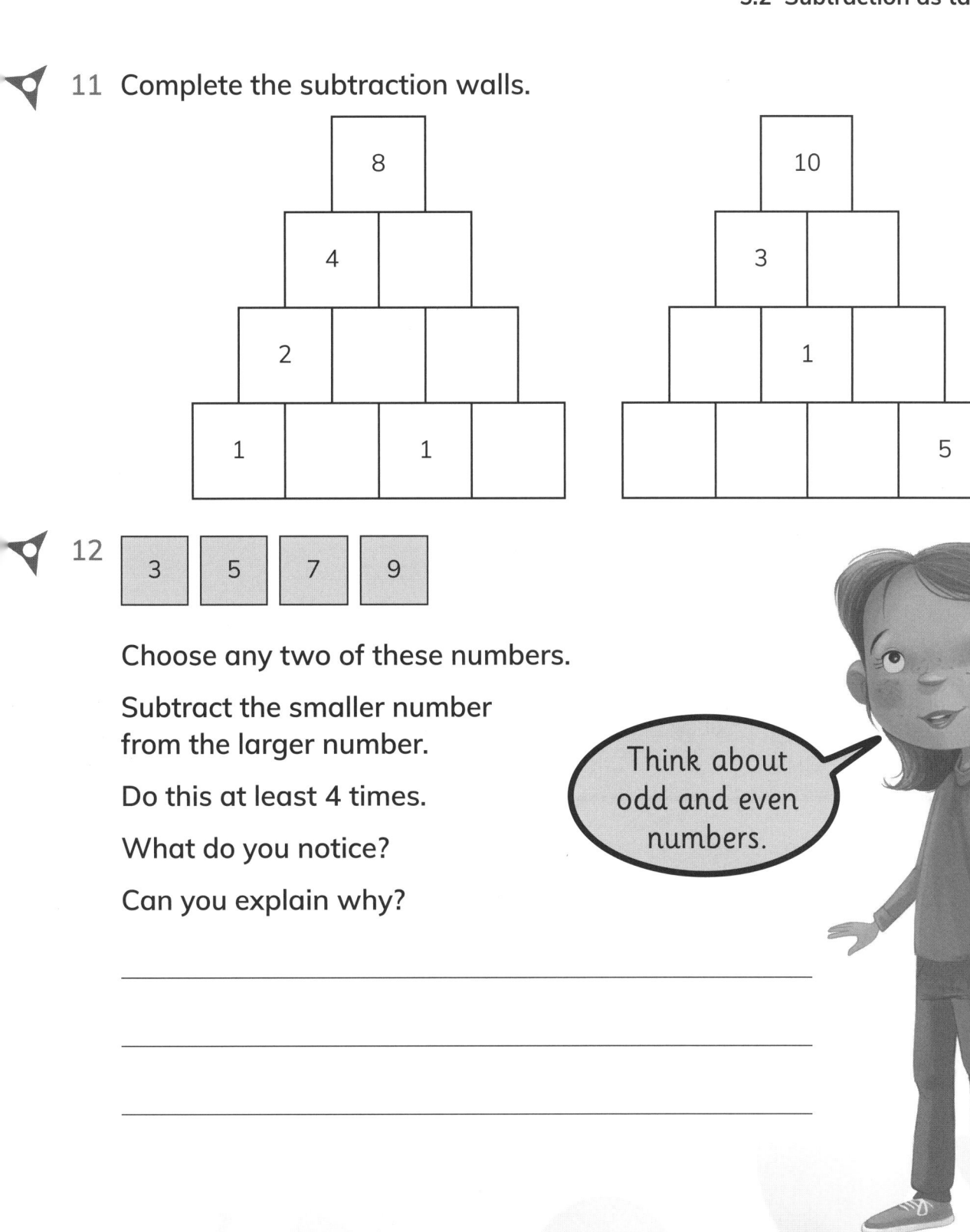

11 Complete the subtraction walls.

```
        [ 8 ]
      [ 4 ][   ]
    [ 2 ][   ][   ]
  [ 1 ][   ][ 1 ][   ]
```

```
        [ 10 ]
      [ 3 ][    ]
    [    ][ 1 ][    ]
  [    ][    ][    ][ 5 ]
```

12 [3] [5] [7] [9]

Choose any two of these numbers.

Subtract the smaller number from the larger number.

Do this at least 4 times.

What do you notice?

Can you explain why?

Think about odd and even numbers.

_____

_____

_____

6 Position

> 6.1 Position

Exercise 6.1

> above   behind   below   beside
> in front of   next to   on
> ordinal   position   under

Worked example 1

Draw a ring around the 1st and 5th bears.

Cross out the 3rd and 8th bears.

Shade the 6th and 10th bears.

1st   2nd   3rd   4th   5th   6th   7th   8th   9th   10th

Answer:

1st   2nd   3rd   4th   5th   6th   7th   8th   9th   10th

The 2nd, 4th, 7th and 9th bears are left.

70

6.1 Position

Focus

1. Draw a ball **next to** the boy.

   Draw a spider **under** the table.

   Draw a cloud **above** the tree.

   Draw a cat **beside** the fence.

   Draw a girl **under** the umbrella.

| Ball | Spider | Cloud | Cat | Girl |

6 Position

2 Colour the fourth snail to the right.

Colour the elephant to the left of the third elephant.

Colour the third cat.

1st

Colour the sixth car.

1st

6.1 Position

3 Write the **ordinal** number of the shaded object.
   The first one has been done for you.

   [Trees row, 7th shaded] → 7th
   1st

   [Tulips row, 5th shaded] →
   1st

   [Pine trees row, 8th shaded] →
   1st

   [Flowers row, 6th shaded] →
   1st

   [Bushes row, 2nd shaded] →
   1st

4 Colour the 2nd and 7th scarves yellow.
   Colour the 9th and 1st scarves blue.
   Colour the 3rd and 10th scarves red.
   Colour the 5th and 6th scarves green.

   Which scarves are not coloured? ☐ ☐

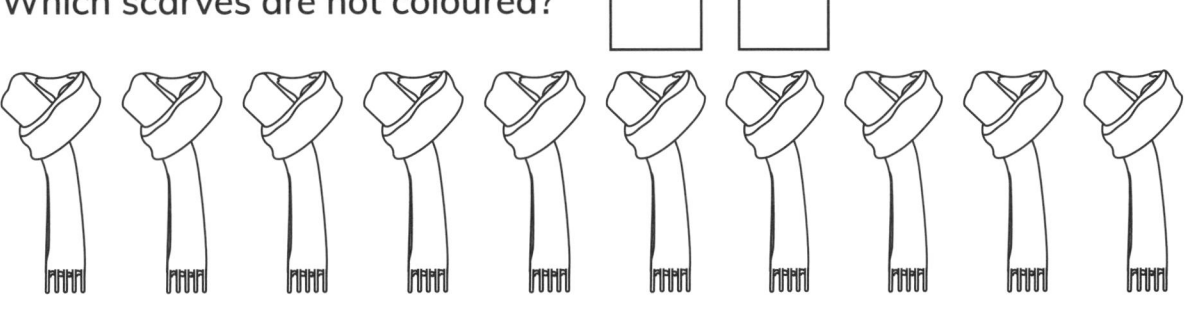

   1st   10th

6 Position

Practice

5   Write the missing ordinal numbers.

1st _____ _____ _____ _____ 6th _____ _____ _____ _____

6   Draw lines to match the ordinal number with the ordinal number word.

1st   seventh

3rd   first

5th   tenth

7th   third

10th   fifth

6.1 Position

7 Here is a set of insects.

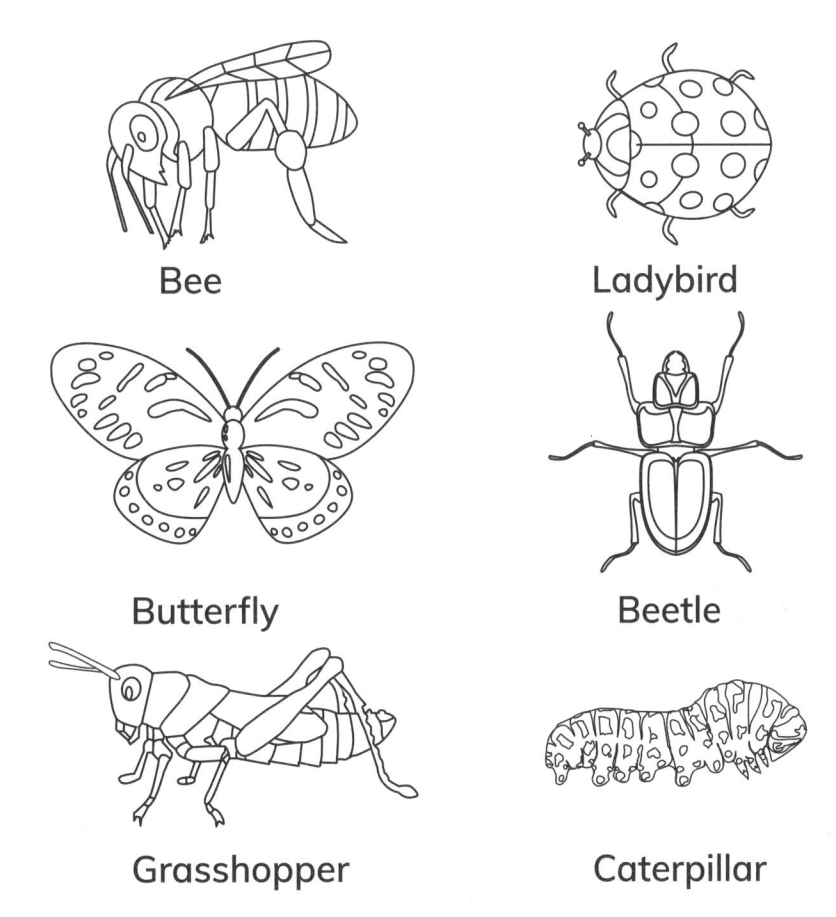

Bee

Ladybird

Butterfly

Beetle

Grasshopper

Caterpillar

Draw a ring around the insect above the butterfly.

Draw a cross ✗ through the insect below the beetle.

Draw a ring around the insect above the beetle.

Colour the insects between other insects.

Colour the insect that is left a different colour.

8 Draw a worm between the birds.

75

6 Position

Challenge

9   Colour the shape between the squares yellow.

Colour the shape between the triangles green.

Colour the shapes above the squares blue.

Colour the shape below the circle red.

Add a row or column of shapes to the pattern.

Colour the shapes to match the pattern.

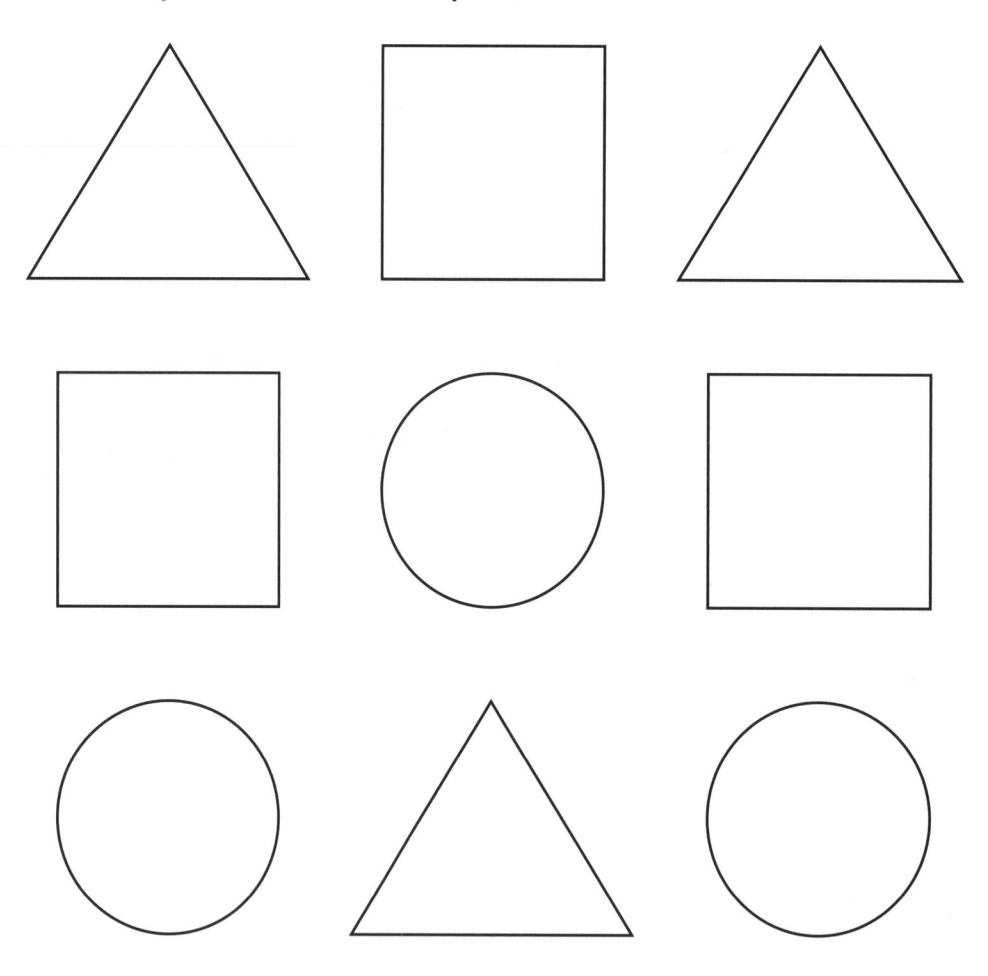

6.1 Position

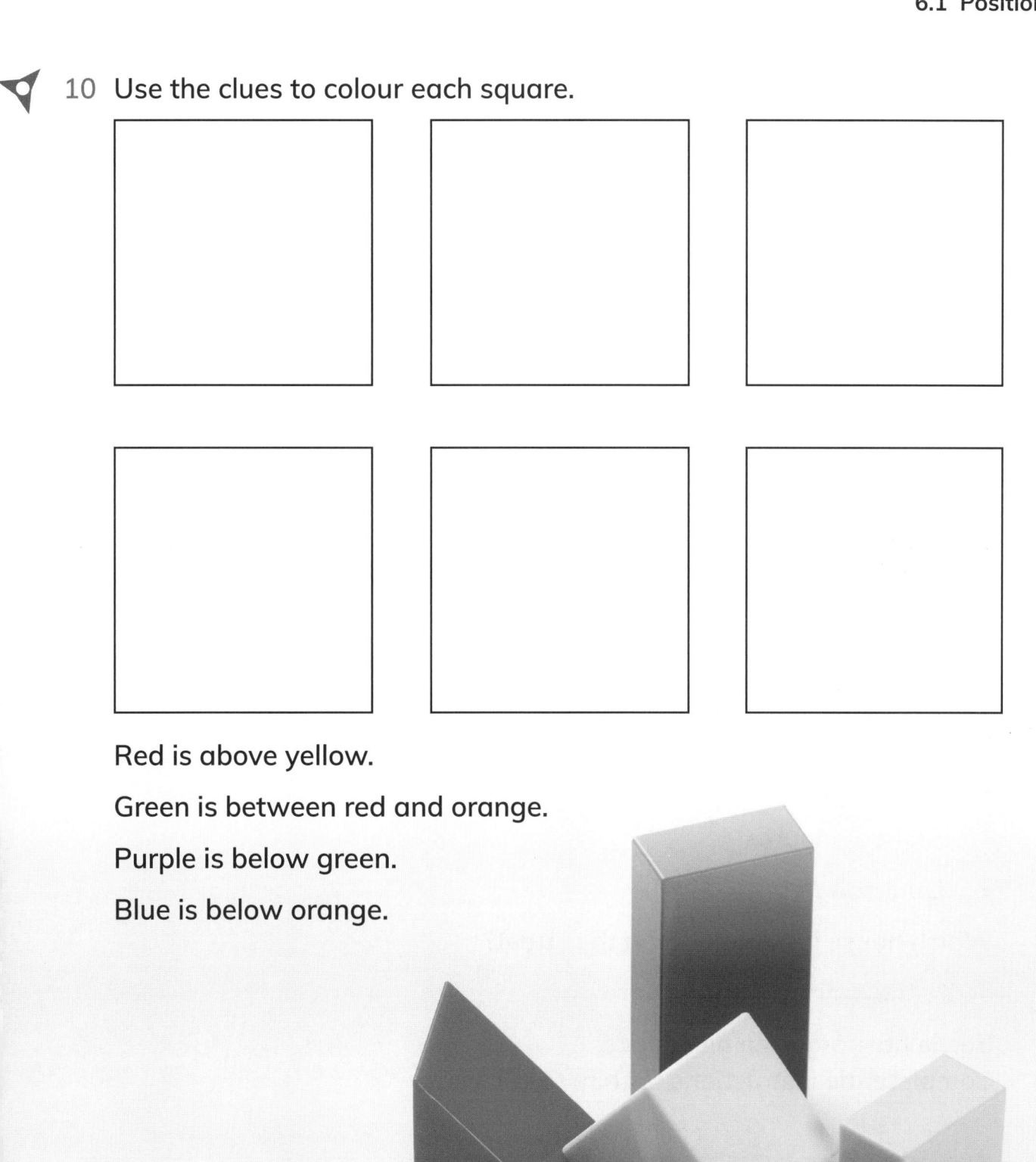

10 Use the clues to colour each square.

Red is above yellow.

Green is between red and orange.

Purple is below green.

Blue is below orange.

6 Position

11

Bertie the tortoise travels the following route:

- Up 1 square
- Right 3 squares
- Up 2 squares

Which house is he visiting on the street?

Write the ordinal number word. _____

Bertie has forgotten his lettuce.
Complete the instructions for him to collect it.

_____

_____

_____

7 Statistics

> 7.1 Sets

Exercise 7.1

Focus

> data   group   set   sort

Worked example 1

Sort the stars.

Draw lines to show where each star belongs.

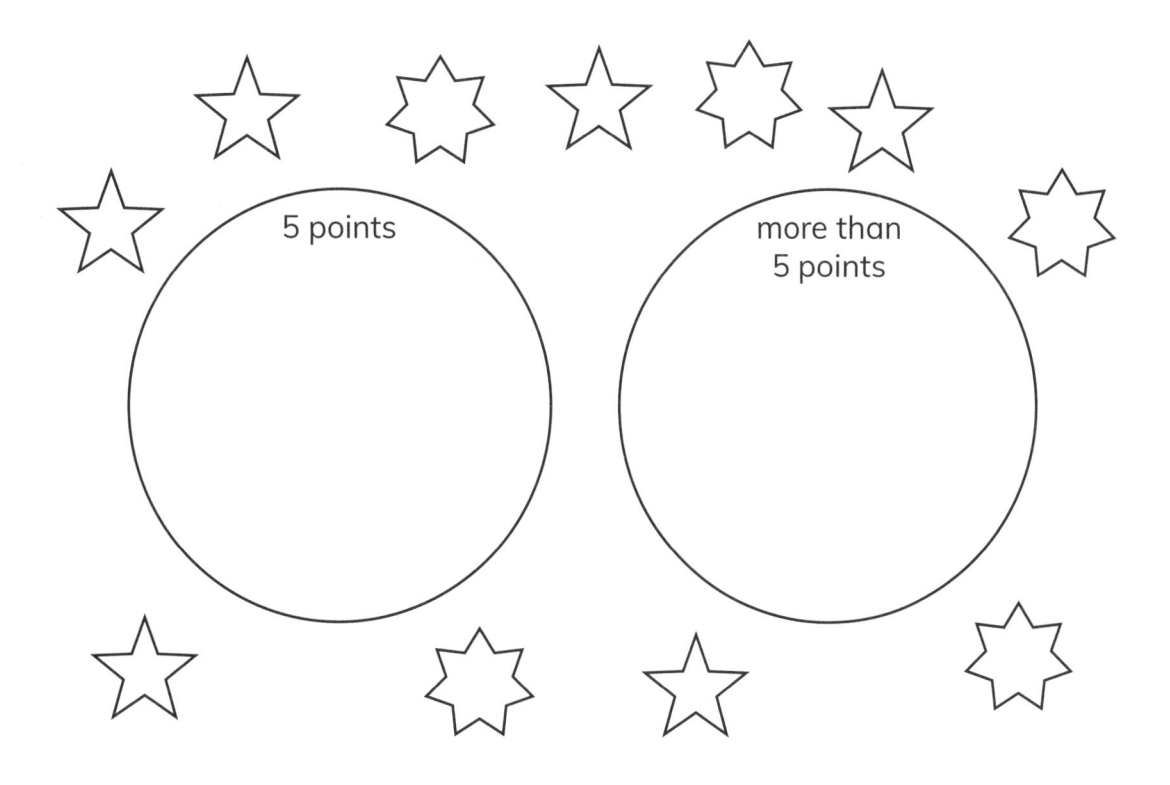

- 5 points
- more than 5 points

79

7 Statistics

Continued

Answer:

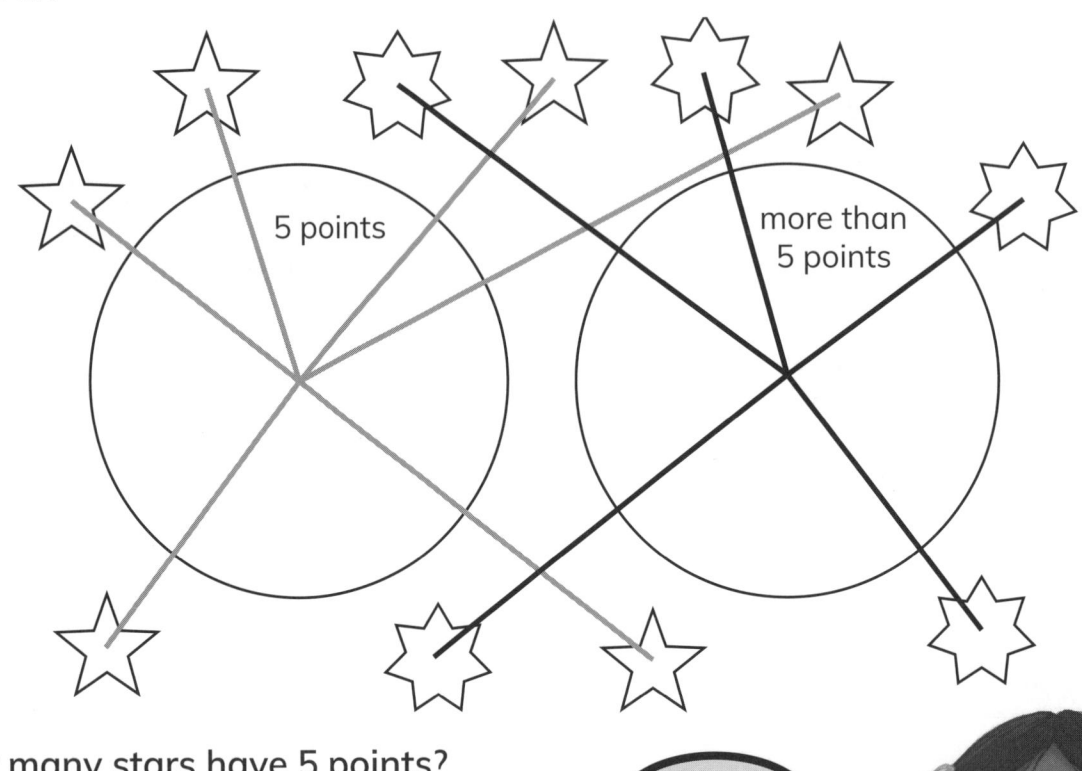

How many stars have 5 points?   6!

How many stars have more than 5 points?   5!

There are more stars with 5 points.

There are fewer stars with more than 5 points.

7.1 Sets

1. Draw lines to sort each pair of shoes into the 2 sets.

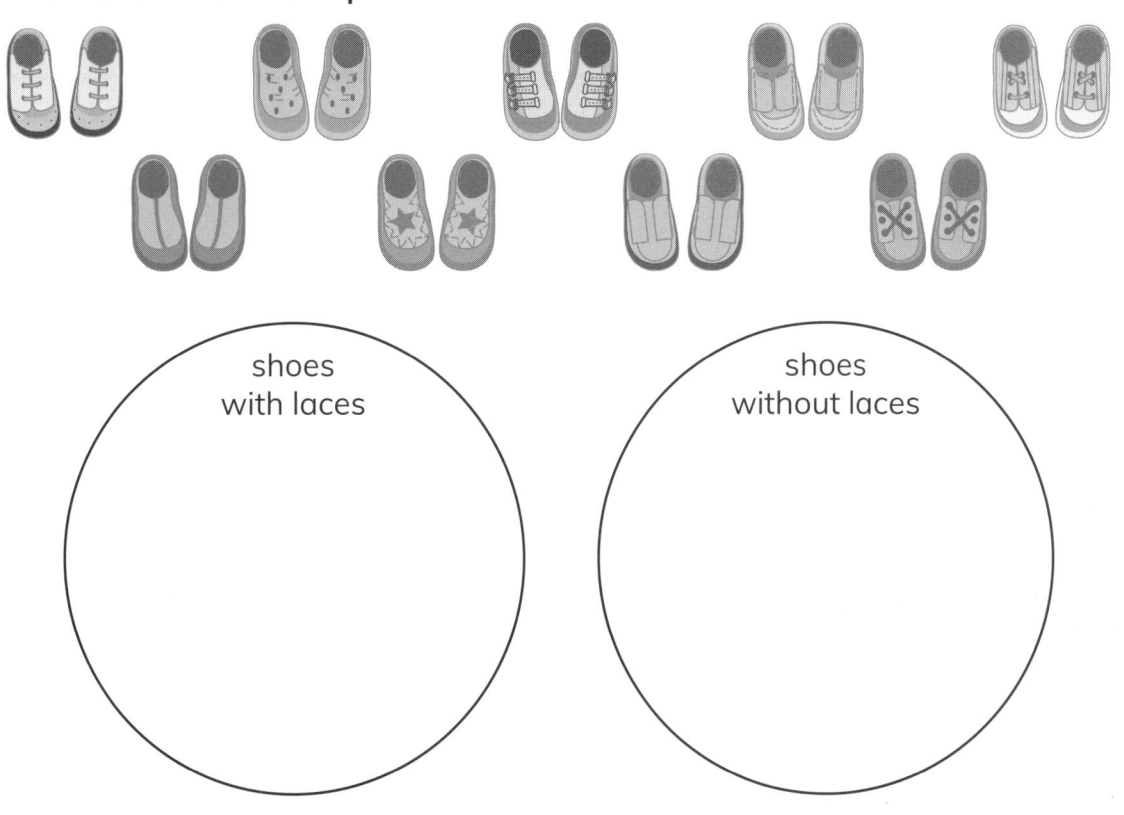

shoes with laces

shoes without laces

2. Draw the buttons in the correct set.

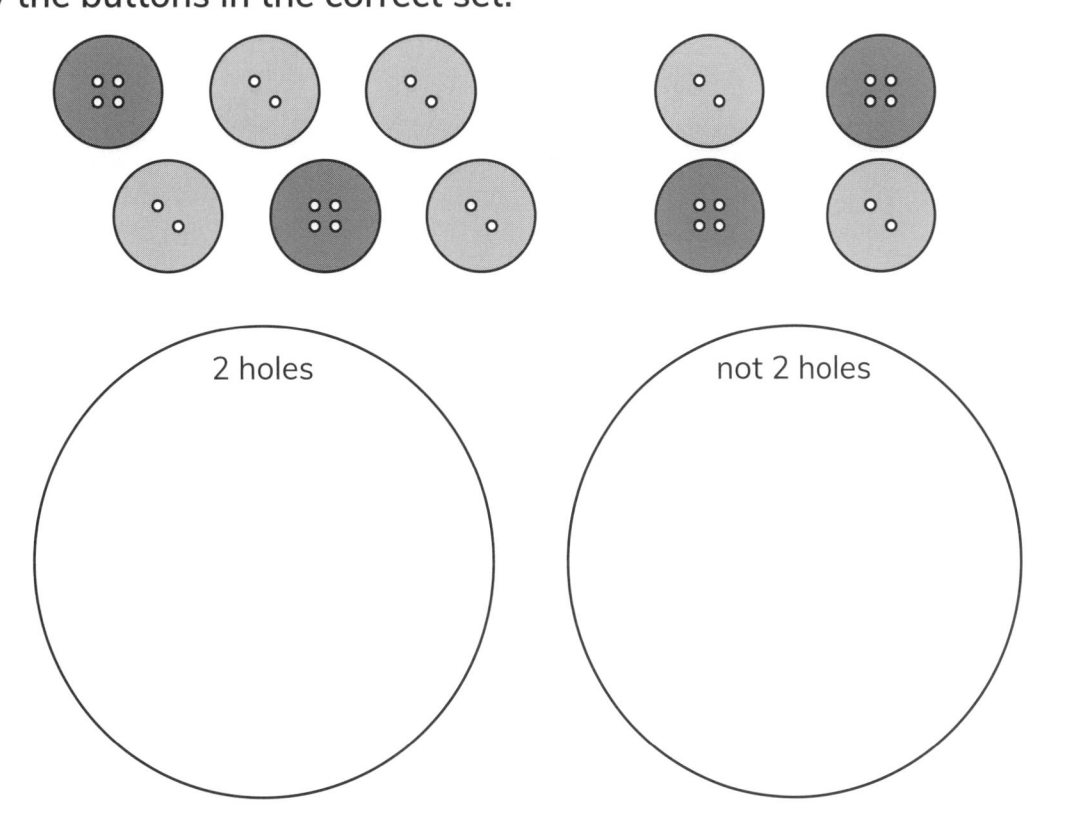

2 holes

not 2 holes

7 Statistics

3   Ask at least 3 people what their favourite fruit is.
    Write their names and draw their favourite fruit.

Practice

4   The cats are sorted into two sets.

    sitting   not sitting

    How many cats are sitting? ☐

    How many cats are not sitting? ☐

    How many cats are there altogether? ☐

    Don't forget to add your labels.

7.1 Sets

Find a different way to sort this group of cats. Write the label for each circle. Then write the letter for each cat in the correct circle.

A B C

D E F

83

7 Statistics

5 How do you get to school?

A group of children come to school by car, bike, bus or on foot. Sort these ways into 2 sets.

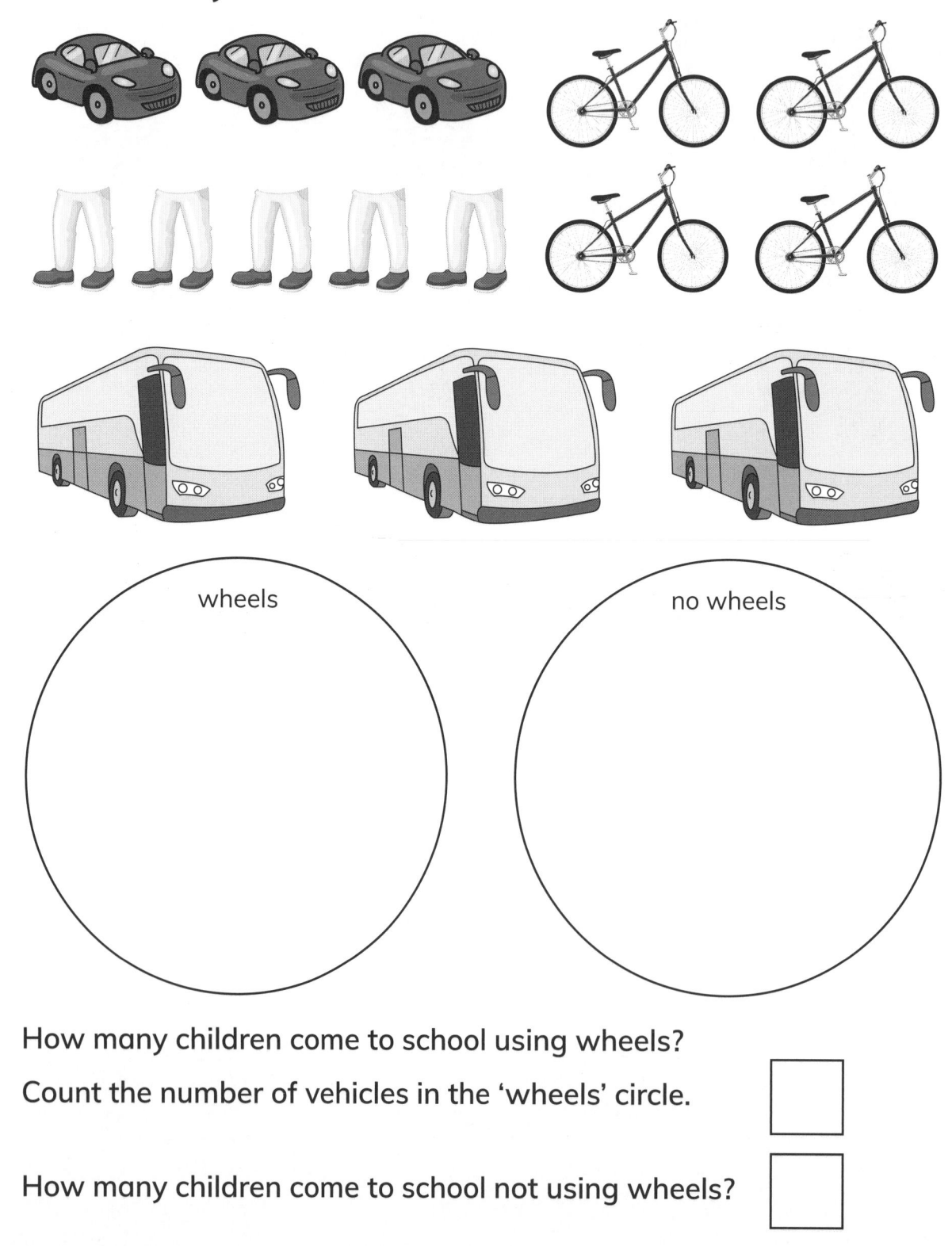

wheels

no wheels

How many children come to school using wheels?

Count the number of vehicles in the 'wheels' circle.

How many children come to school not using wheels?

6   Zara asks her family for their favourite animals.

Mum likes [zebra]

Dad likes [cat]

Grandma likes [cat]

Grandpa likes [zebra]

Her brother likes [lion]

Her sister likes [zebra]

Draw a ring around the correct answers.

Which animal is liked by the most people?

[zebra]   [cat]   [lion]

Which animal is liked by the fewest people?

[zebra]   [cat]   [lion]

7 Statistics

Challenge

7 Find 2 different ways to sort this group of socks into 2 sets.

Don't forget to write your labels.

8 Draw lines to sort these objects into 2 sets.

Write labels to show how they are sorted.

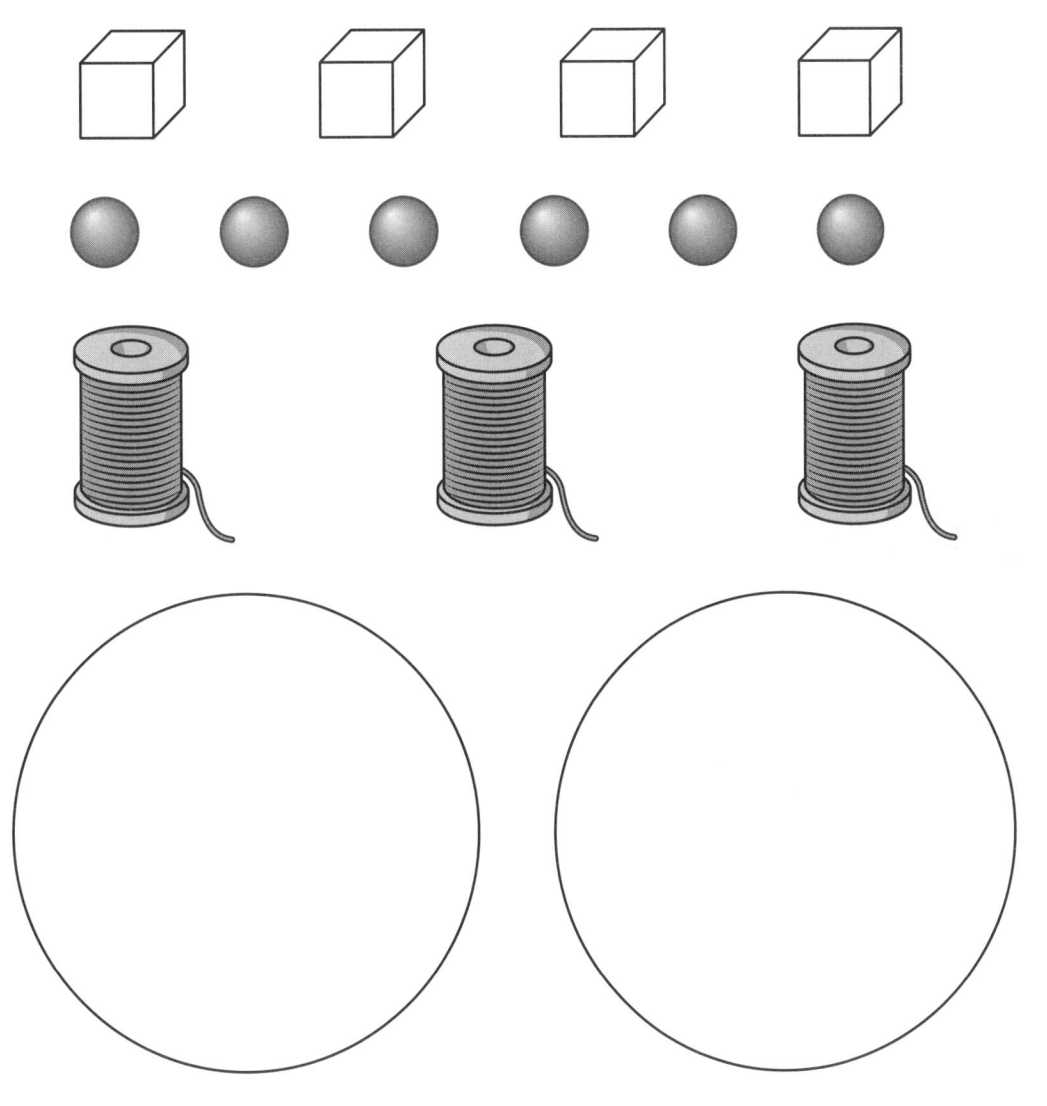

How else could you sort the objects?
Talk to a parent or carer about your answer.

7 Statistics

9 Sort these animals into 2 sets. Write labels for each circle. Then write each letter into the correct circle.

Tell a parent or carer about 2 things that the sorting activity has shown you. Try to use the words **most, least, more than** and **less than**.

> 7.2 Venn diagrams

Exercise 7.2

Focus

Venn diagram

> **Worked example 2**
>
> Sort the flowers into the Venn diagram.
>
> flowers with only 3 leaves

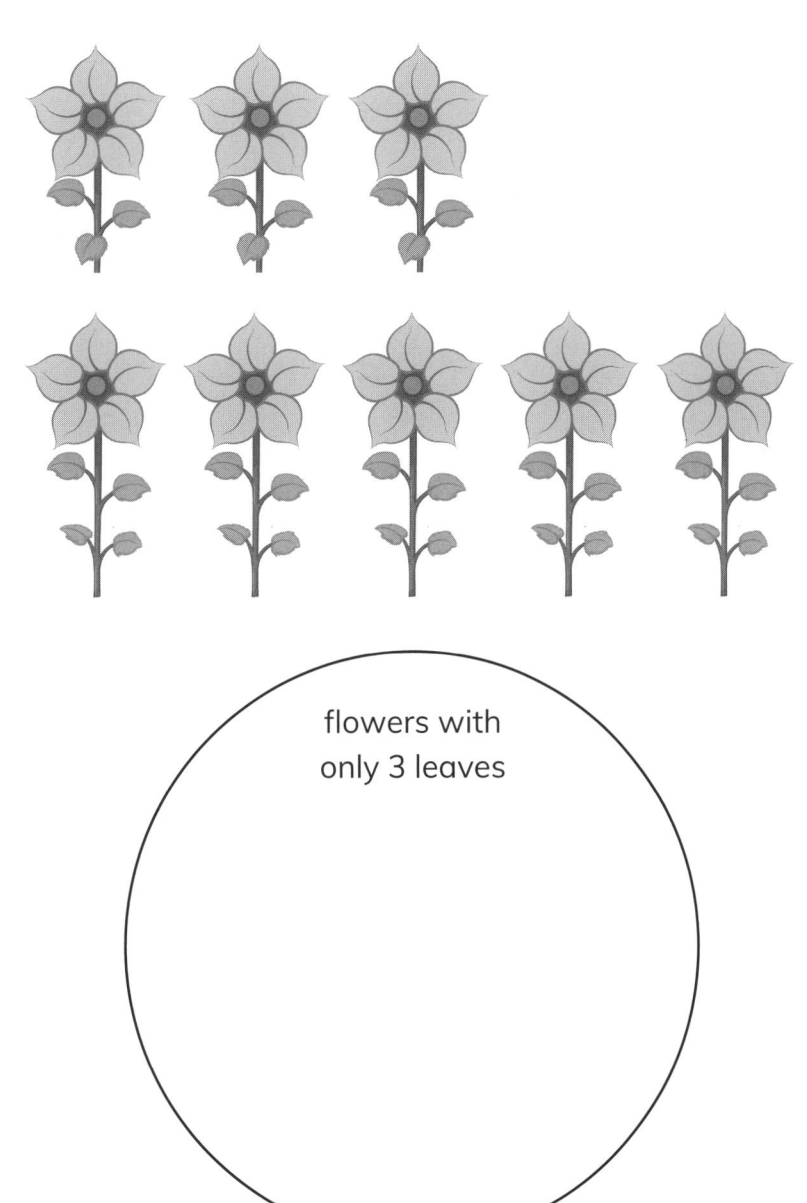

89

7 Statistics

Continued

Answer:

flowers with only 3 leaves

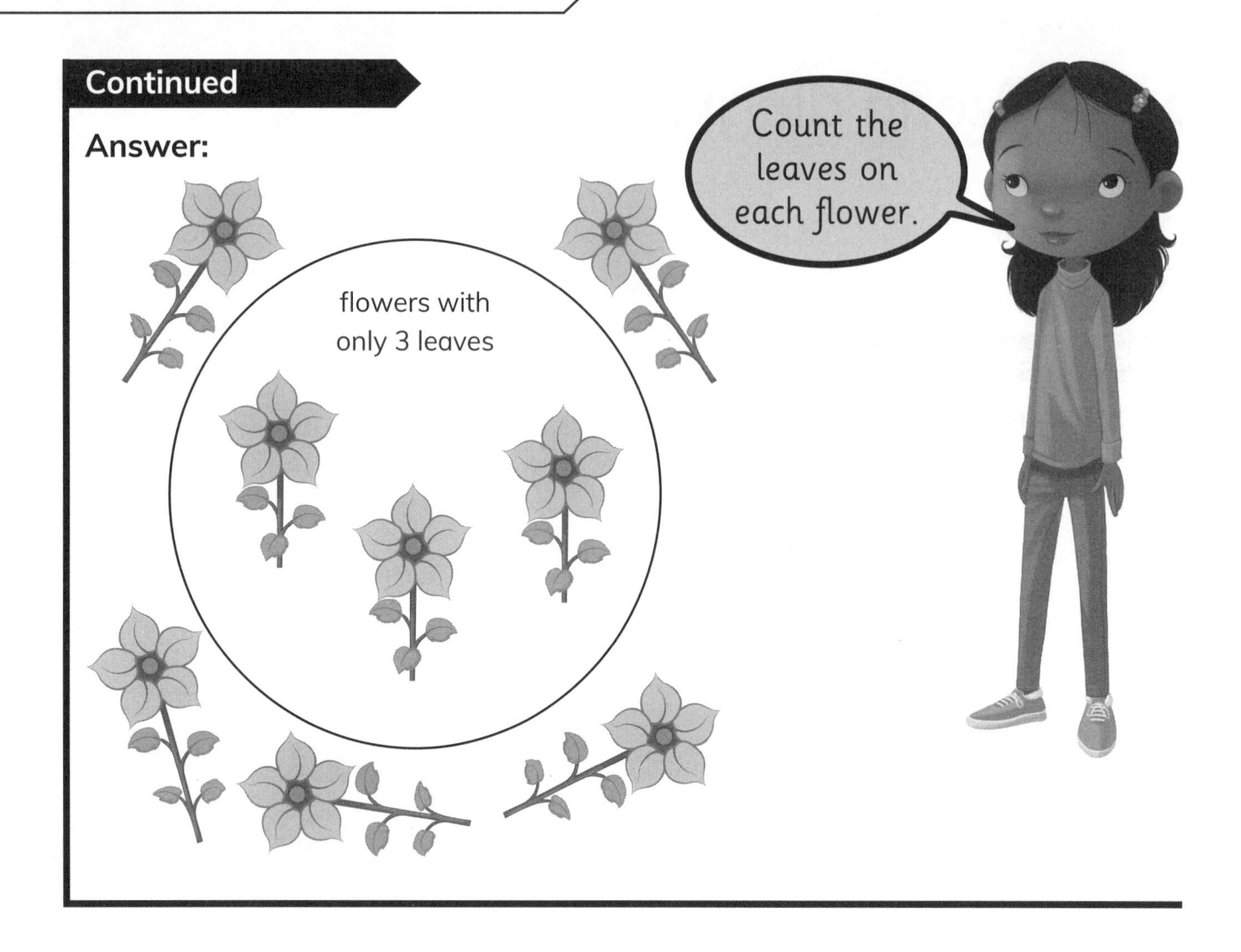

Count the leaves on each flower.

1 Look at the Venn diagram in Worked example 1 and answer these questions.

How many flowers with only 3 leaves?

How many flowers with more than 3 leaves?

Draw a ring around the correct word.

There are **more / fewer** flowers with 3 leaves than flowers with 4 leaves.

7.2 Venn diagrams

2 Label the circles.

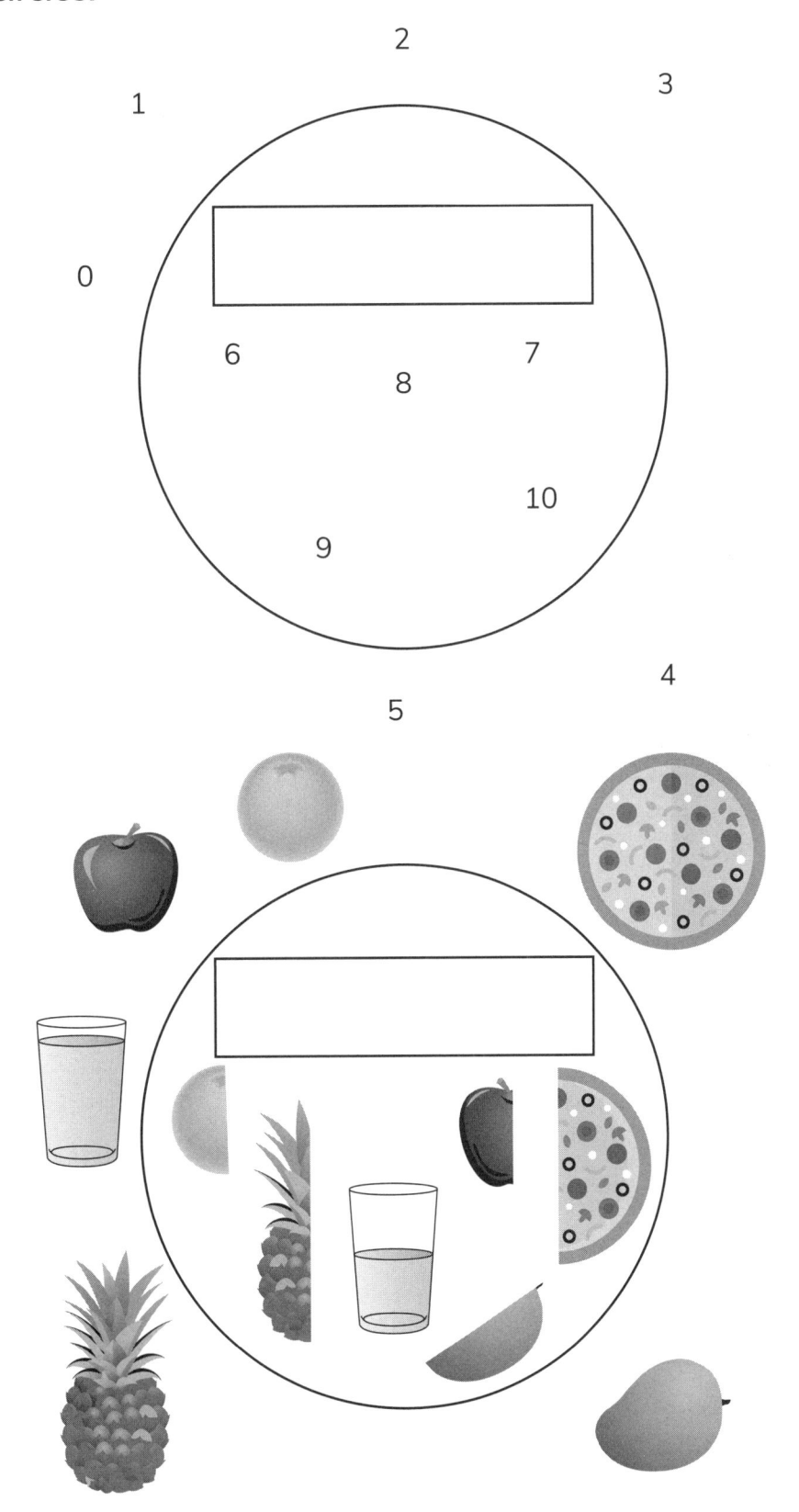

7 Statistics

Practice

3   Draw lines to sort the vehicles into the Venn diagram.

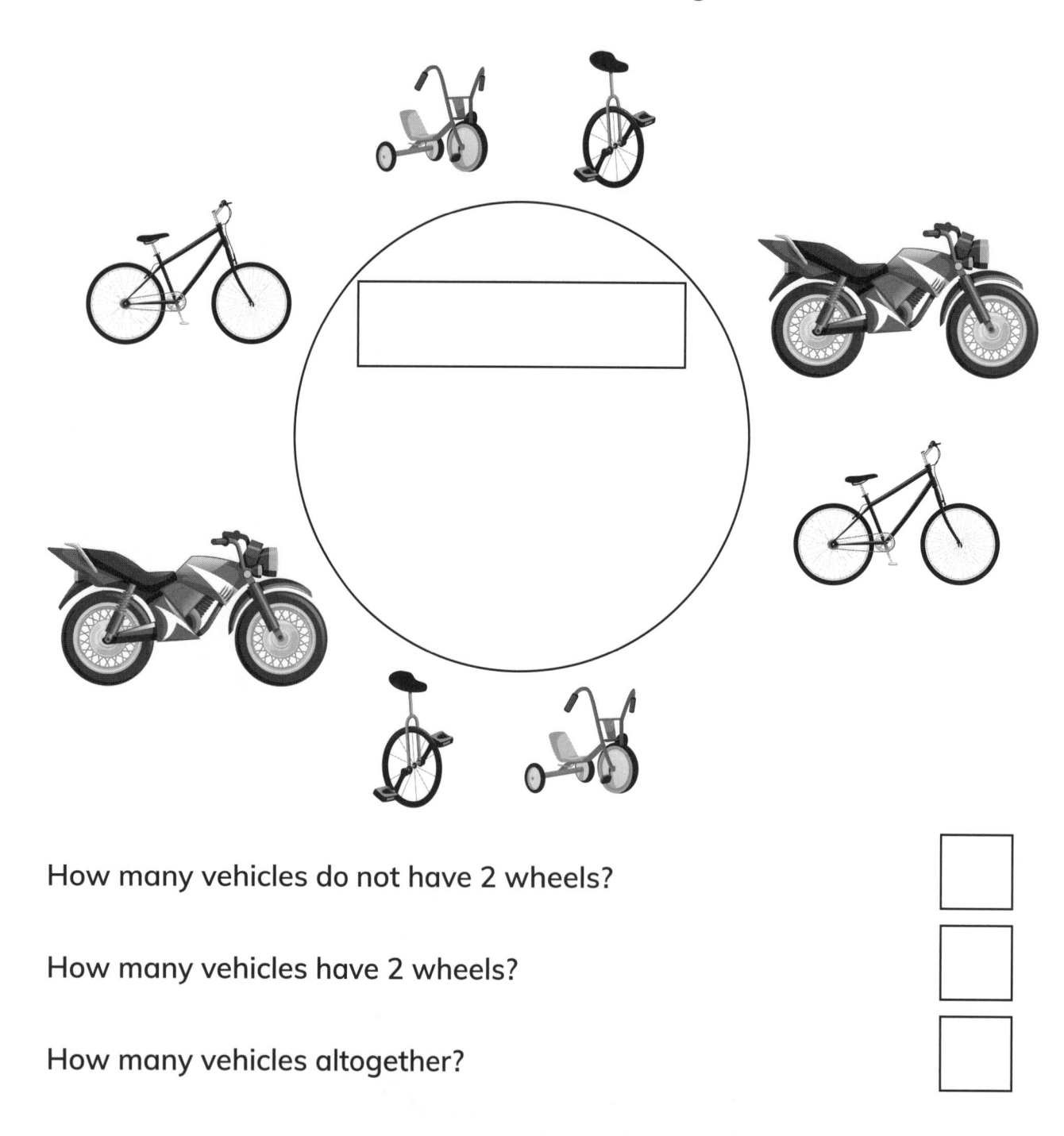

How many vehicles do not have 2 wheels?

How many vehicles have 2 wheels?

How many vehicles altogether?

4 Look at the shapes.

Some have straight sides. Some have curved sides.

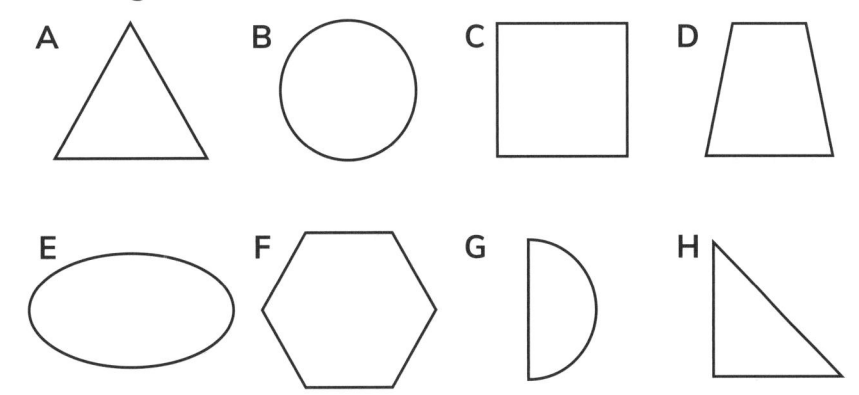

A △   B ○   C □   D ▱

E ⬭   F ⬡   G ⌓   H ◿

Draw and label a Venn diagram.

Sort the shapes into the correct place on the Venn diagram based on whether they have curved or straight sides.

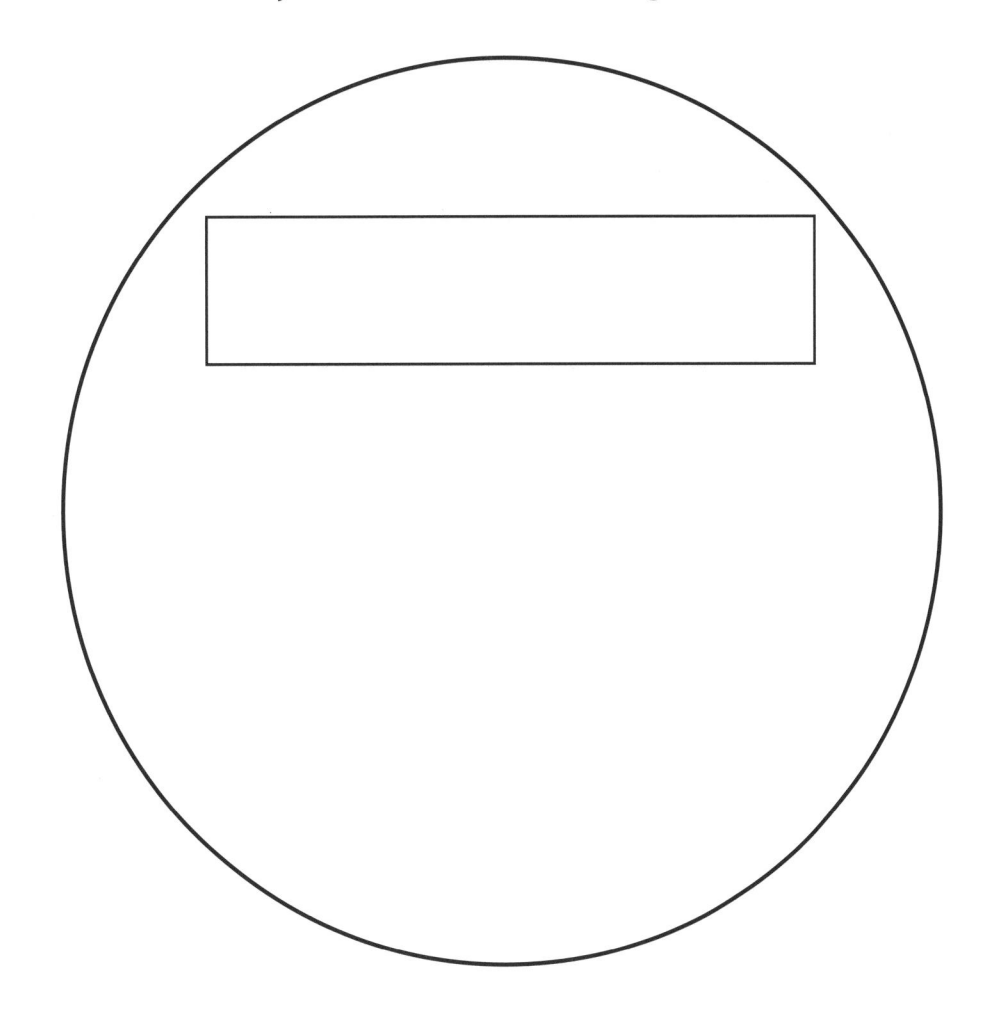

7 Statistics

Challenge

5 Select 2 labels for the Venn diagram from the box. Draw lines to sort the children into the Venn diagram based on the labels you have chosen.

plays tennis	does not play tennis
plays sports	plays football
plays baseball	does not play baseball
does not play sports	does not play football

7.2 Venn diagrams

6 Select 2 labels for the Venn diagram from the box. Draw lines to sort the animals into the Venn diagram based on the labels you have chosen.

animals	cannot swim
can fly	can walk
cannot fly	cannot walk
can swim	not animals

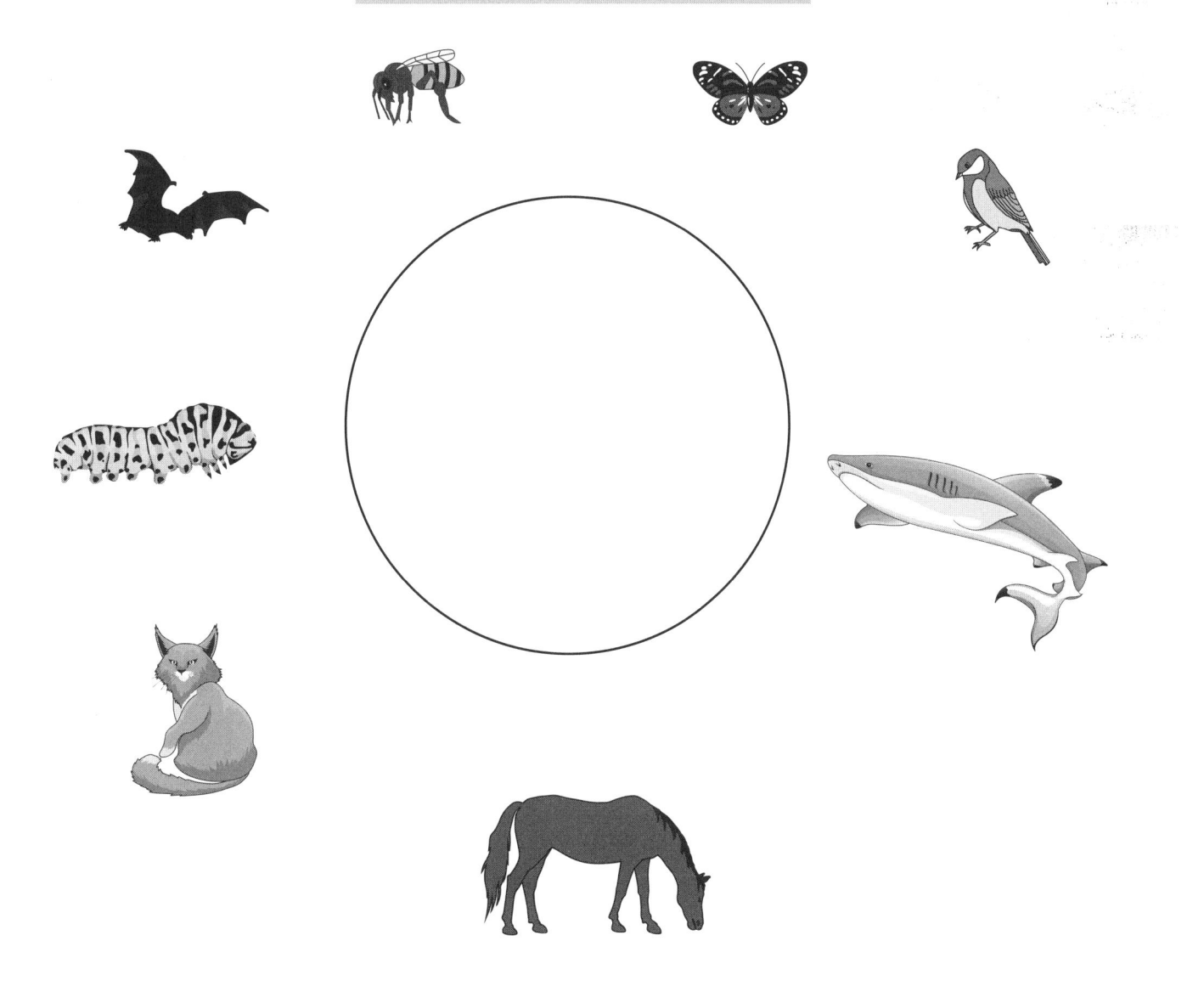

7 Statistics

7. Use this group of objects to make your own Venn diagram.

8 Time

> 8.1 Time

Exercise 8.1

> afternoon   clock   evening   half past
> hands   hour   minute   o'clock   today
> tomorrow   week   yesterday

Focus

1 Write **morning**, **afternoon** or **evening** next to the pictures.

Travel to school

_____

Eat your lunch

_____

Go to bed

_____

Draw something you did yesterday.

8 Time

2. A clock has numbers and hands.

   The long hand is the minute hand.

   The short hand is the hour hand.

   The long minute hand is pointing to 12.

   The short hour hand is pointing to 2.

   This clock shows 2 o'clock.

   What are the times on these clocks?

   _____ o'clock   _____ o'clock

3. The minute hand has moved to 6.

   The clock now says half past.

   Write the times.

   Half past _____   Half past _____

4   Write the times these clocks show.

_____   _____   _____

5   Colour the days.

Monday: yellow

Tuesday: orange

Wednesday: blue

Thursday: green

Friday: purple

Saturday: pink

Sunday: red

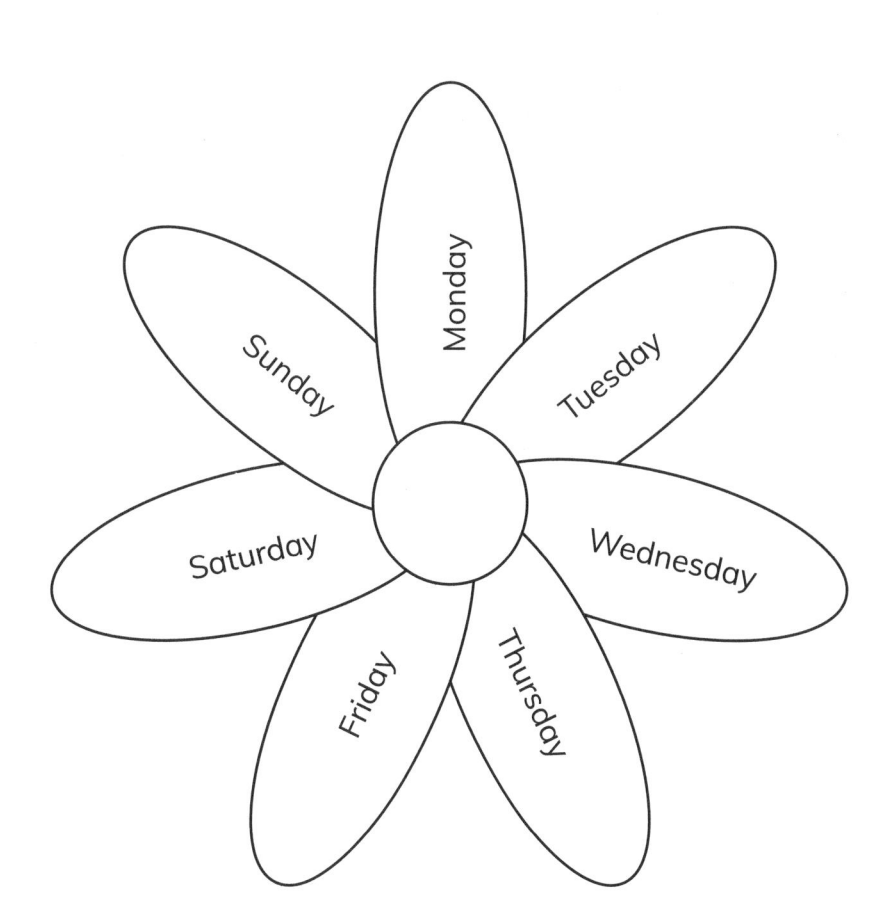

8 Time

6   Here are the days of the week.

Monday   Tuesday   Wednesday   Thursday   Friday   Saturday   Sunday

What day is it today? Draw a ring around your answer.

Draw what you are going to do tomorrow at school.

Practice

7   Write the numbers on the clock.

8.1 Time

8 Draw a ring around the clock that matches the words.

Hickory Dickory Dock,
The mouse ran up the clock.
The clock struck 1,
The mouse ran down,
Hickory Dickory Dock.

9 Draw a ring around the clock that matches the words.

Hickory Dickory Dock,
The mouse ran up the clock.
The clock struck 4,
He ran out of the door,
Hickory Dickory Dock.

10 Draw a ring around the clock that matches the words.

Hickory Dickory Dock,
The mouse ran up the clock.
The clock struck 2,
The mouse lost a shoe,
Hickory Dickory Dock.

11 Draw a ring around the clock that matches the words.

Hickory Dickory Dock,
The mouse ran up the clock.
The clock struck 6,
Oh, fiddlesticks!
Hickory Dickory Dock.

8 Time

12 Draw the hour hand on the clock to show the time in the rhyme.

Hickory Dickory Dock,
The mouse ran up the clock.
The clock struck 7,
The cat tried to get him,
Hickory Dickory Dock.

13 Draw the hands on the clock to show the time in the rhyme.

Hickory Dickory Dock,
The mouse ran up the clock.
The clock struck 8,
He ran out the gate,
Hickory Dickory Dock.

14 Write the times these clocks show.

_____   _____   _____

15 Write the correct day in each empty space.

Monday   Tuesday   Wednesday   Thursday   Friday   Saturday   Sunday

| Sunday | Monday | |

| | Tuesday | Wednesday |

| Thursday | | Saturday |

| | Friday | Saturday |

16 Draw and write about something that happens once a year.

8 Time

Challenge

17 Draw the hands on the clocks to match the times.

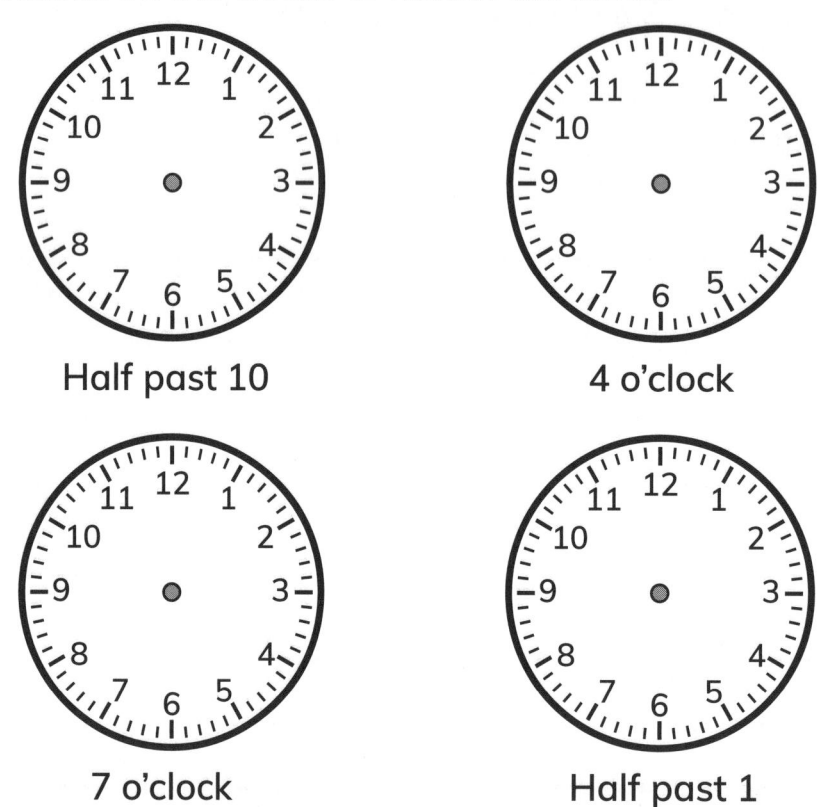

Half past 10   4 o'clock

7 o'clock   Half past 1

18 What time will it be in 1 hour? Draw the new time on the clock.

19
> It is eight o'clock in the evening. In three hours, it will be tomorrow.

Is Marcus correct? Explain your answer to a parent or carer.

9 Numbers to 20

> 9.1 Counting to 20

Exercise 9.1

> place value cards   teen numbers

Focus

1 Write the missing numbers.

1	2	3	4	5	6	7	8	9	10
11	12	13		15	16		18		20

2 Write the missing numbers.

| 14 | |

| 12 | | |

| 18 | | |

3 Which numbers can you make with these place value cards?

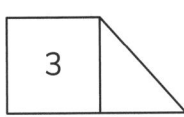

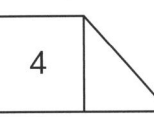

   1 0   3   4   5

9 Numbers to 20

4 Complete these part-whole diagrams.

```
    12              17
   ↙ ↘            ↙ ↘
  ○   10         7   ○
```

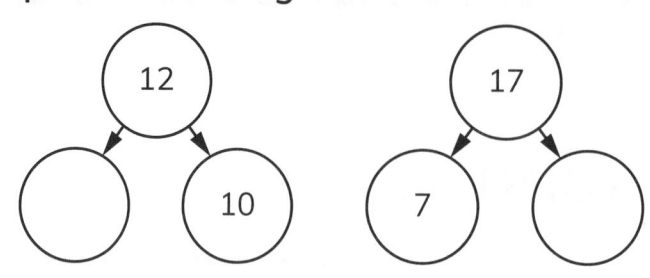

5 Write these numbers in words.

Use these words to help you.

| six seven eight |

16	
17	
18	

Practice

6 Write the missing numbers.

| | 16 | | | | 12 | | | | | 14 |

7 All the odd numbers are missing from a set of place value cards.

Which numbers between 10 and 20 can you make?

8 Complete these part-whole diagrams.

```
     10               ○
    ↙ ↘             ↙ ↘
  10   ○          10   10
```

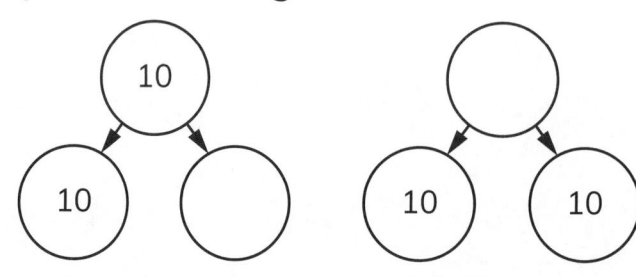

9 Write these numbers in words.

12	
14	
19	

Challenge

10 Count back from 20.

What is the fourth teen number you say? ☐

11 Write the missing numbers.

14 = ☐ tens and ☐ ones   17 = ☐ tens and ☐ ones

1 ten and 6 ones = ☐   2 tens and 0 ones = ☐

12

> I need one each of the digits 0, 1, 2, 3, 4, 5, 6, 7, 8 and 9 and an extra 10 ones to write all the numbers from 10 to 20.

Is Sofia right?

How do you know?

_____

_____

9 Numbers to 20

> 9.2 Counting, comparing, ordering and estimating

Exercise 9.2

> digit   number line

Focus

1   How many objects are there?

Use your ten and some ones strips to help you write the numbers.

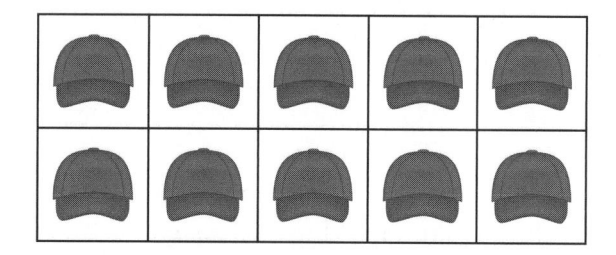

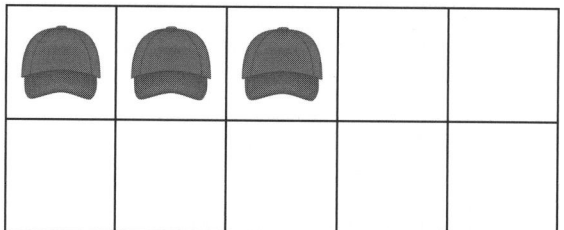

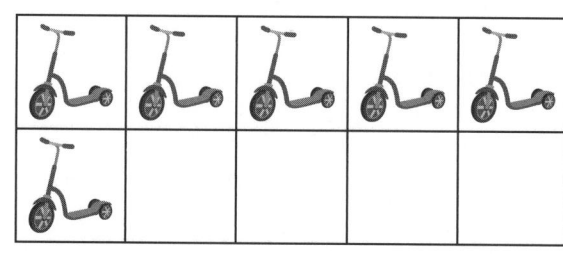

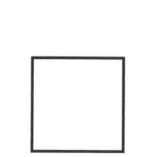

2   Draw some more beads on the bead string so that there are 14 beads altogether.

Complete the place value cards for the bead string.

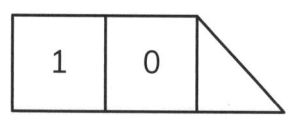

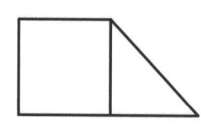

1 0   1 4

9.2 Counting, comparing, ordering and estimating

Worked example 1

Are there fewer pencils or books? Estimate then count to check.

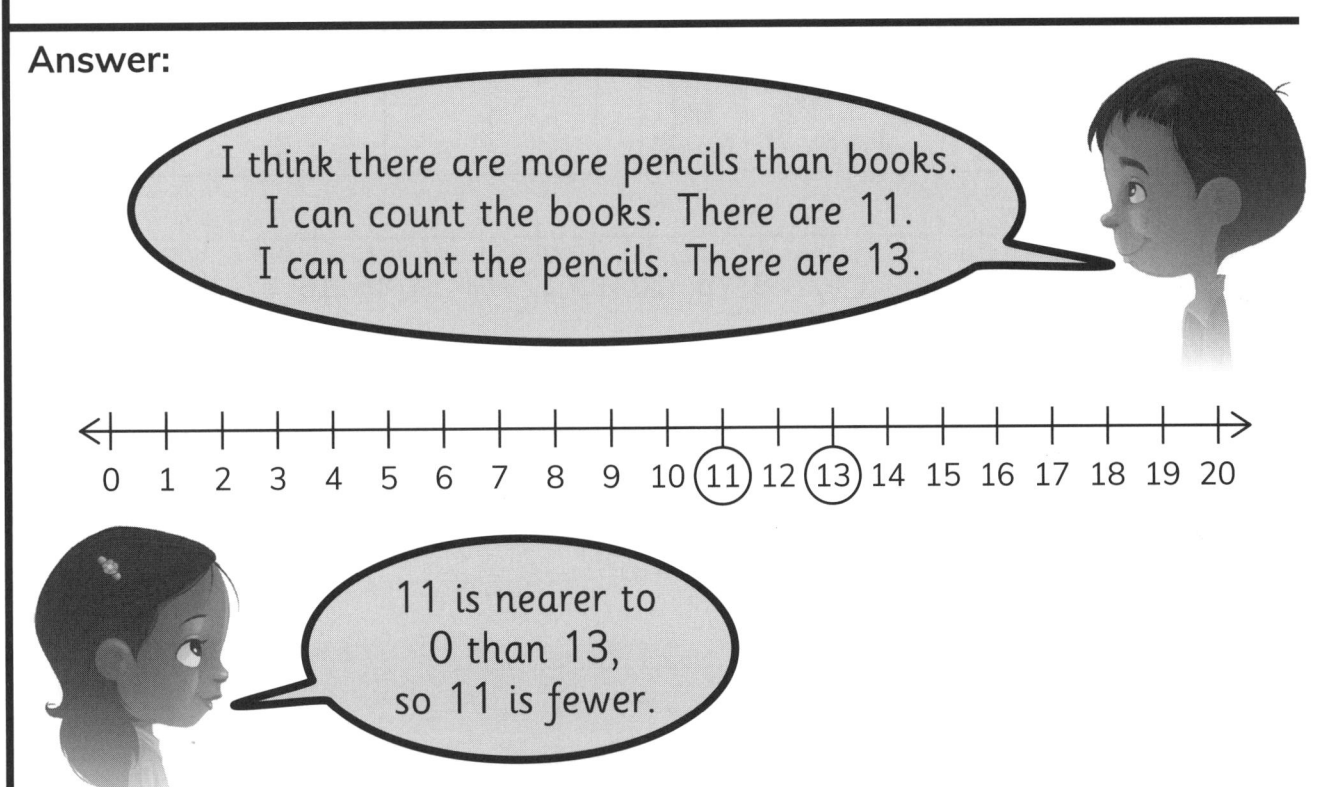

Answer:

> I think there are more pencils than books.
> I can count the books. There are 11.
> I can count the pencils. There are 13.

0 1 2 3 4 5 6 7 8 9 10 (11) 12 (13) 14 15 16 17 18 19 20

> 11 is nearer to 0 than 13, so 11 is fewer.

There are fewer books than pencils.

9 Numbers to 20

3   Are there fewer teddy bears or dolls?

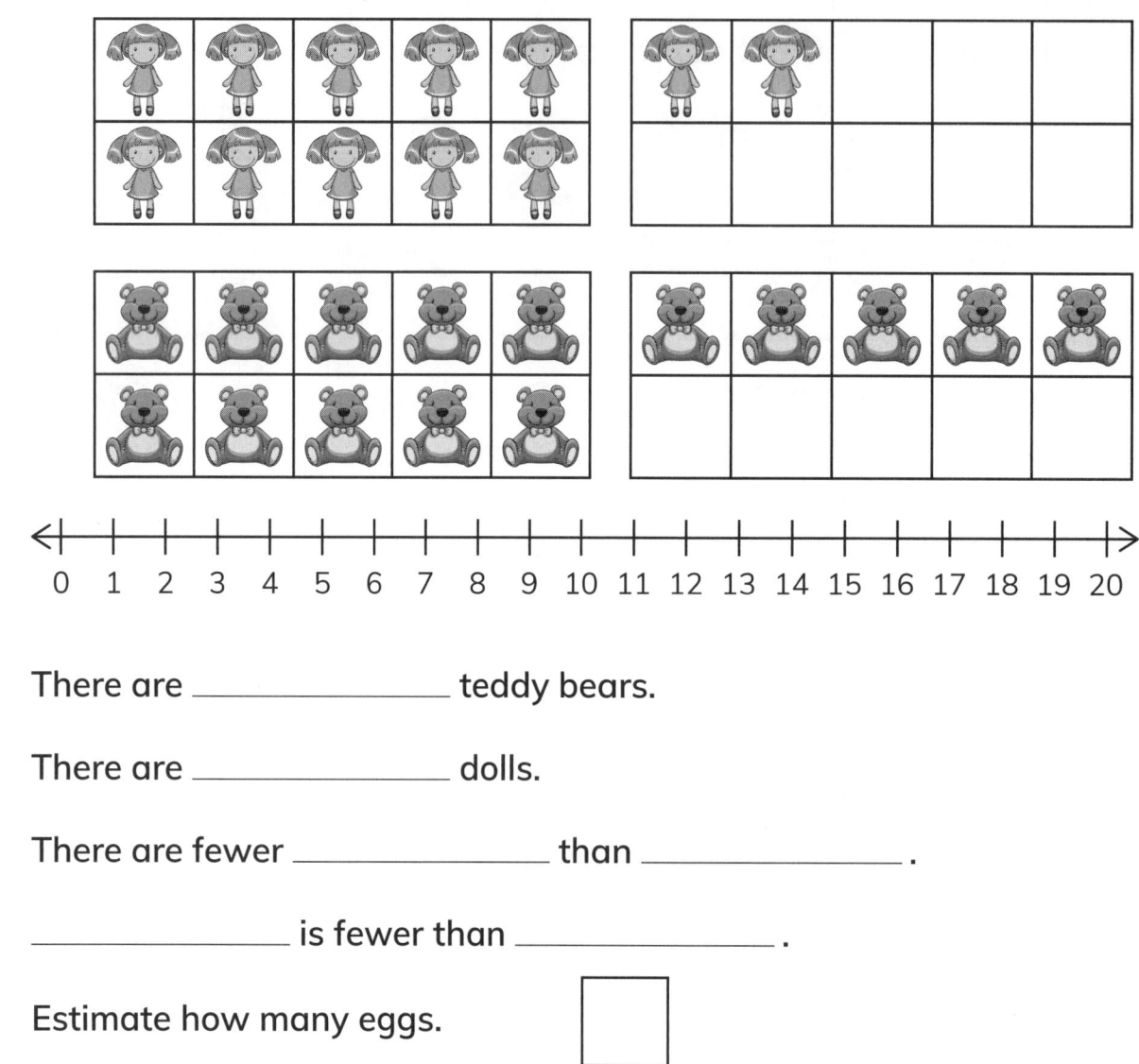

There are _____ teddy bears.

There are _____ dolls.

There are fewer _____ than _____ .

_____ is fewer than _____ .

4   Estimate how many eggs. ☐

    Estimate how many egg cups. ☐

Is there an egg cup for every egg?

Count the eggs and count the egg cups to see if you were correct.

9.2 Counting, comparing, ordering and estimating

5   Mark 6 and 15 on the number line.

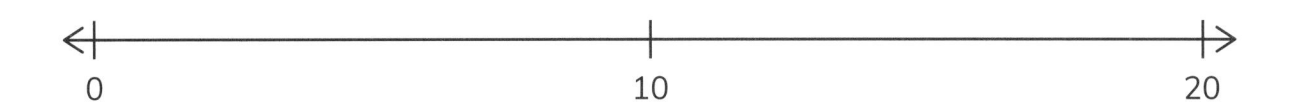

```
<----|--------------------------------|--------------------------------|---->
     0                                10                               20
```

6   Count out 10 pasta shapes.

Then count out 20 pasta shapes.

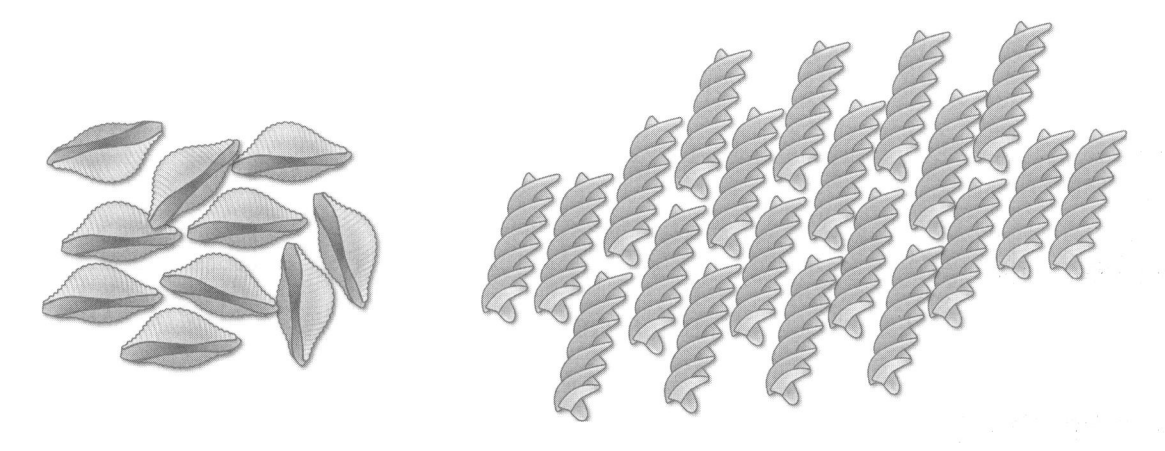

Now take a handful of pasta shapes.

Compare your handful with the piles.

Estimate how many in your handful.

Estimate:

| Fewer than 10 | 10 to 20 | Number |

Now count the pasta shapes in your handful. ☐

9 Numbers to 20

Practice

7   Draw the correct number of counters.

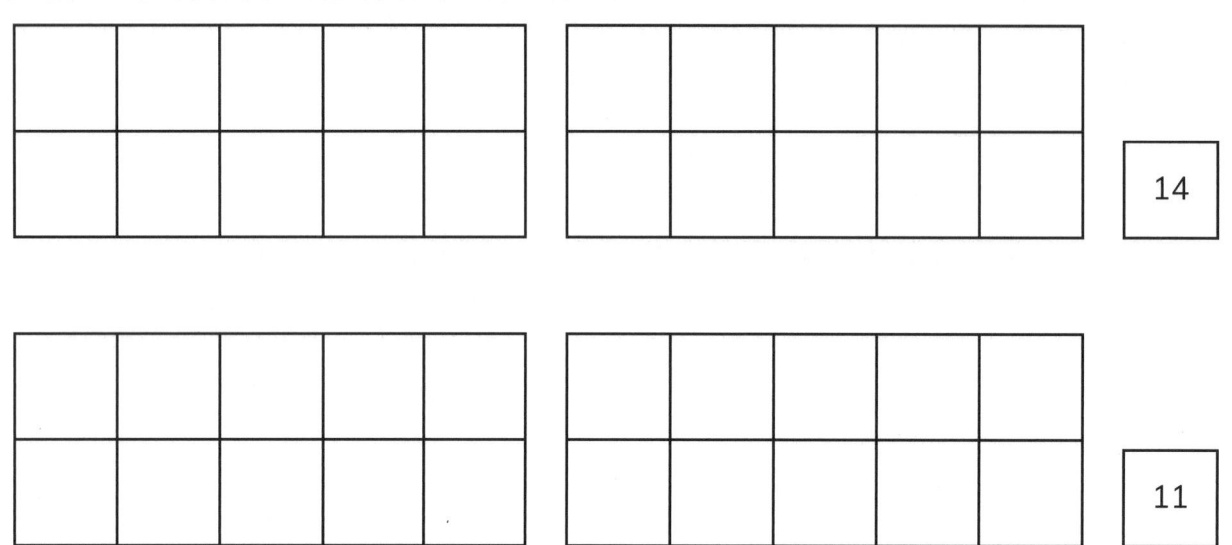

	14

	11

Tick ✓ the set that has the greater number of counters.

8   Estimate if there is a spoon for every bowl.

Then count the bowls and the spoons and compare.

Are there fewer bowls or spoons?

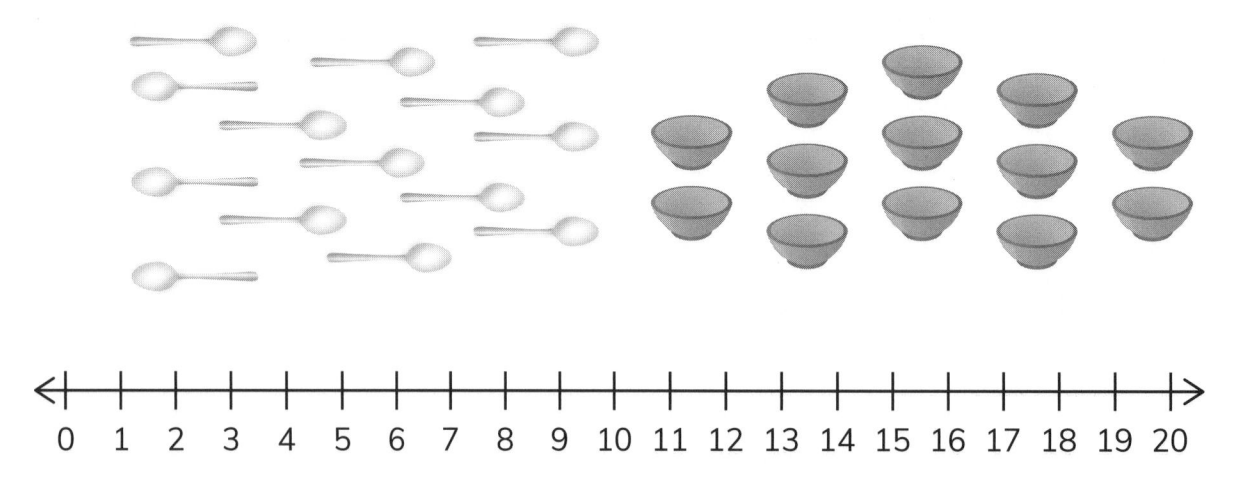

There are _____ spoons.

There are _____ bowls.

112

9.2 Counting, comparing, ordering and estimating

There are fewer _____ than _____ .

_____ is fewer than _____ .

Now that you have counted the bowls and spoons, is there a spoon for every bowl?

9 ⟵|—|—|—|—|—|—|—|—|—|—|—|—|—|—|—|—|—|—|—|—|⟶
   0 1 2 3 4 5 6 7 8 9 10 11 12 13 14 15 16 17 18 19 20

Write **less**, **fewer**, **more** or **greater** to complete the sentences.

19 is _____ than 15.

15 is _____ than 19.

17 is _____ than 15.

15 is _____ than 17.

Put the numbers 19, 15 and 17 in order, from smallest to greatest.

smallest		greatest

10 Mark 4 and 17 on the number line.

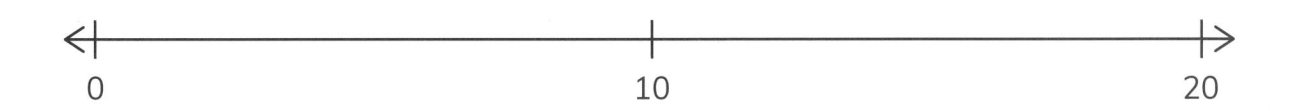

⟵|—————————————|—————————————|⟶
0   10   20

9 Numbers to 20

11 Estimate how many rabbits. ☐

Estimate how many carrots. ☐

Is there a carrot for every rabbit?

Count the carrots and count the rabbits to see if you were correct.

9.2 Counting, comparing, ordering and estimating

12 Look at one dragonfly.

Imagine what 10 dragonflies might look like.

Then imagine what 20 dragonflies might look like.

Estimate how many dragonflies are in the picture.

Do the same for butterflies.

Dragonflies

Estimate:

| Fewer than 10 | 10 to 20 | Number |

Count: ☐

Butterflies

Estimate:

| Fewer than 10 | 10 to 20 | Number |

Count: ☐

115

9 Numbers to 20

Challenge

13 There are 8 cars parked in the car park.
7 more cars park in the car park.

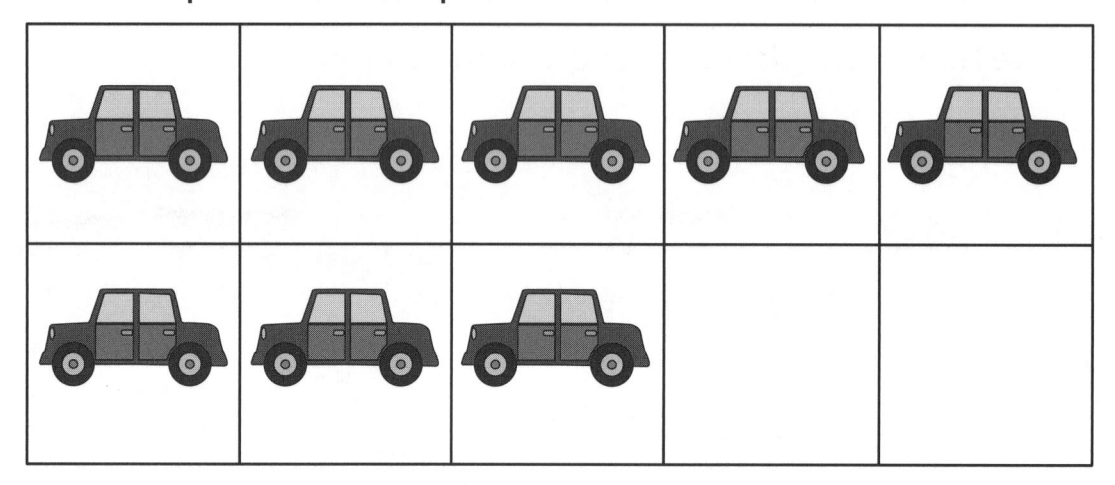

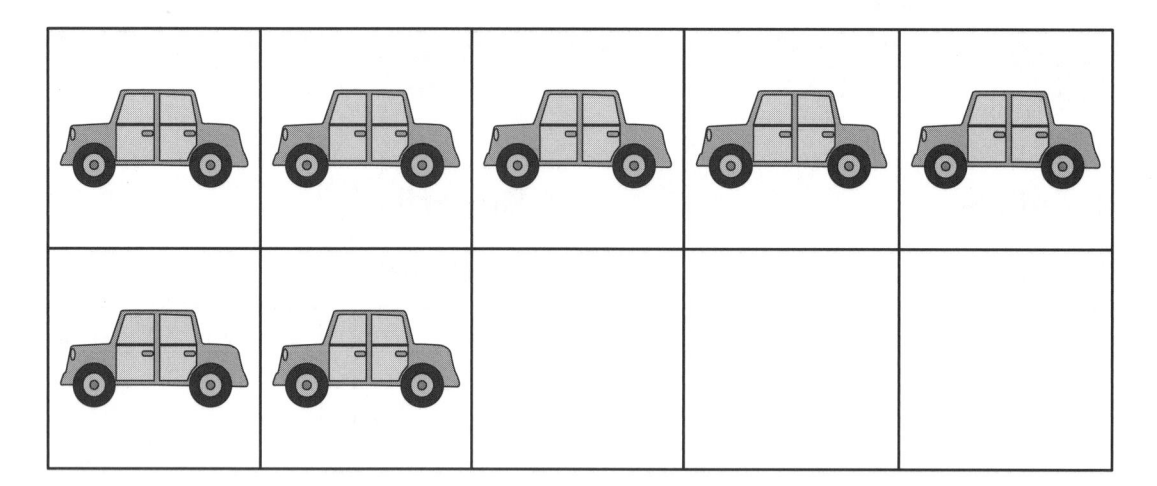

Complete the place value cards to show the total number of cars in the car park.

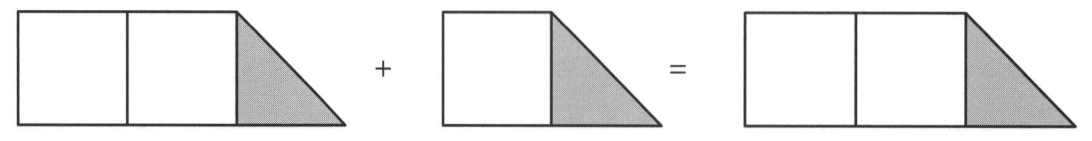

9.2 Counting, comparing, ordering and estimating

14 Estimate how many balls. ☐

Estimate how many bats. ☐

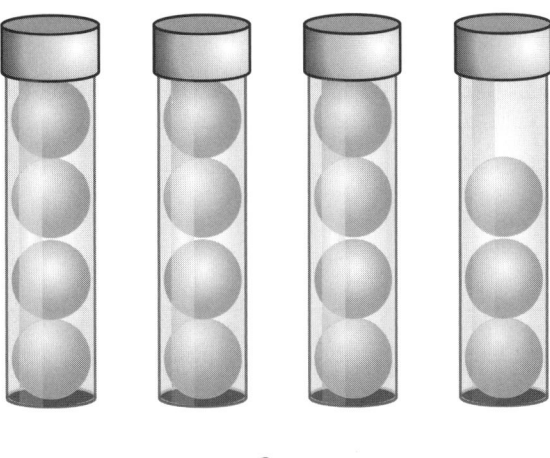

Is there a ball for every bat?

Count the bats and count the balls to see if you were correct.

15 There are fewer frogs than lily pads.

There are more than 10 frogs but fewer than 20 lily pads.

There are 4 more lily pads than frogs.

How many frogs and lily pads could there be?

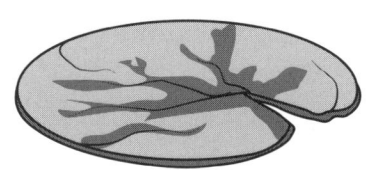

117

9 Numbers to 20

16 Put the numbers 15, 12 and 18 in order from smallest to greatest.

| smallest | | greatest |

Put the numbers 10, 20 and 15 in order from greatest to smallest.

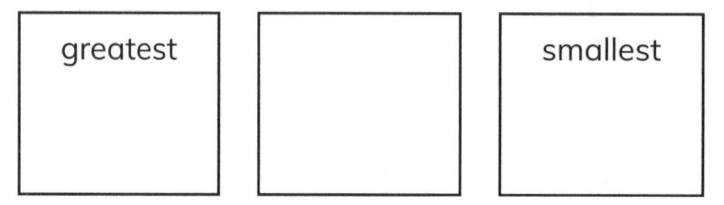

| greatest | | smallest |

17 Mark 13 and 18 on the number line.

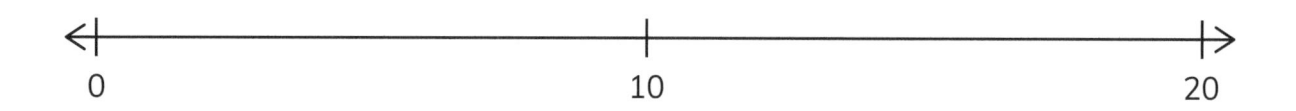

0 — 10 — 20

> 9.3 Number patterns

Exercise 9.3

counting back   counting on

Focus

1 Sort each number into the correct circle.

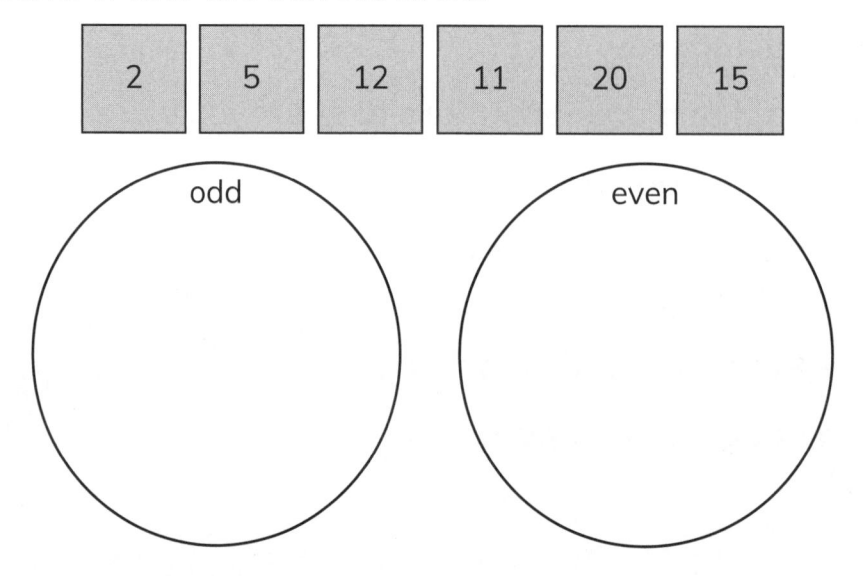

| 2 | 5 | 12 | 11 | 20 | 15 |

odd   even

9.3 Number patterns

Worked example 2

Count on in twos to find out how many cherries.

Answer:

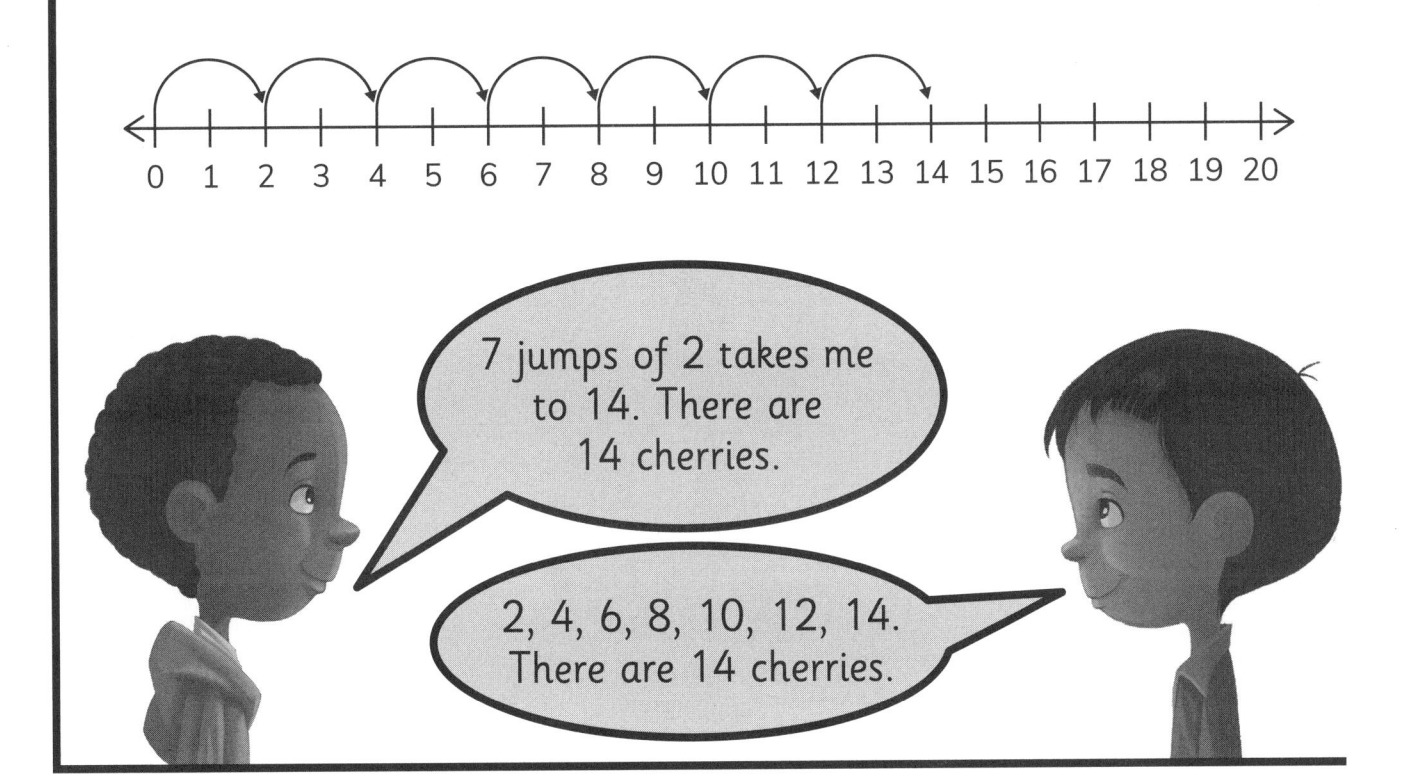

"7 jumps of 2 takes me to 14. There are 14 cherries."

"2, 4, 6, 8, 10, 12, 14. There are 14 cherries."

9 Numbers to 20

2   Count the cherries in twos.

Show your counting in twos on the number line.

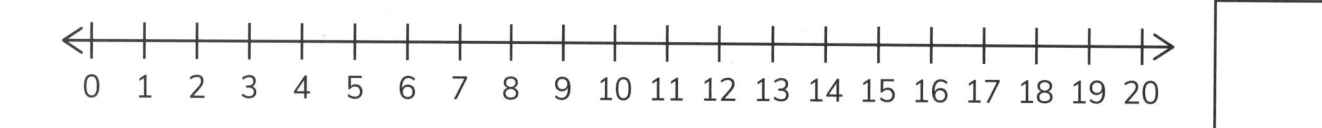

0 1 2 3 4 5 6 7 8 9 10 11 12 13 14 15 16 17 18 19 20

3   2 people can ride in a swing boat.

How many people can ride in 8 swing boats?

Show how you found your answer on the number line.

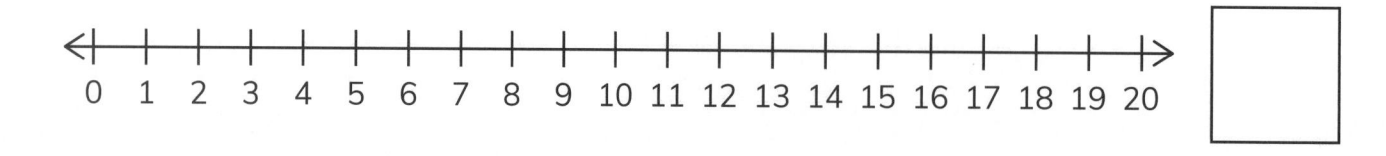

0 1 2 3 4 5 6 7 8 9 10 11 12 13 14 15 16 17 18 19 20

9.3 Number patterns

4 Complete the missing numbers.

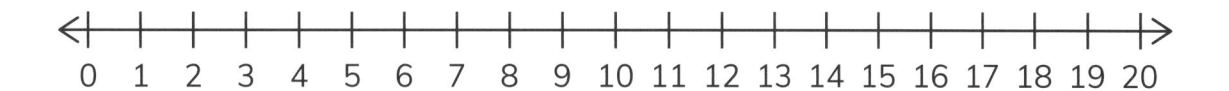

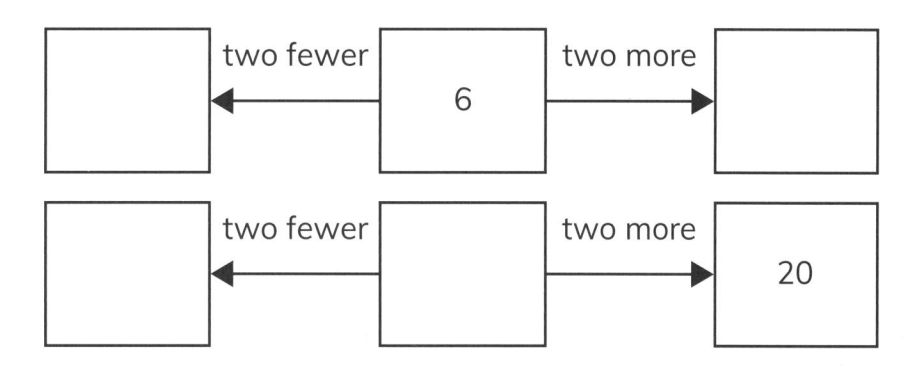

<-+->
0 1 2 3 4 5 6 7 8 9 10 11 12 13 14 15 16 17 18 19 20

[ ] ← two fewer — [6] — two more → [ ]

[ ] ← two fewer — [ ] — two more → [20]

5 Complete the missing numbers.

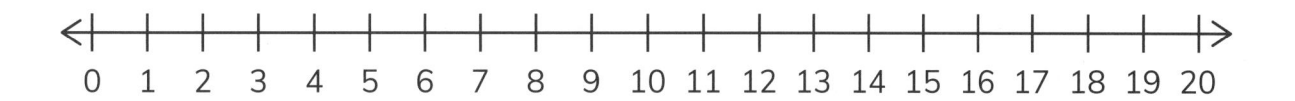

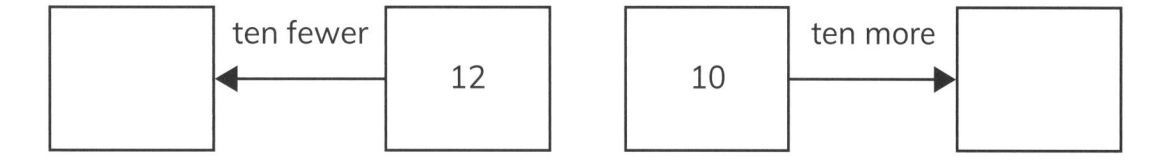

<-+->
0 1 2 3 4 5 6 7 8 9 10 11 12 13 14 15 16 17 18 19 20

[ ] ← ten fewer — [12]   [10] — ten more → [ ]

Practice

6 Zara has 6 pairs of shoes.

Count in twos to find out how many shoes Zara has.

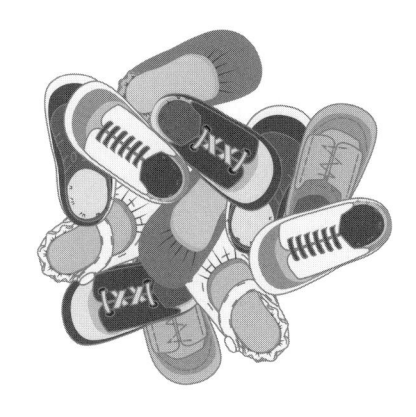

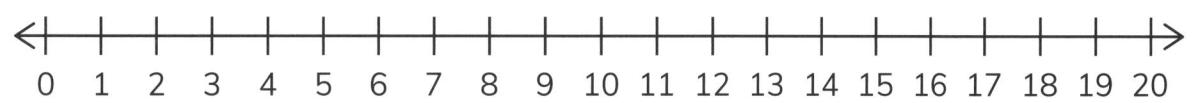

<-+->
0 1 2 3 4 5 6 7 8 9 10 11 12 13 14 15 16 17 18 19 20

7 Complete the missing numbers.

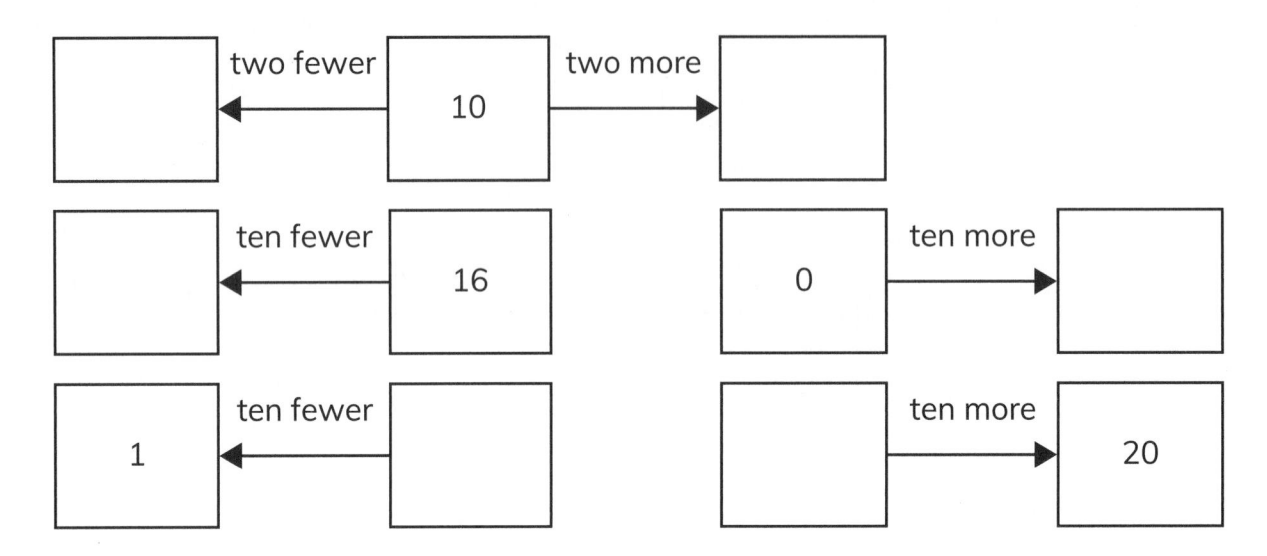

[ ] ← two fewer — [10] — two more → [ ]

[ ] ← ten fewer — [16]   [0] — ten more → [ ]

[1] ← ten fewer — [ ]   [ ] — ten more → [20]

8 Use **odd** or **even** to complete each sentence.

Two more than an even number is an _____ number.

Two fewer than an even number is an _____ number.

Ten fewer than an even number is an _____ number.

Ten more than an even number is an _____ number.

9 16 children are going to work in groups of two.

How many groups of two will there be?

Challenge

10 The Chen family have 10 bicycles. 8 wheels **do not** have a puncture.

How many wheels do have a puncture? [ ]

9.3 Number patterns

11 Arun counted back in twos on a number line.
Write the missing numbers.

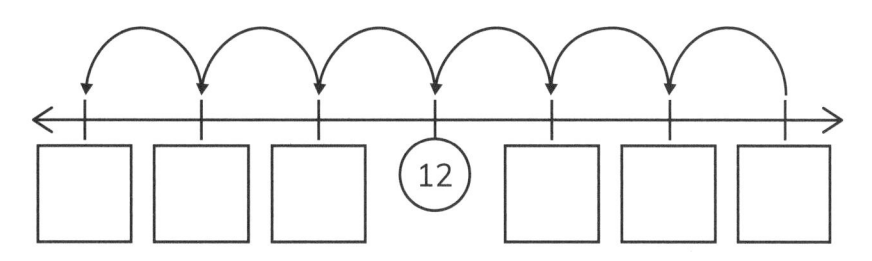

[ ] [ ] [ ] (12) [ ] [ ] [ ]

What was the first number Arun said? [ ]

What was the last number Arun said? [ ]

12 Complete the missing numbers.

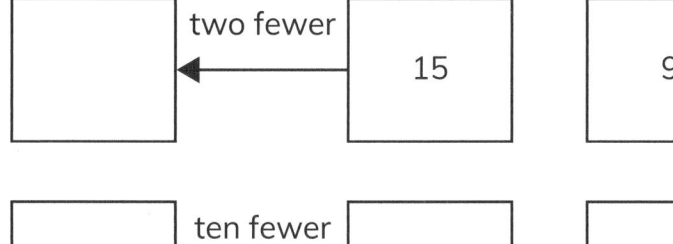

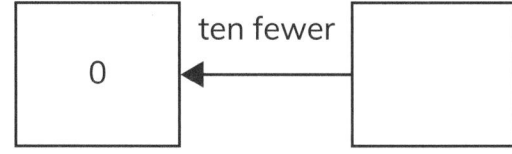

[ ] ← two fewer — 15   9 — two more → [ ]

0 ← ten fewer — [ ]   [ ] — three more → 20

13 Use **odd** or **even** to complete each sentence.

Two more than an odd number is an _____ number.

Two fewer than an odd number is an _____ number.

Ten fewer than an odd number is an _____ number.

Ten more than an odd number is an _____ number.

123

9 Numbers to 20

14 Marcus wants to show that 10 more than 0 is 10 and 10 fewer than 10 is 0.

What advice would you give to Marcus?
Where would you put the 0 card?

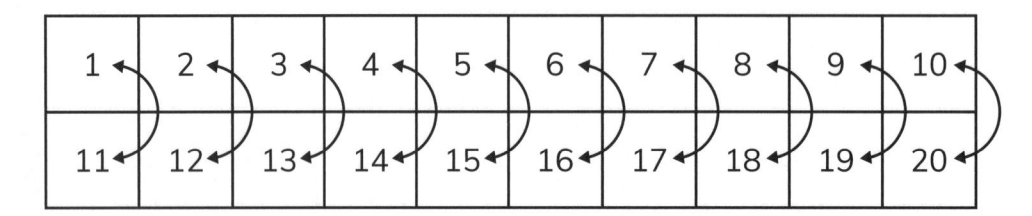

| 0 |

1	2	3	4	5	6	7	8	9	10
11	12	13	14	15	16	17	18	19	20

10 Geometry (2)

> 10.1 3D shapes

Exercise 10.1

cuboid   pyramid

Focus

> **Worked example 1**
>
> Join the dots to make the shapes. 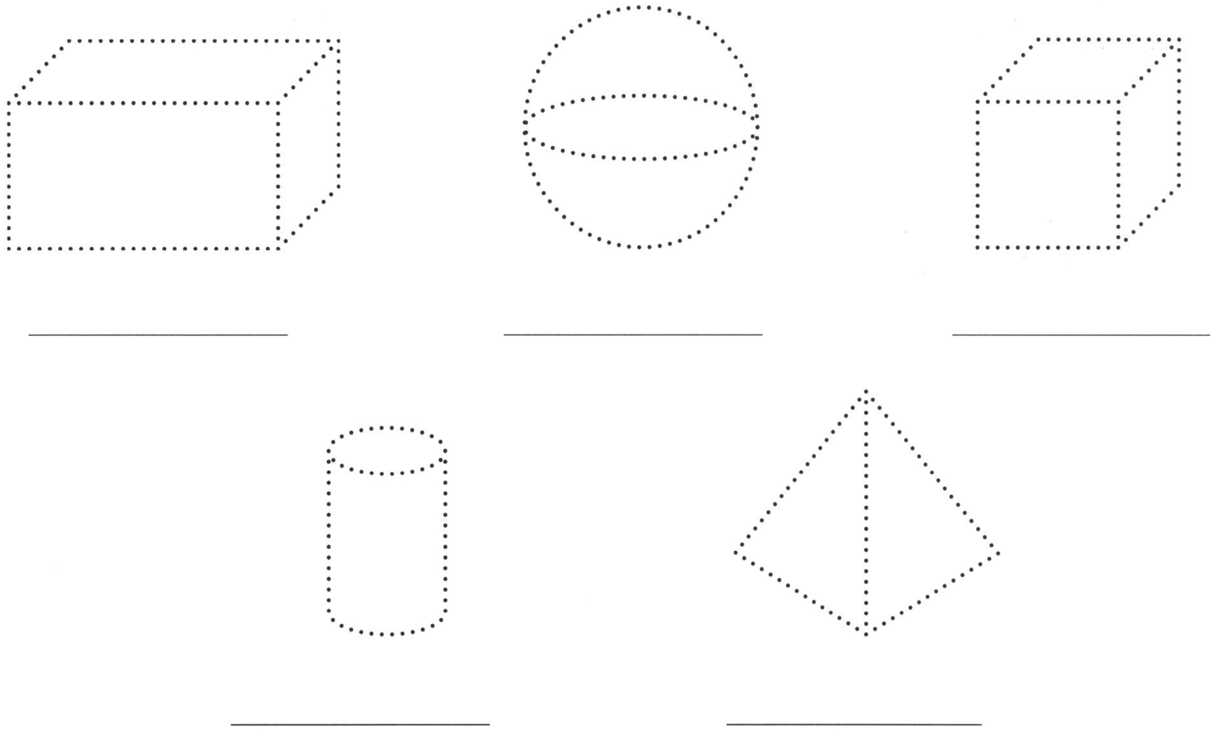
>
> _____   _____   _____
>
> _____   _____
>
> Choose from the list of words and write the name of each shape under your drawing.
>
> cylinder   cuboid   sphere   cube   pyramid

125

10 Geometry (2)

Continued

What will you look for when you are naming your shapes?

> I'm going to look for straight edges, so that will be a cube, a cuboid or a pyramid.

> I'm going to look for curved surfaces, so that will be a cylinder or a sphere.

Answer:

cuboid

sphere

cube

cylinder

pyramid

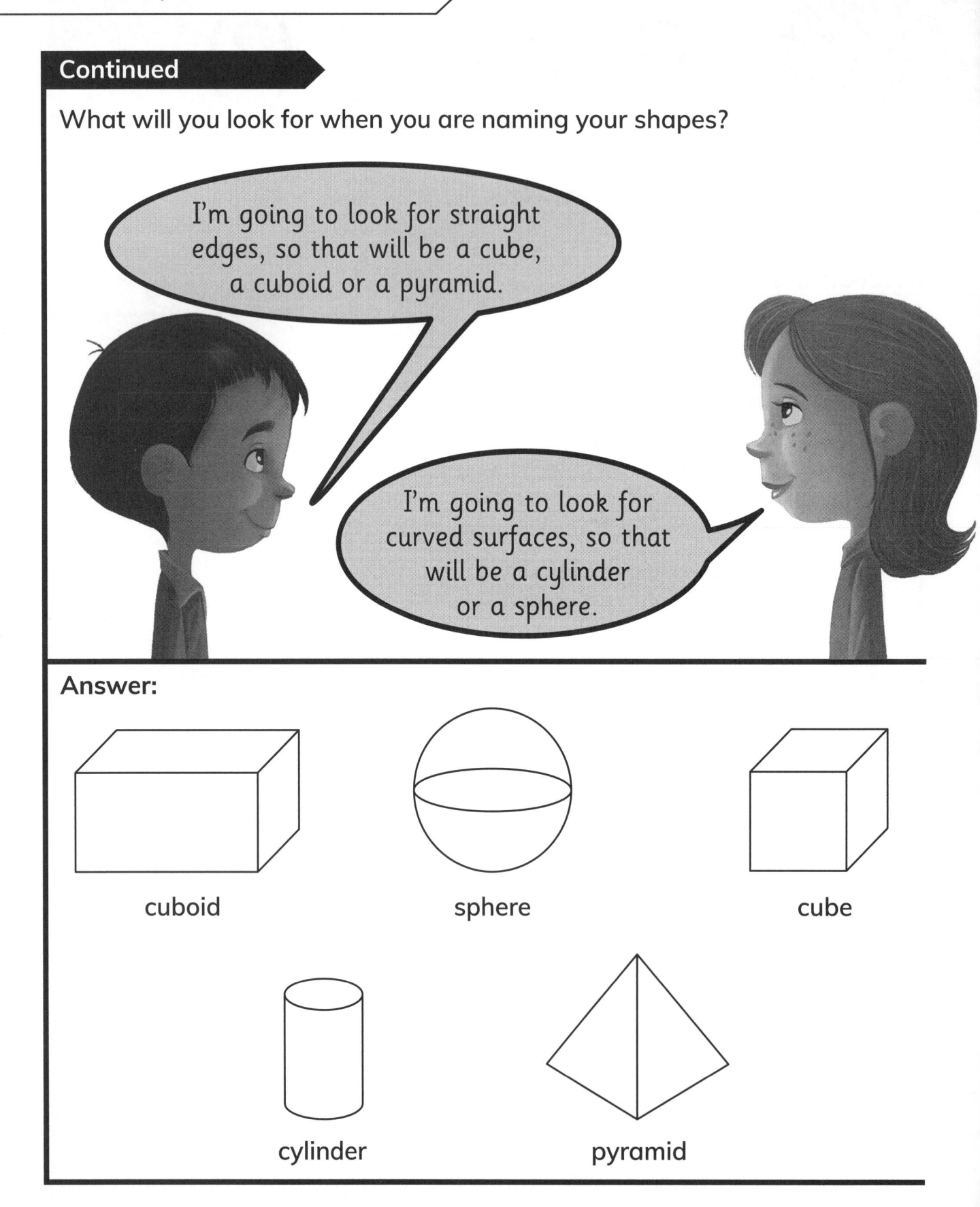

10.1 3D shapes

1. Colour the cylinders blue.

   Colour the pyramids red.

   Describe all of the red shapes.

   Describe the shapes that are not coloured.

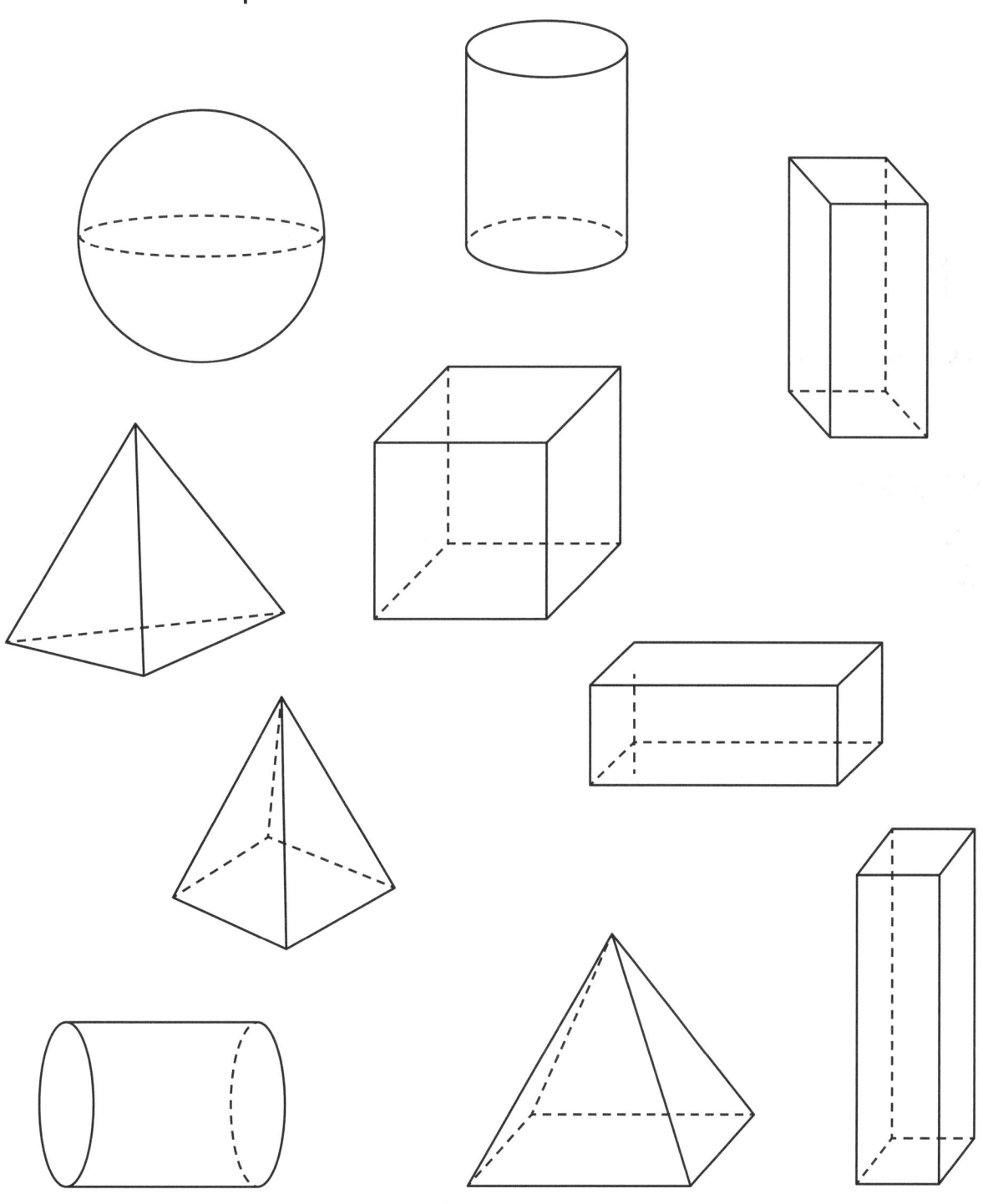

10 Geometry (2)

2 Draw a ring around the correct shape in each pair.

cube

pyramid

cuboid

cylinder

3   Sort the shapes into the table.

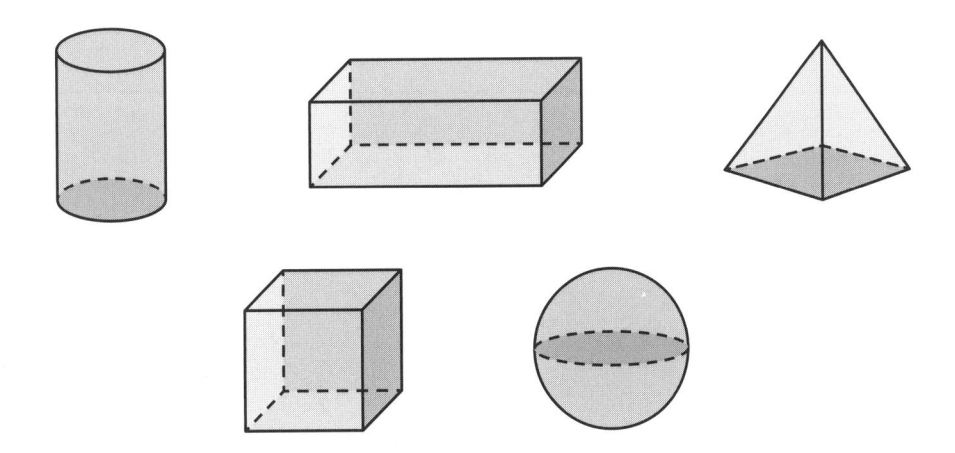

Shape	Number of faces	Number of edges	Flat or curved?
	5	8	flat
	2	2	both
	6	12	flat
	6	12	flat
	0	0	curved

10 Geometry (2)

Practice

4   How many faces does each shape have?

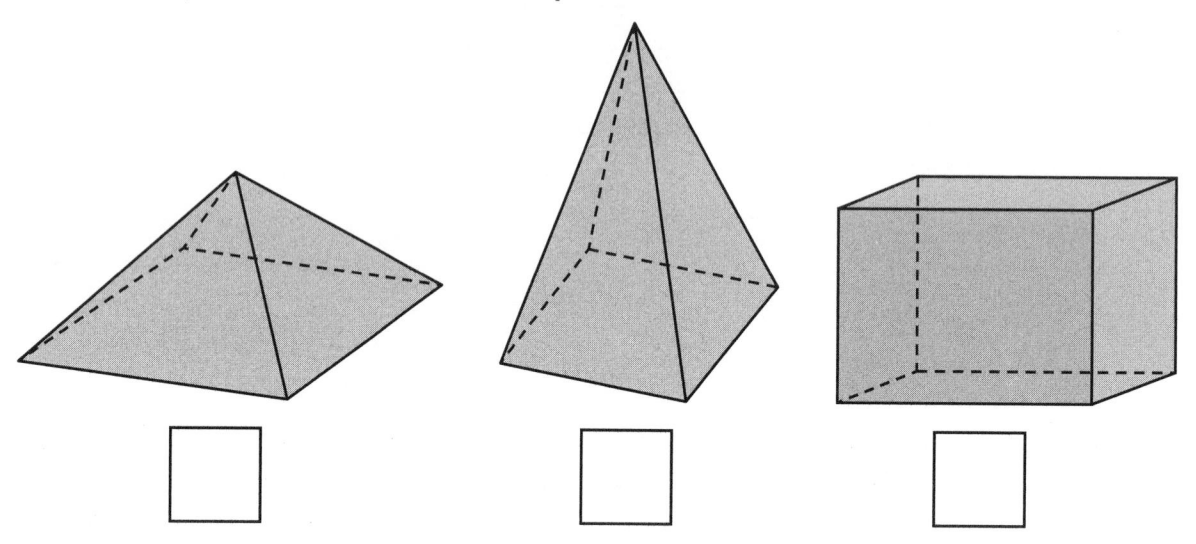

☐   ☐   ☐

5   Draw a ring around the correct answer.

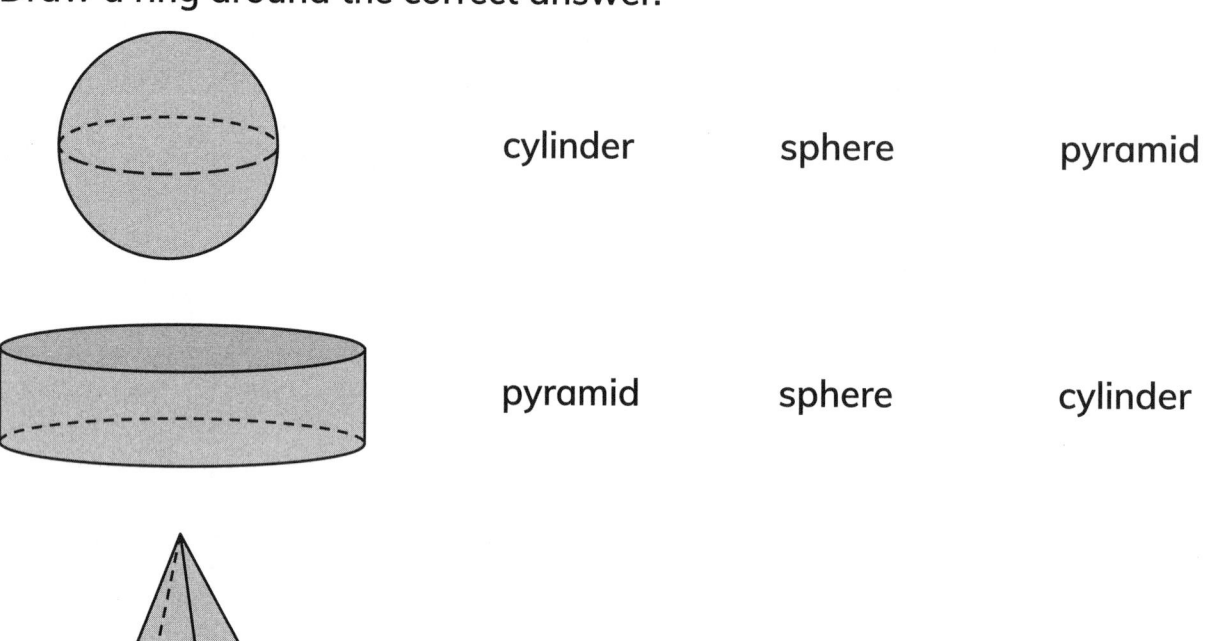

cylinder   sphere   pyramid

pyramid   sphere   cylinder

sphere   cuboid   pyramid

10.1 3D shapes

6 a Draw a ring around the correct shape in each pair.

This is a cube.

This is a pyramid.

This is a cuboid.

This is a square-based pyramid.

b Describe these shapes:

Cube _____

Pyramid _____

Cuboid _____

Draw and describe a sphere.

10 Geometry (2)

Challenge

7 Complete the table.

Shape	Number of faces	Number of edges	Flat or curved?
(triangular pyramid)			
(cube)			
(square pyramid)			
(cuboid)			
(sphere)			
(cylinder)			

Find an example of one of the shapes.

Name it. Draw it. Describe it.

8   Draw a ring around the shape with the most faces.

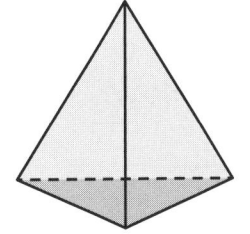

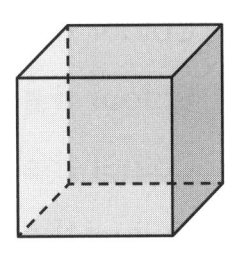

9   Draw a ring around the shape with the most edges.

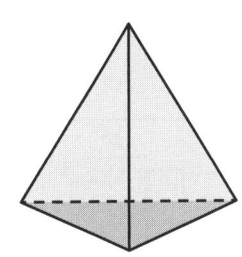

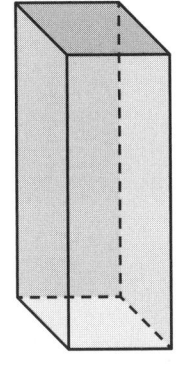

> ## 10.2 2D shapes

Exercise 10.2

Focus

> hexagon   pentagon   rectangle   rotate

1   Colour the circles red.

    Colour the squares blue.

10 Geometry (2)

2 Colour the circles green.

Colour the triangles yellow.

Colour the squares blue.

Colour the rectangles red.

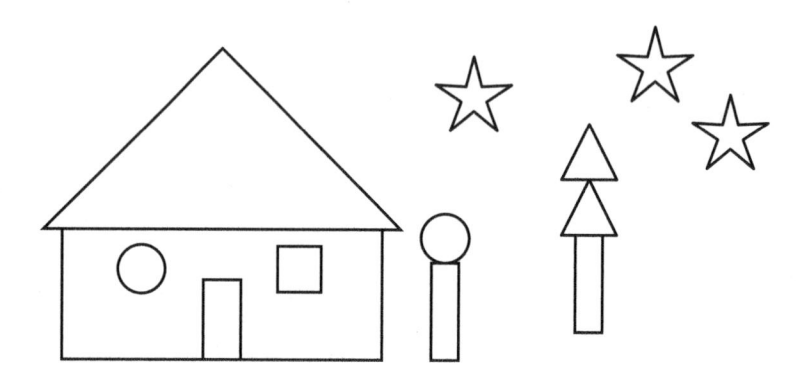

3 Here is a pattern made using triangles. Draw the next triangle.

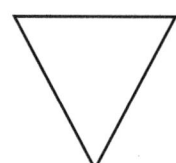

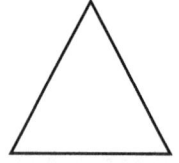

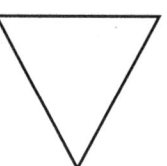

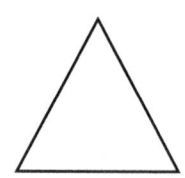

4 Rotating a shape means moving it round a fixed point.

The shape stays the same, but its position will change.

Draw a ring around the shapes that are the same as the first shape.

10.2 2D shapes

5   2D or 3D? Draw a ring around the correct answer.

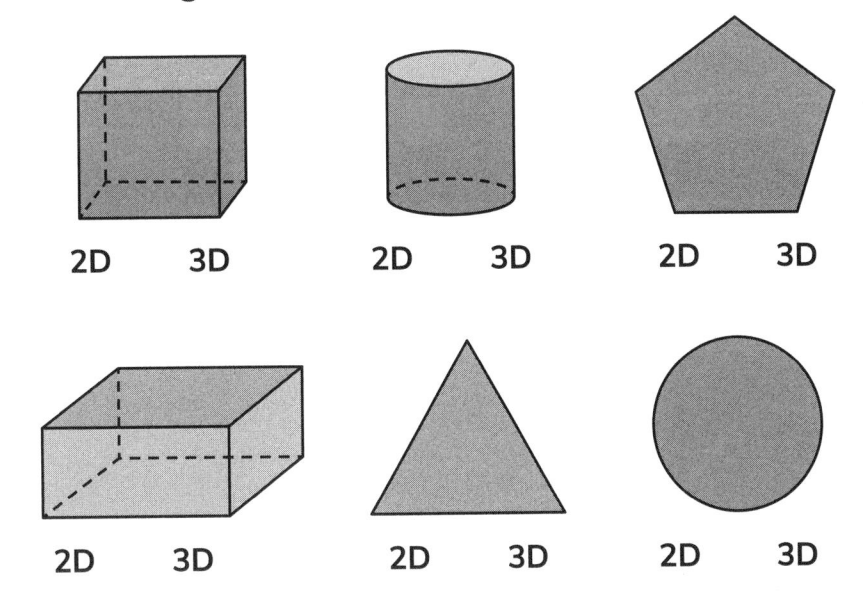

   2D   3D   2D   3D   2D   3D

   2D   3D   2D   3D   2D   3D

6   Draw a line to match the shapes with their description.

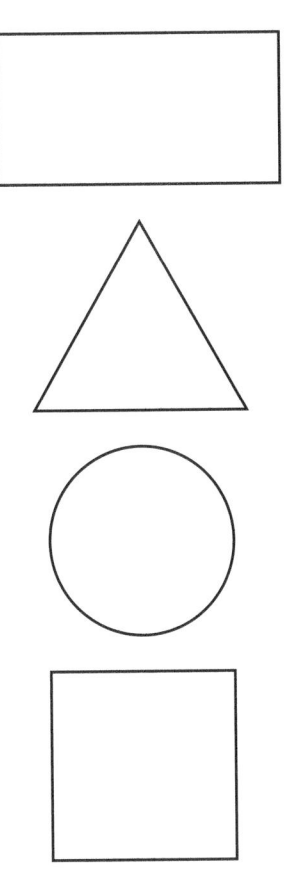

   This 2D shape has 3 straight sides.

   It is a _____.

   This 2D shape has 4 straight sides all the same length.

   It is a _____.

   This 2D shape has 4 straight sides. 2 of them are long and 2 are shorter.

   It is a _____.

   This 2D shape has no straight sides.

   It is a _____.

   Which 2 shapes have the same number of sides? _____

   Which shape has the fewest number of sides? _____

   135

10 Geometry (2)

Practice

7 Join the shape to its name.

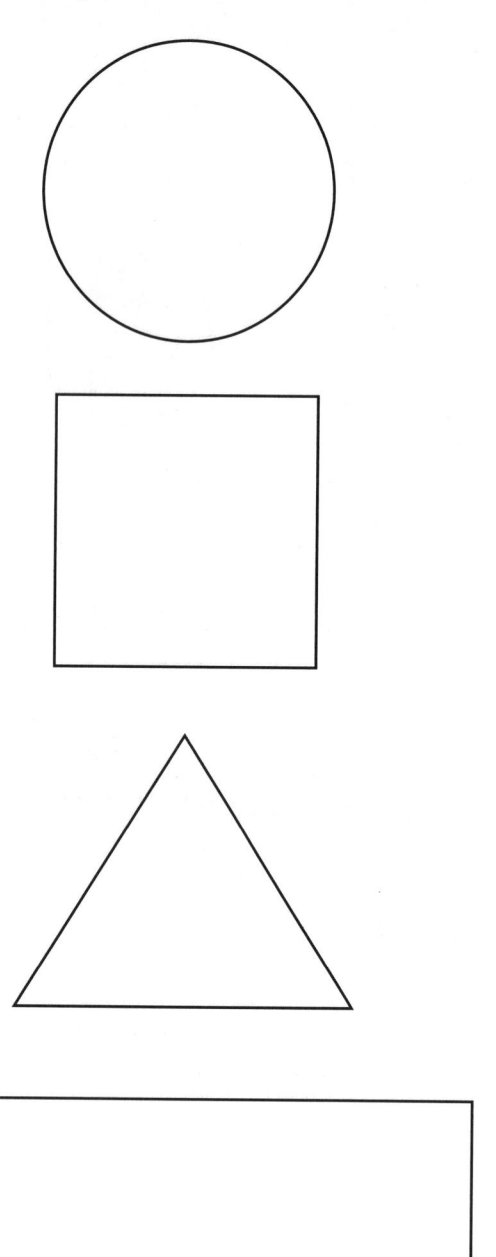

triangle

circle

rectangle

square

10.2 2D shapes

8 Draw an animal using these shapes.

You can use the shapes as many times as you like.

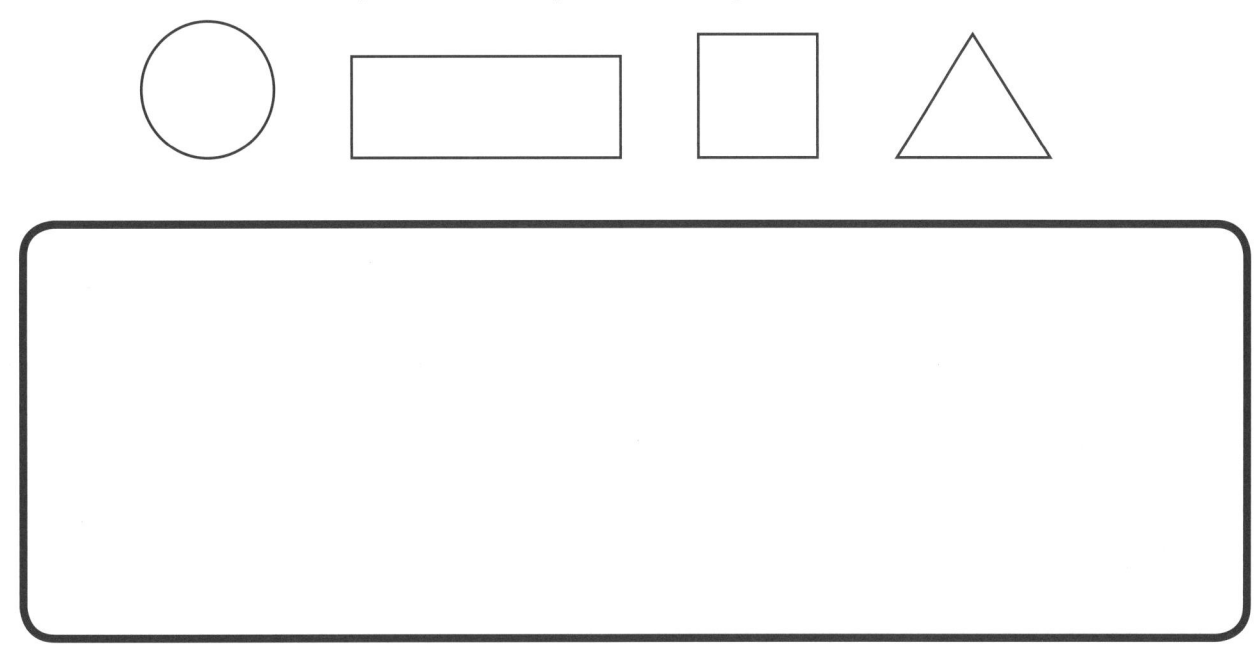

How many shapes did you use?

I used _____ ◯.   I used _____ ▭.

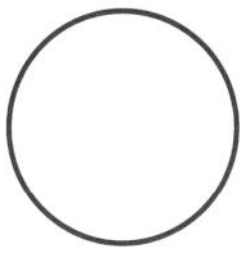

I used _____ □.   I used _____ △.

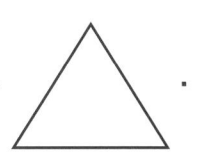

137

10 Geometry (2)

9 Draw a ring around the shape that is **not** the same as the first one.

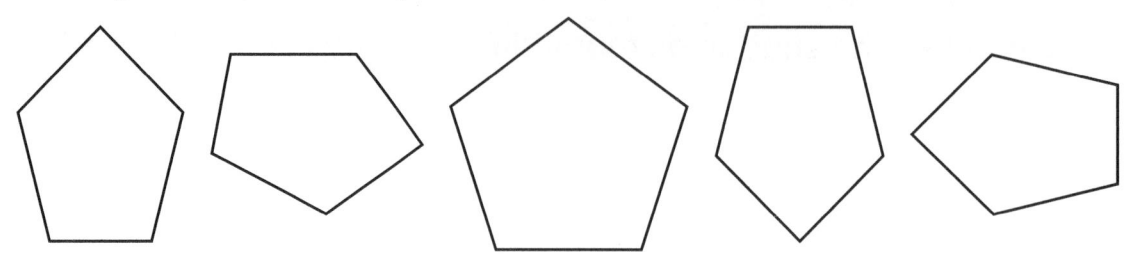

Choose your own shape.

Draw the shape and then draw 3 different rotations.

10 Write a description for each shape.

This 2D shape is a _____.

It has _____

_____

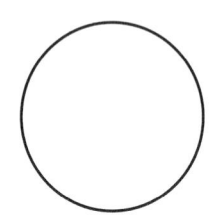

This 2D shape is a _____.

It has _____

_____

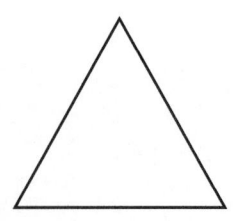

This 2D shape is a _____.

It has _____

_____

10.2 2D shapes

This 2D shape is a _____ .

It has _____

_____

11 Sort the shapes into 2D or 3D.

Write the name of each shape in the correct column.

2D shapes	3D shapes

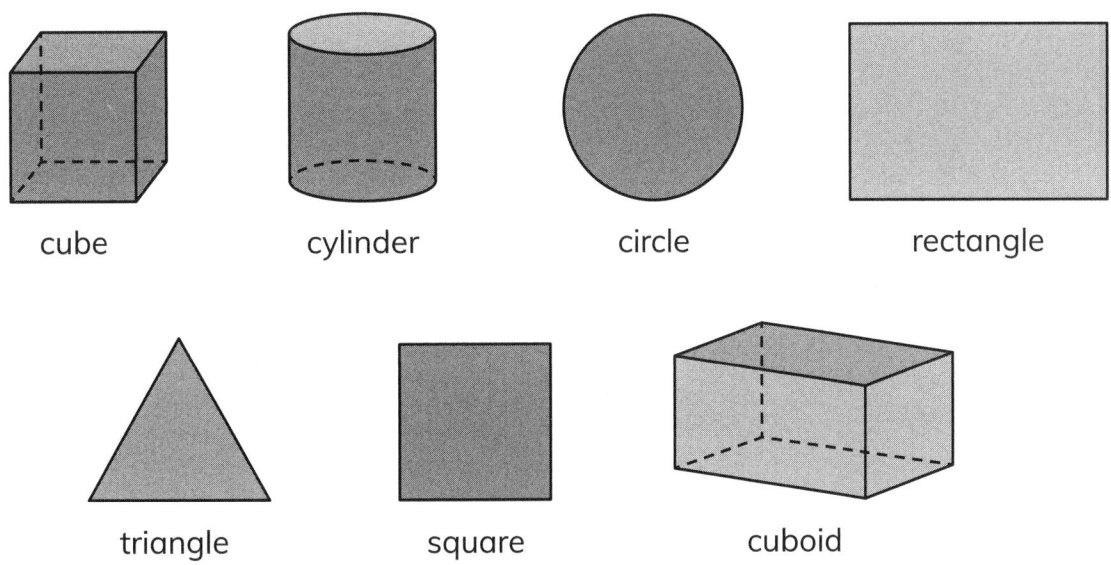

cube   cylinder   circle   rectangle

triangle   square   cuboid

139

10 Geometry (2)

Challenge

12 Have a look around the room.

Draw things that are the same as these shapes.

circle　　square　　triangle　　rectangle

13 1 square

4 squares

Draw the next biggest square using just squares.

I used _____ squares.

10 Geometry (2)

14 Choose 3 of these shapes.

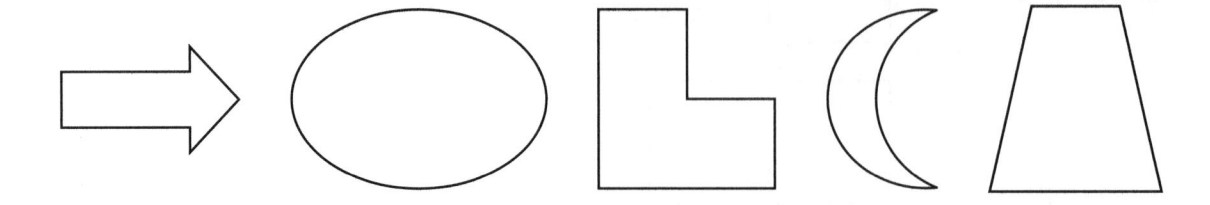

Draw 4 different rotations of each shape you choose.

15 Complete the table.

Name of 2D shape	Number of straight sides	Number of curved sides
square		0
rectangle		
circle		
triangle		0

16 Describe a circle.

A circle has _____ .

17 What is the same and what is different in each pair?

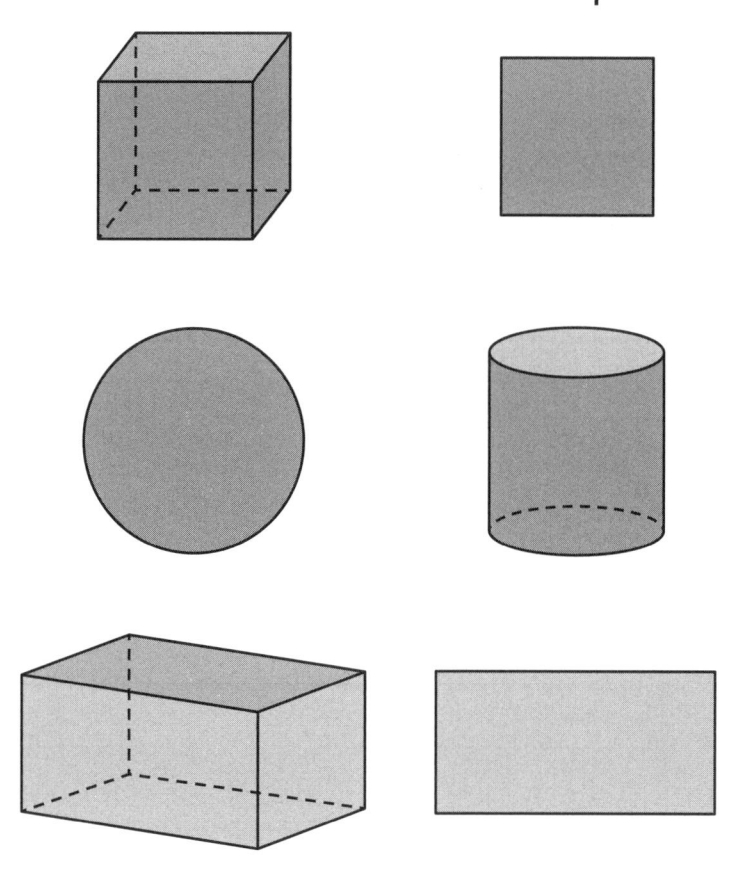

_____

_____

11 Fractions (2)

> 11.1 Halves

Exercise 11.1

$\frac{1}{2}$ halve

Focus

> **Worked example 1**
>
> A half is when there is the same in both parts of the whole.
>
> Draw a ring around one half of these objects.
>
> Answer:
>
> There are 4.
> There are 2 in each half.
> Half of 4 is 2.

144

11.1 Halves

1 Draw a ring around one half of each set.

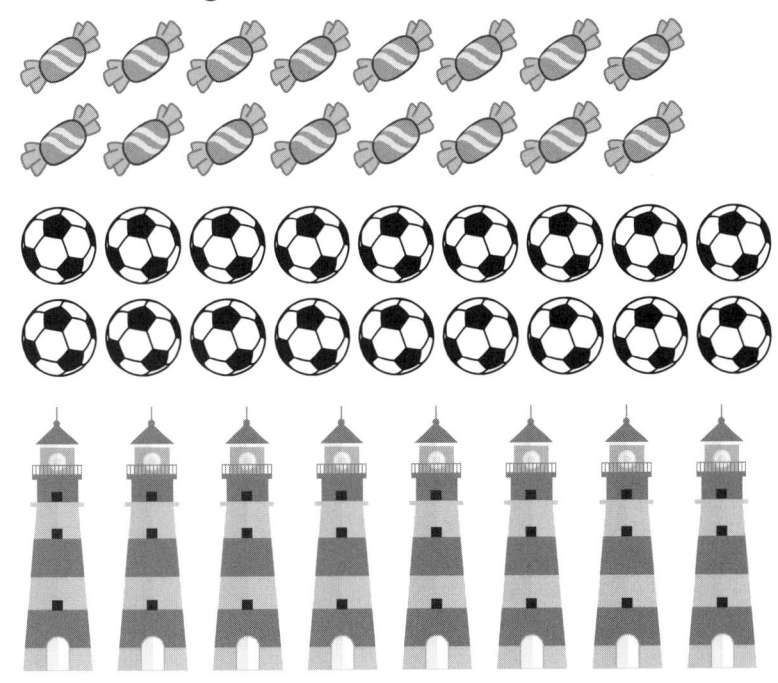

2 For each box:
   - Draw the correct number of balls in the box.
   - Halve the balls into two equal groups by drawing a ring around each half.
   - Complete the number sentence to find the answer:

   Half of _____ is _____.

   | 18 | 14 |

   Half of 18 = ☐   Half of 14 = ☐

145

11 Fractions (2)

12

Half of 12 = ☐

20

Half of 20 = ☐

16

Half of 16 = ☐

Draw a box of your own. Draw an even number of balls. Halve them. Write how many are in each group.

11.1 Halves

3 Draw a ring around each shape that shows 2 halves.

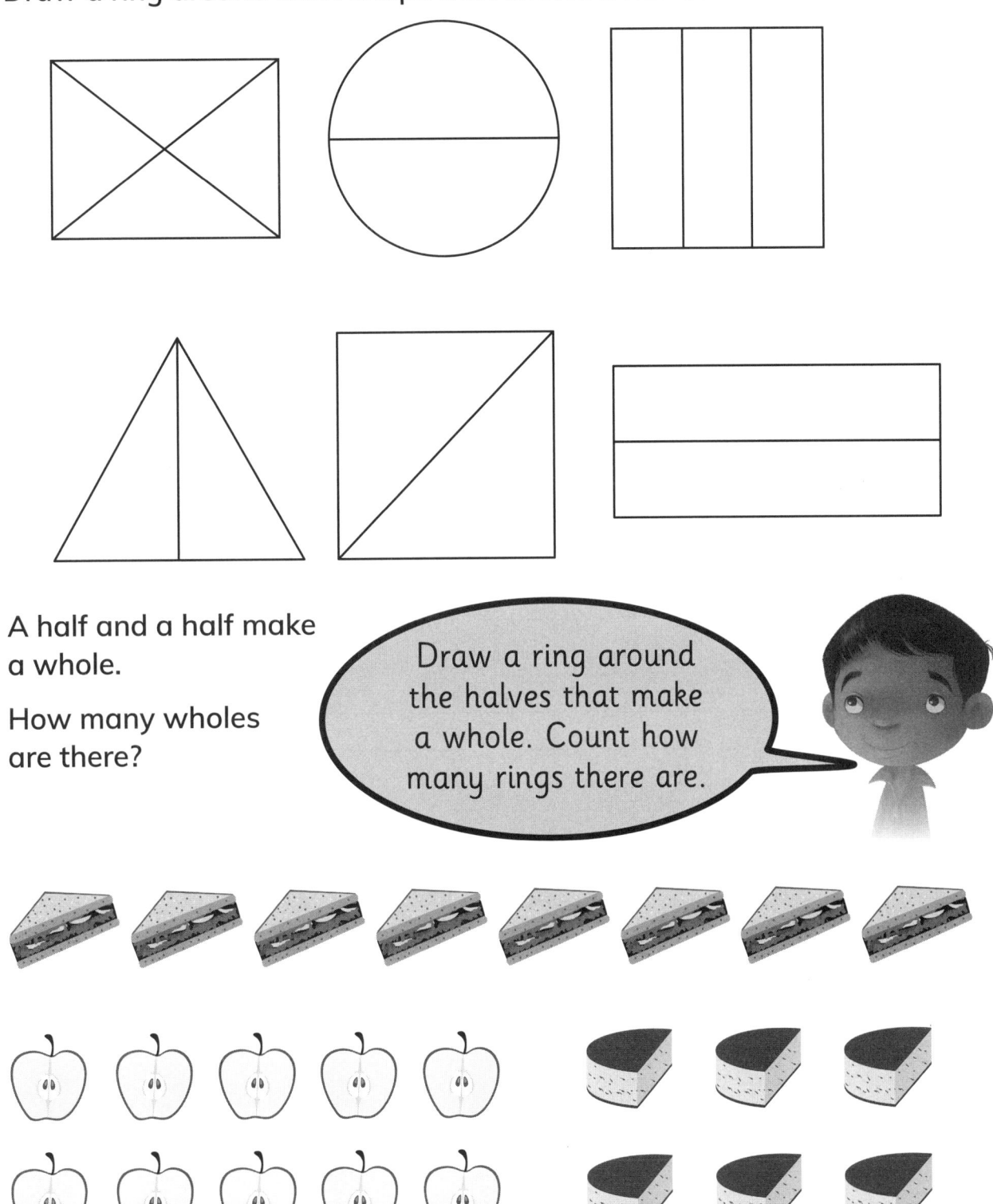

4 A half and a half make a whole.

How many wholes are there?

Draw a ring around the halves that make a whole. Count how many rings there are.

147

11 Fractions (2)

Practice

5   Colour half of each set of shapes.

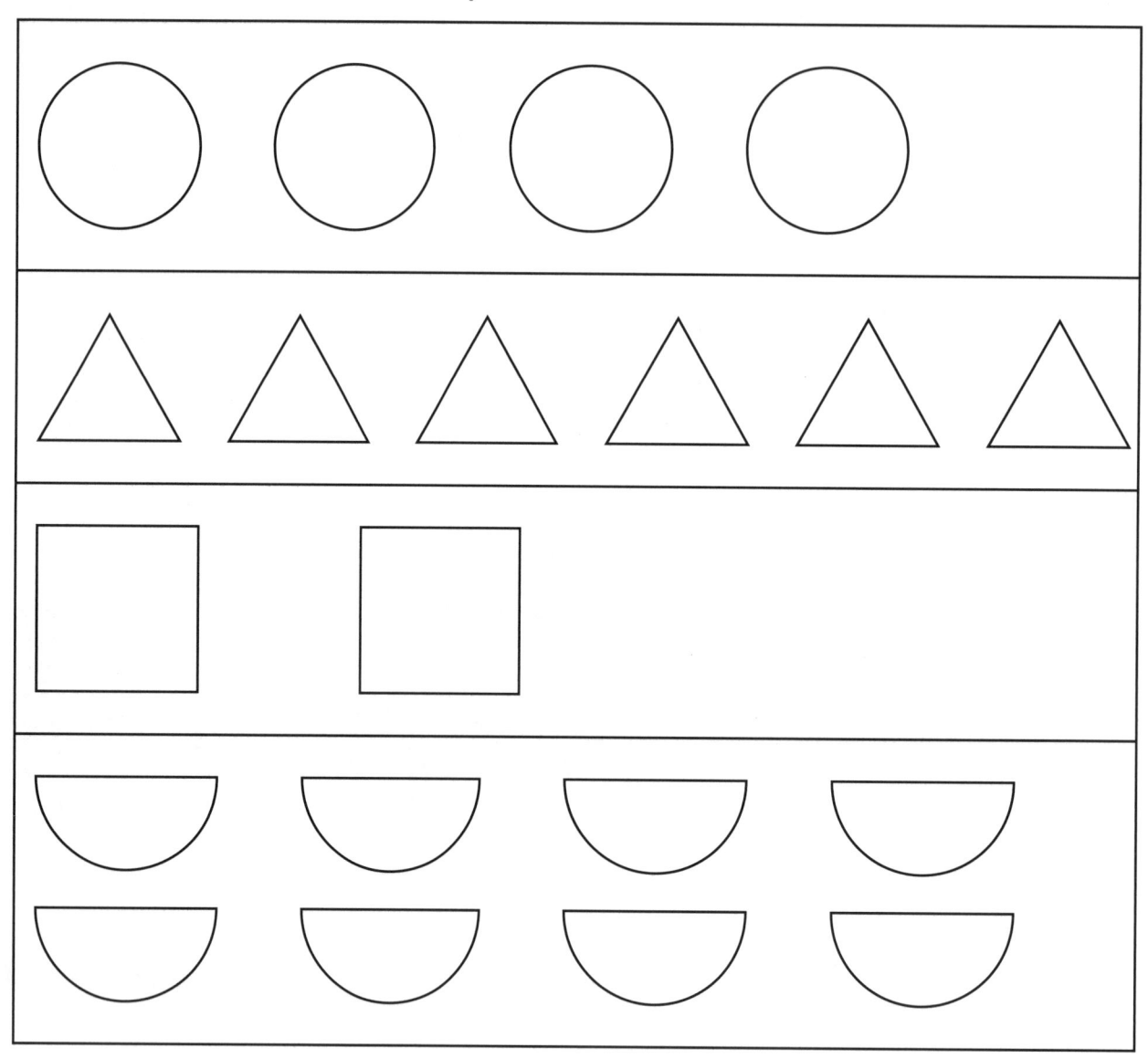

6 Draw half the number of objects.

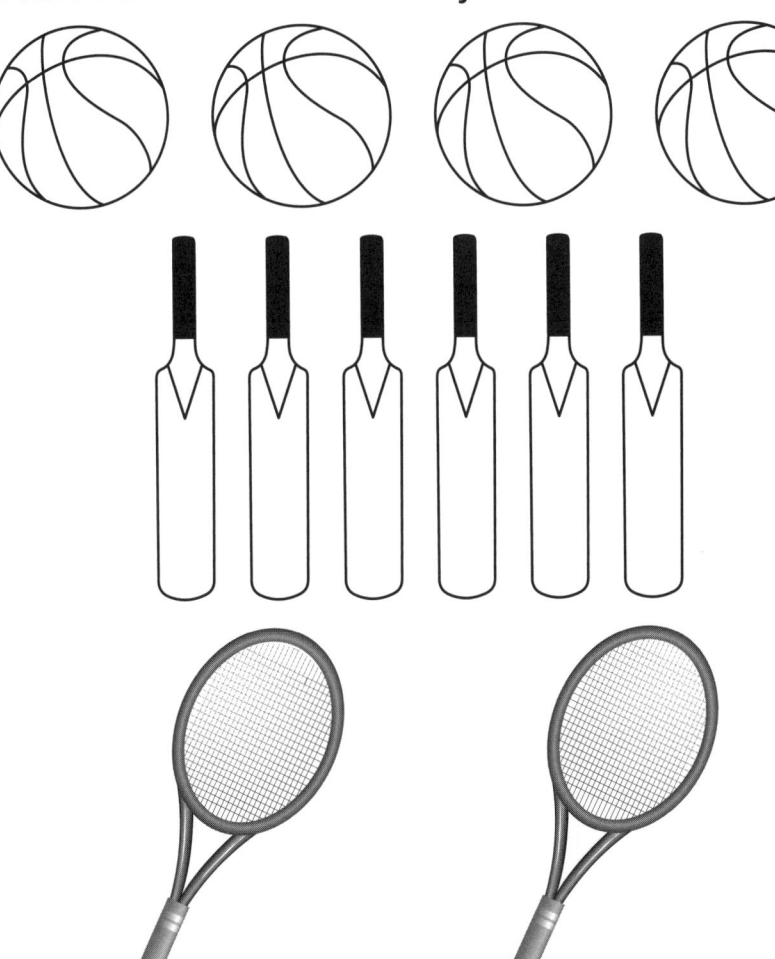

Tip

If you don't want to draw pictures, you can draw a ring around half of the objects.

11 Fractions (2)

7 Find half of each set.

☐

☐

☐

8 How many whole objects are there in each set?

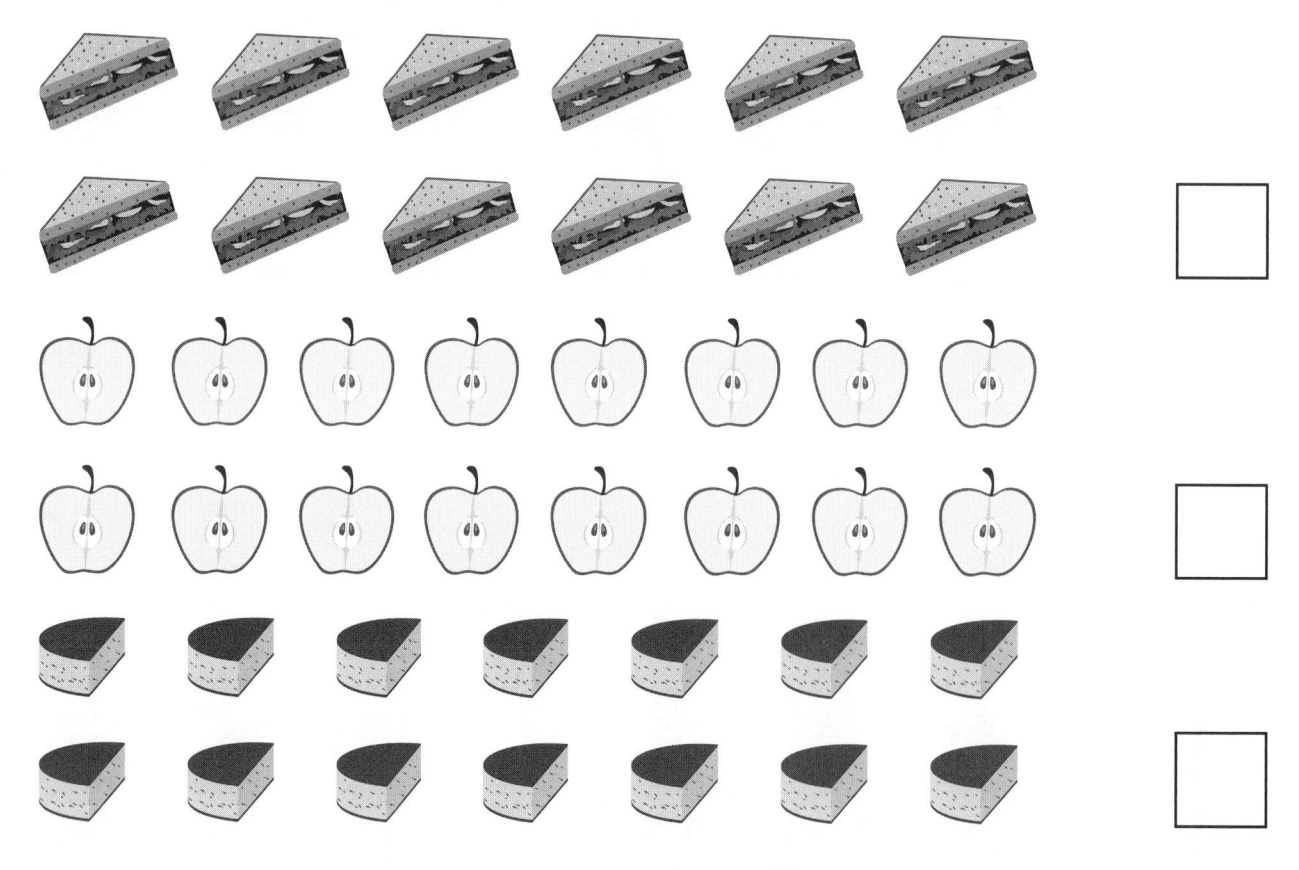

☐

☐

☐

11.1 Halves

9 Draw the number of balls in each box.

Halve that amount. Write a number sentence for each box.

The first one has been done for you.

10 (ten balls drawn)	12
Half of 10 = 5	_____

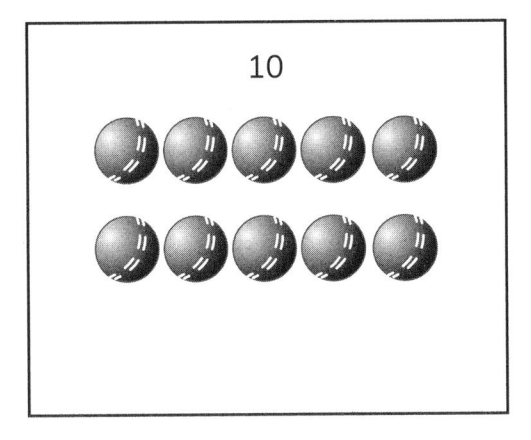

14	16
_____	_____

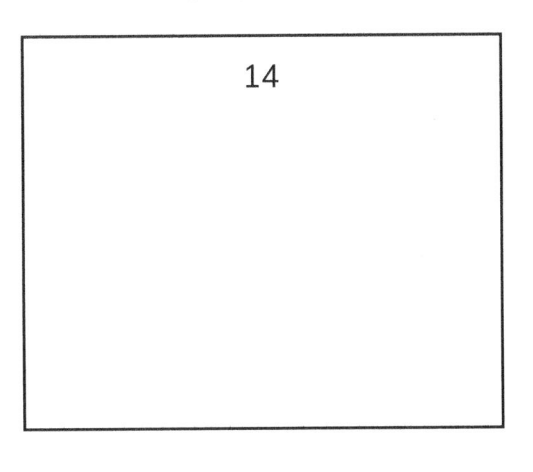

18	20
_____	_____

11 Fractions (2)

Challenge

10 The bar of chocolate has 8 squares.

Share the whole bar **equally** between 2 people.

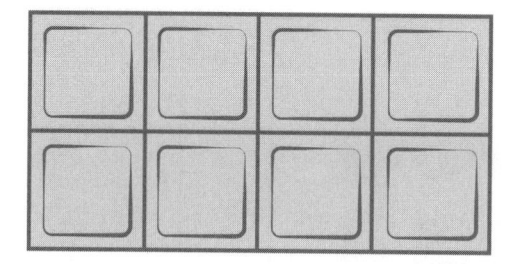

Here is one way to cut it in half.

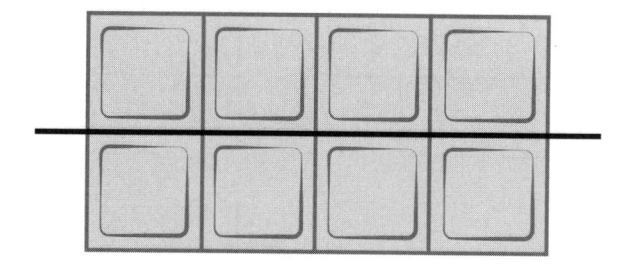

Here is another way to cut it in half.

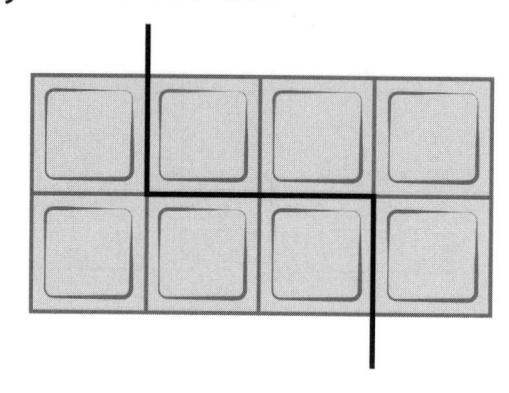

Find 2 more ways to cut it in half.

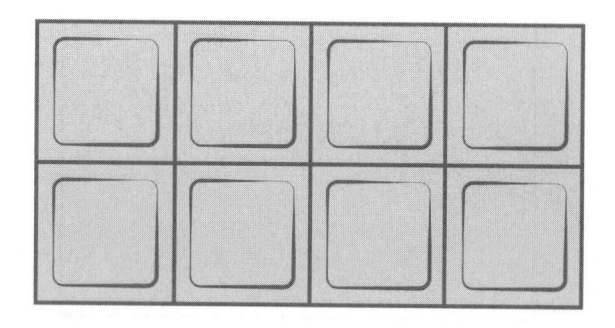

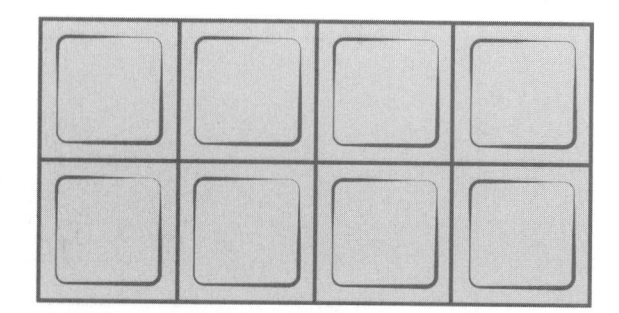

11.1 Halves

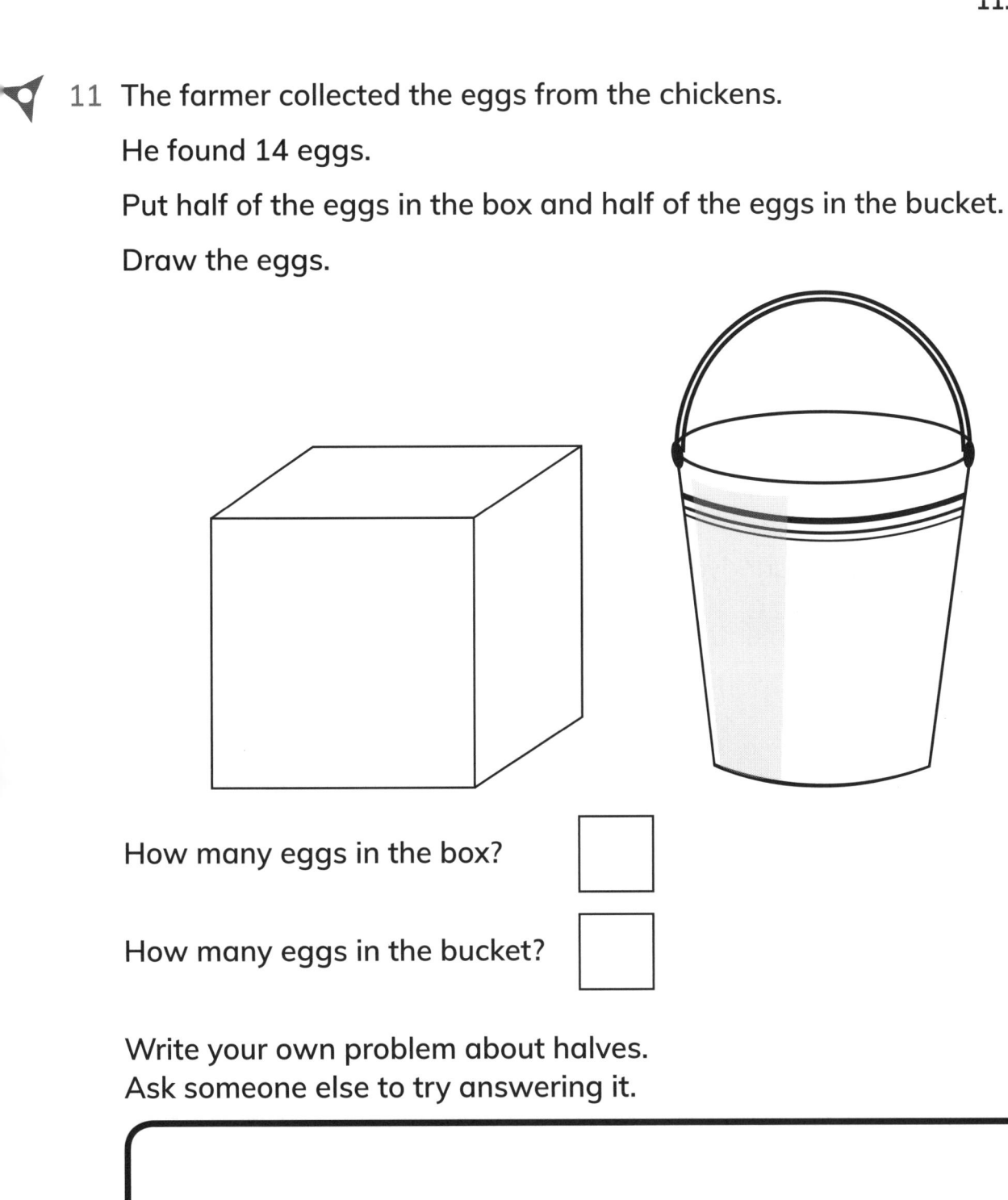

11 The farmer collected the eggs from the chickens.

He found 14 eggs.

Put half of the eggs in the box and half of the eggs in the bucket.

Draw the eggs.

How many eggs in the box? ☐

How many eggs in the bucket? ☐

Write your own problem about halves.
Ask someone else to try answering it.

153

11 Fractions (2)

12 What do you notice about the numbers that are half of all even numbers to 20?

Write 4 examples.

_____

_____

_____

13 There were 6 whole sandwiches.

How many have been eaten? _____

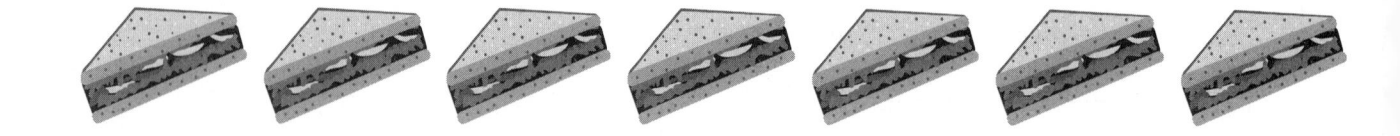

There were 4 whole apples.

How many have been eaten? _____

11.1 Halves

There were 8 whole cakes.

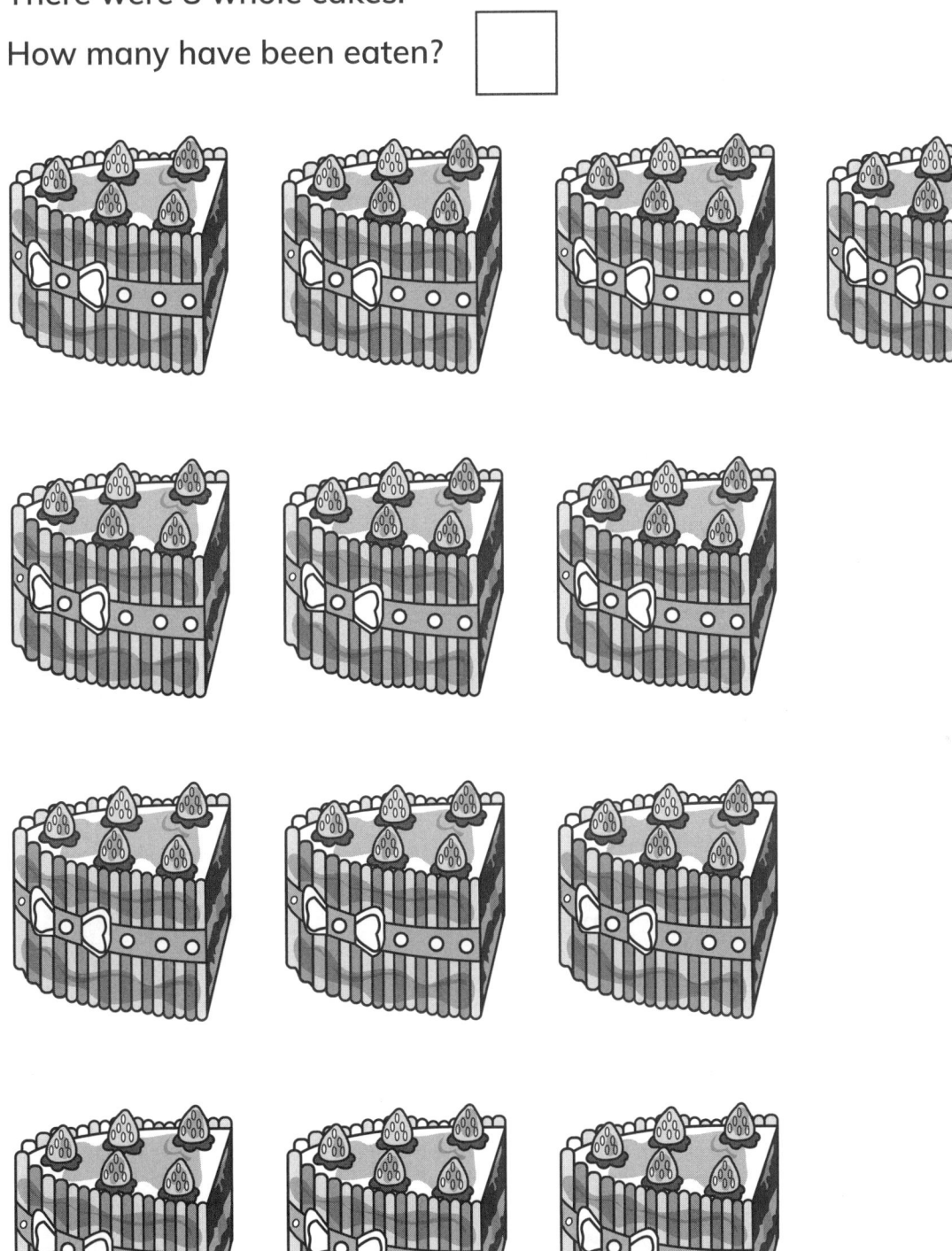

How many have been eaten? ☐

12 Measures (2)

> 12.1 Mass and capacity

Exercise 12.1

Focus

> balance scales   capacity   empty
> full   heavy   light   mass

Worked example 1

Draw a ring around the container that holds more in each pair.

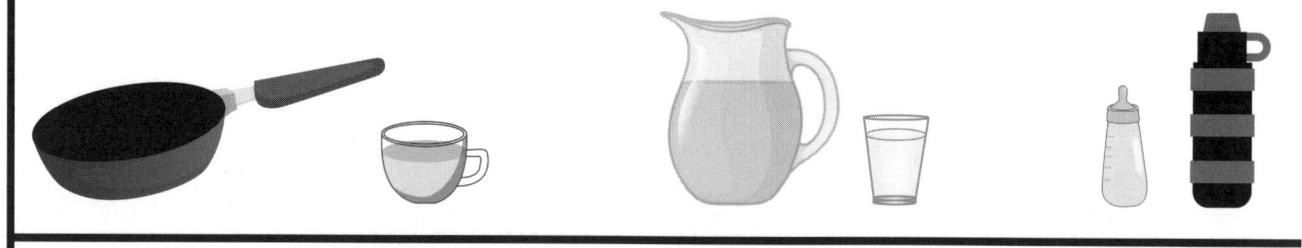

Answer:

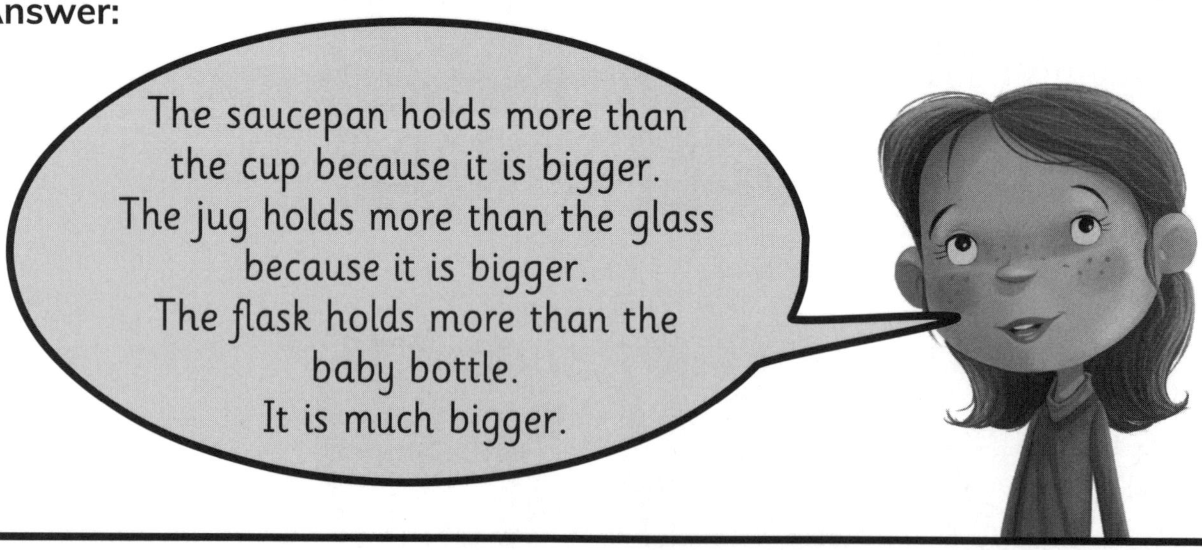

> The saucepan holds more than the cup because it is bigger.
> The jug holds more than the glass because it is bigger.
> The flask holds more than the baby bottle.
> It is much bigger.

12.1 Mass and capacity

1   Draw a ring around the heavier object on each balance scale.

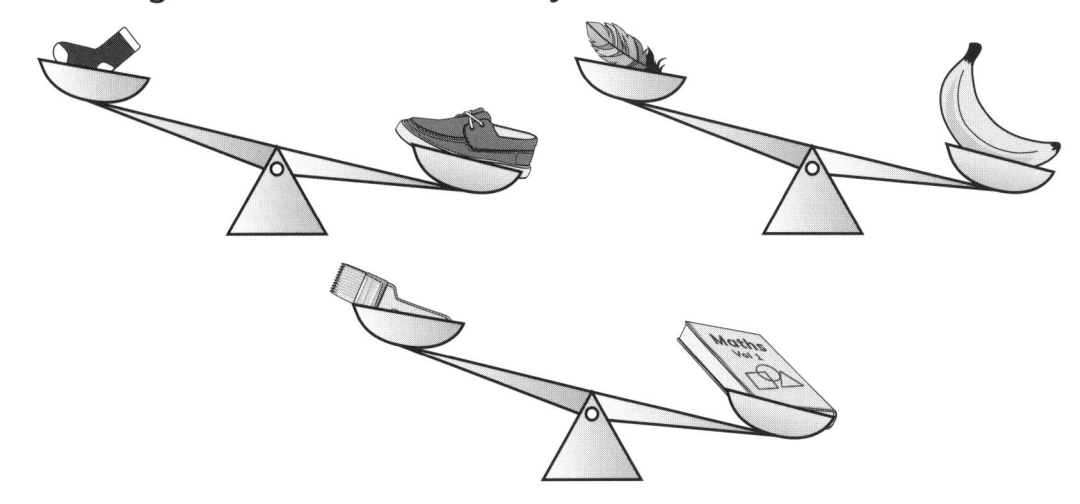

Draw or write the three heavy objects.

Draw or write the three lighter objects.

12 Measures (2)

2. Draw a ring around the container in each pair that has less in it.

Draw 2 bottles. One has less in it than the other.

Draw 2 buckets. One has more in it than the other.

Label them **more** and **less**.

Practice

3. How many things can you hold in your hand?

    Write the capacity of your hands next to each drawing.

    I can hold ☐ marbles.

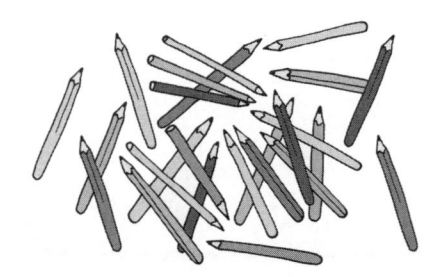

    I can hold ☐ pencils.

12.1 Mass and capacity

I can hold _____

4   Fill in the missing words.

Use the words **heavier, lighter, balance**.

The apple is _____ than the pear.

The pear is _____ than the apple.

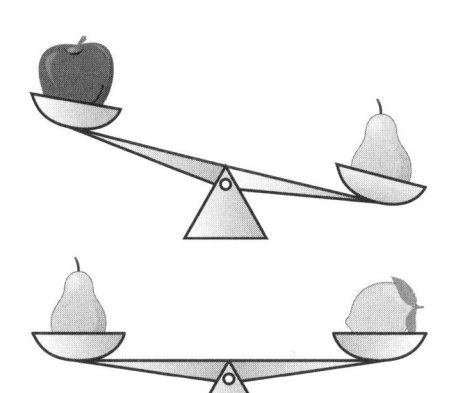

The pear and the lemon _____ .

The strawberry is _____ than the grapes.

The grapes are _____ than the strawberry.

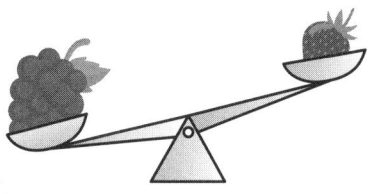

5   Colour the pictures to show what the words mean.

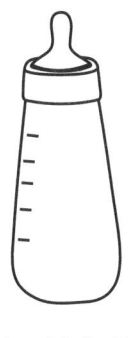

full   half full   empty

159

12 Measures (2)

Challenge

6 Look at the balance scales.

   The apple has the same mass as 10 cubes.

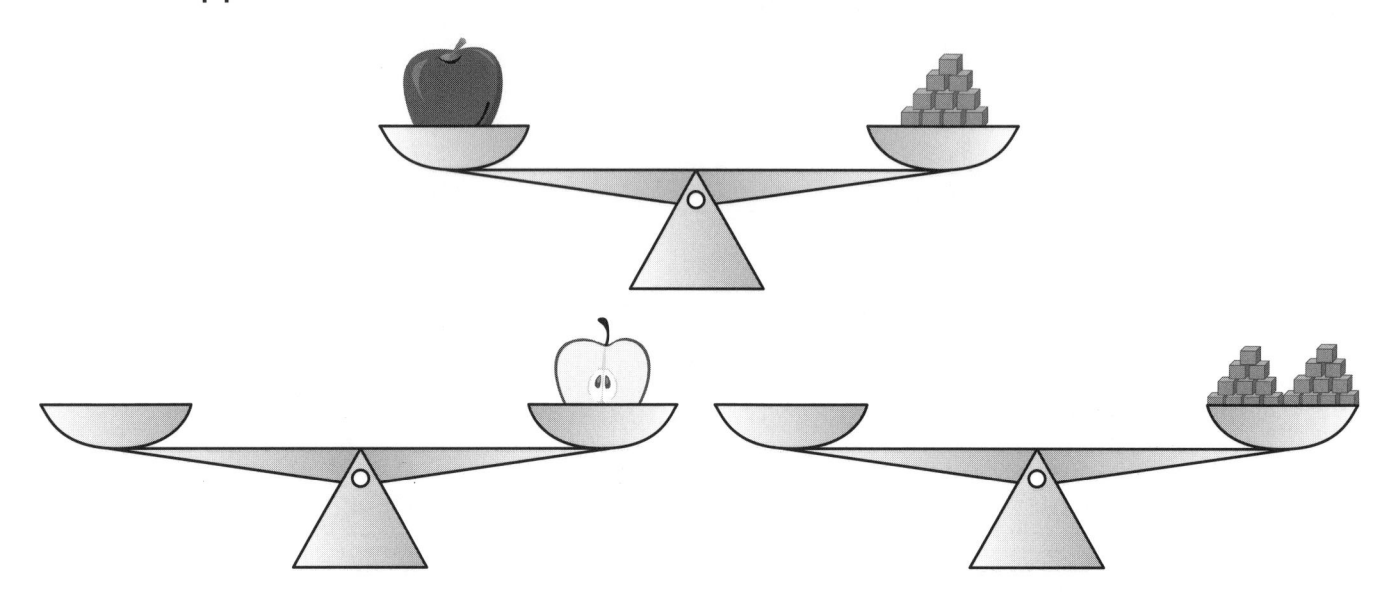

   Draw the cubes that will balance half an apple.

   Draw the apples that will balance 20 cubes.

   Draw three sets of scales to show **heavier than**, **lighter than** and **balanced**.

   Write a sentence for each of them.

12.1 Mass and capacity

7   Read the clues below. Work through each clue before moving
    to the next one.

    The glasses below are in the wrong order.

    Use the clues to find the correct order.

    Write the correct position in the box below each glass.

    There is one glass which is left over.

    | empty | juice | water | juice | water | water | empty | juice |

    Clues:

    The 7th glass is tall and half full of juice.

    The 6th glass is half full of water.

    The 5th and the 4th glasses are empty.

    The 3rd and the 2nd glasses are full of juice.

    The 1st glass is short.

    Draw a ring around the glass that is left. Is it full, half full or empty?

12 Measures (2)

> 12.2 How do we measure?

Exercise 12.2

temperature   thermometer

Focus

1 Draw a ring around the instrument you would use to measure length.

Draw a picture of something that is long.

Draw a picture of something that is short.

12.2 How do we measure?

2 Draw a ring around the instrument you would use to measure temperature.

Draw something that would make you hot.

Draw something that would make you cold.

163

12 Measures (2)

3. Draw a ring around the instrument you would use to measure height.

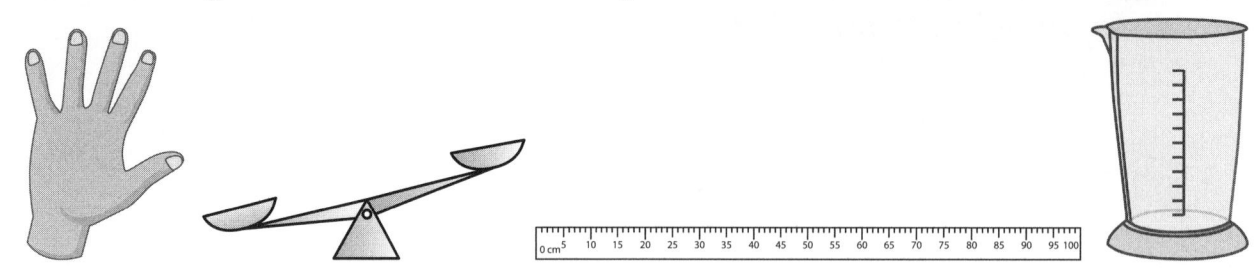

Draw the tallest thing you know.

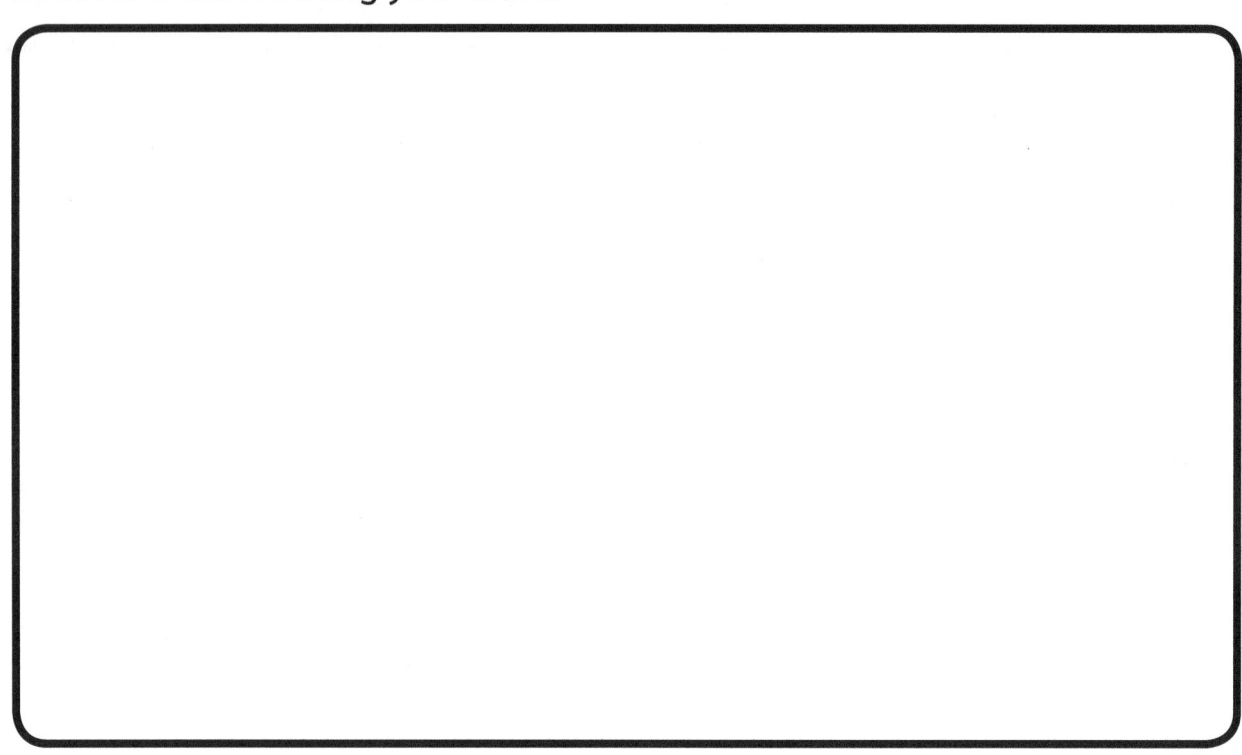

Draw the shortest thing you know.

Practice

4 Draw a ring around the thermometer that shows the highest temperature.

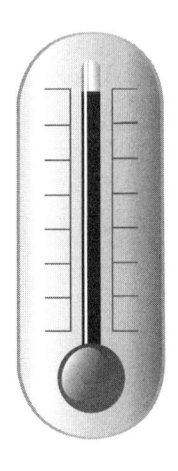

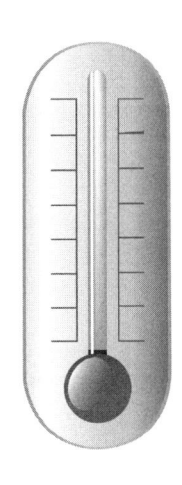

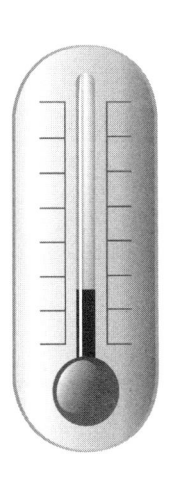

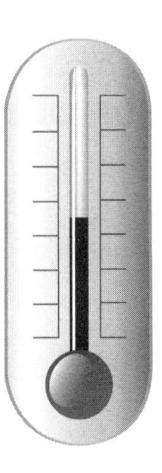

Colour these thermometers to match the words.

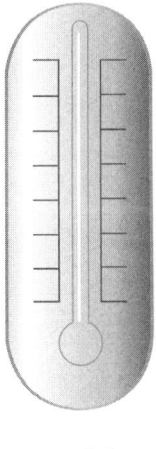

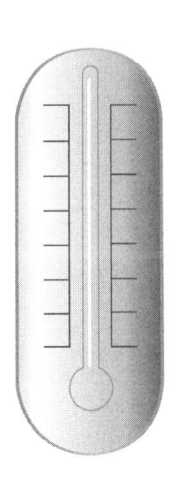

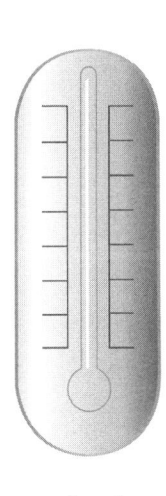

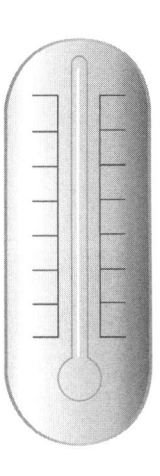

cold warm hot freezing

12 Measures (2)

5   When you measure your height and length they will be the same.

Find three things that you can measure.

Draw them to show their height and length.

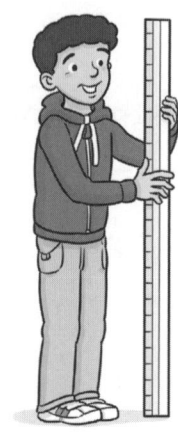

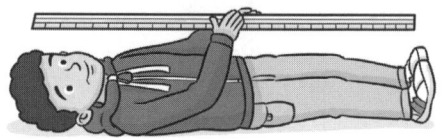

Remember, the height and length must be the same.

12.2 How do we measure?

6 Draw a ring around the thermometer that goes with each picture.

12 Measures (2)

Challenge

7   Match the words with the thermometers.

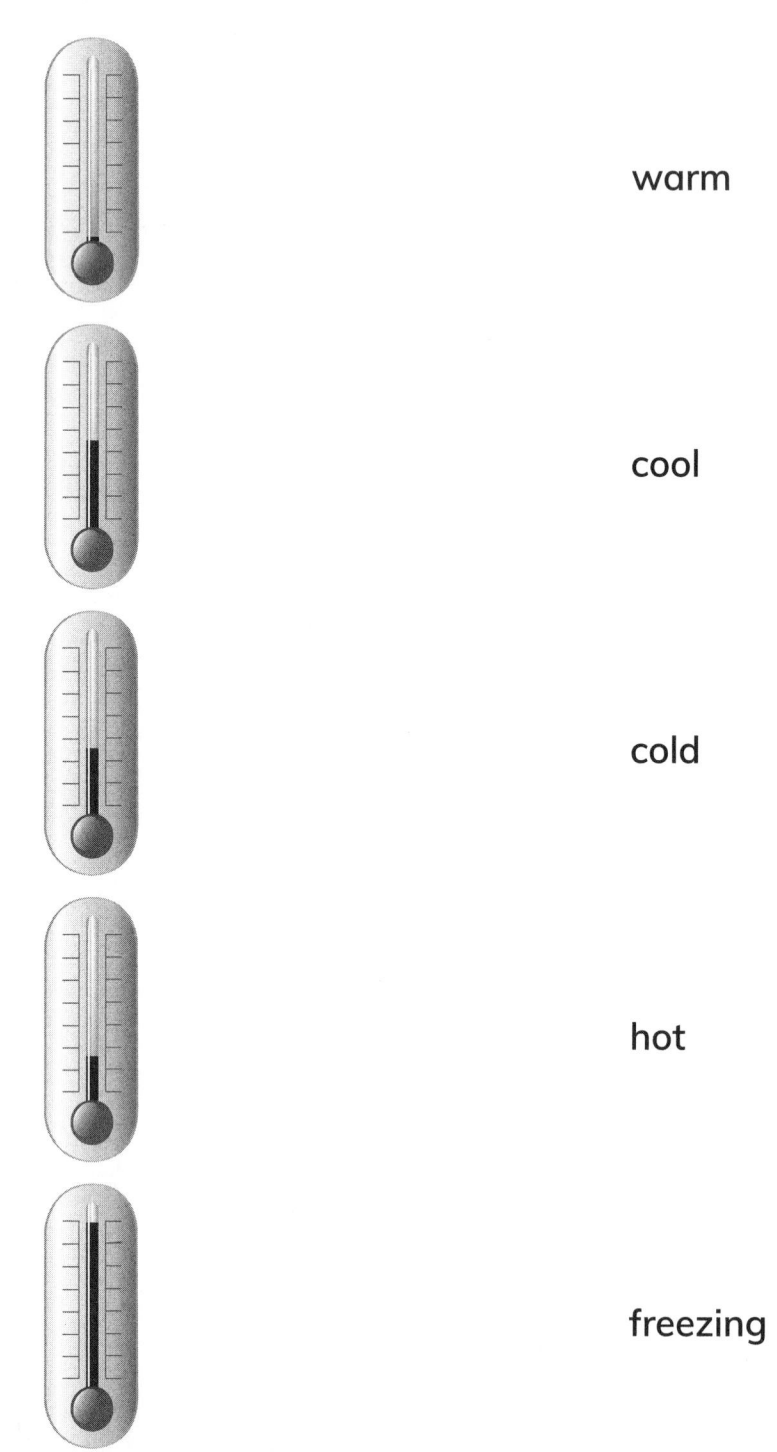

warm

cool

cold

hot

freezing

Explain to a parent or carer how you matched each word and thermometer.

168

12.2 How do we measure?

8   Which would you use to measure the length of each object?

Draw a ring around the answer.

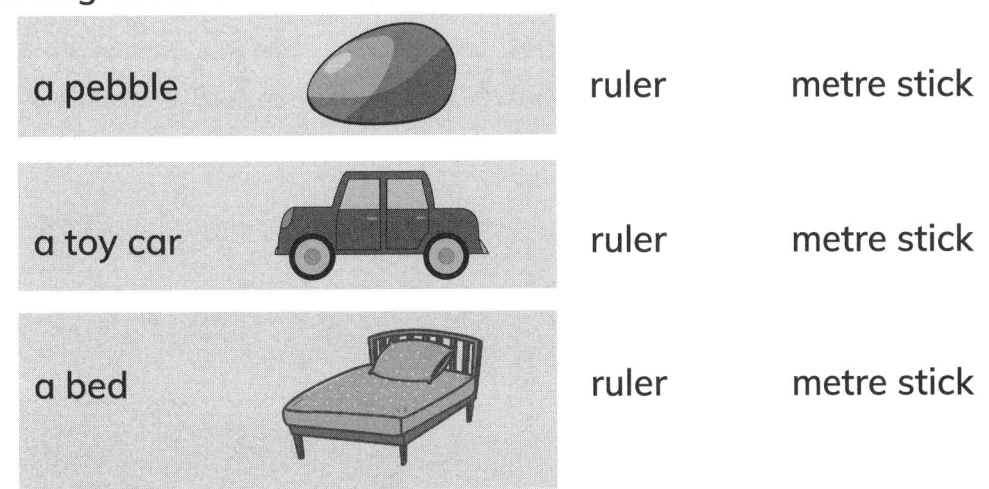

a pebble	ruler	metre stick
a toy car	ruler	metre stick
a bed	ruler	metre stick

9   Which would you use to measure the height of the following objects?

Draw a ring around the answer.

a tree	ruler	metre stick
a giraffe	ruler	metre stick
a flower	ruler	metre stick
a vase	ruler	metre stick

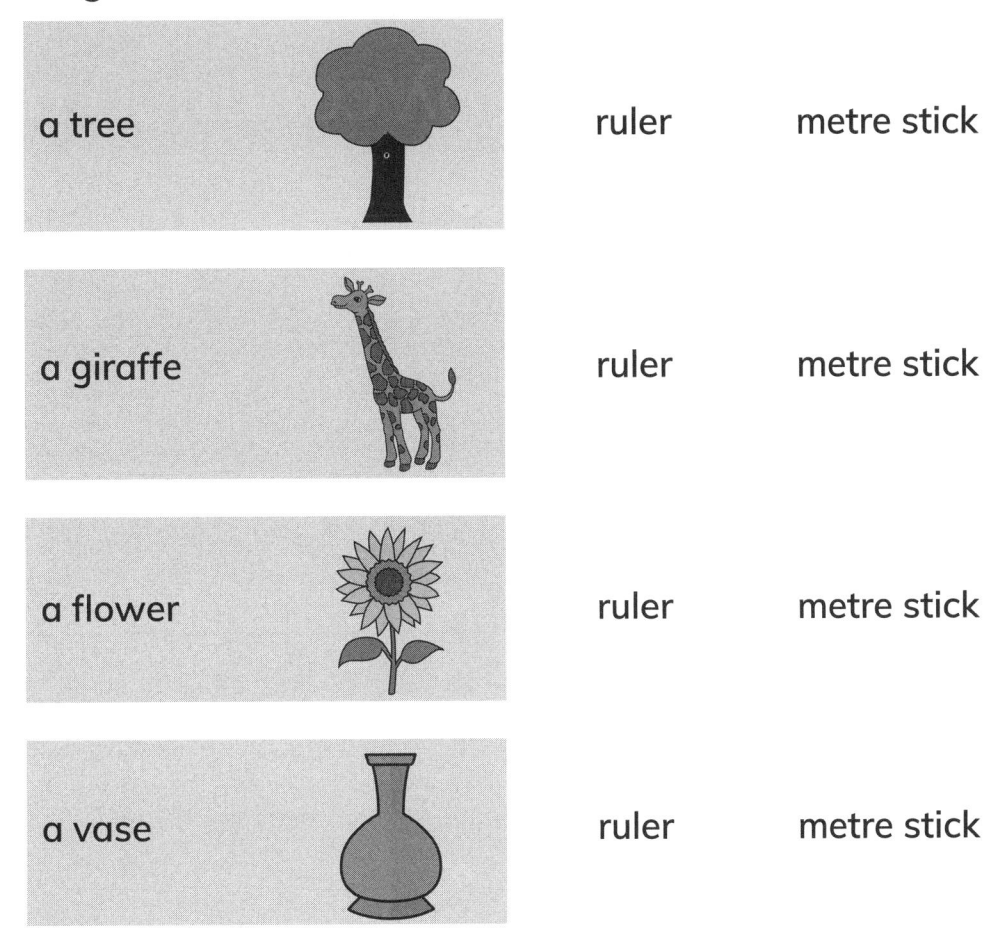

13 Working with numbers to 20

> 13.1 Addition by counting on

Exercise 13.1

> calculation   complement
> method   regroup   solve

Focus

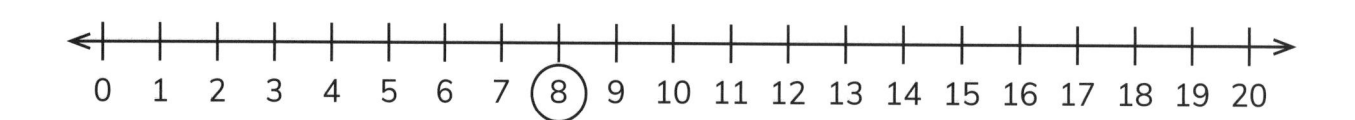

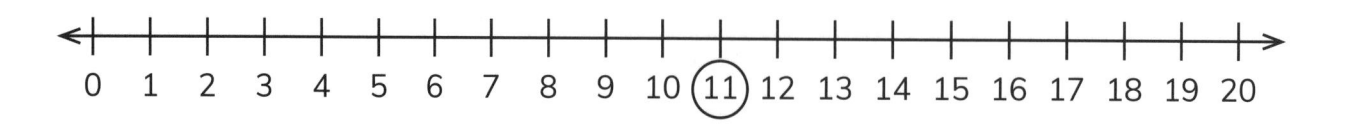

1   Count on in ones.

   Draw and label your jumps. Then write the missing total.

   8 + 5 = ☐

   0 1 2 3 4 5 6 7 ⑧ 9 10 11 12 13 14 15 16 17 18 19 20

   11 + 3 = ☐

   0 1 2 3 4 5 6 7 8 9 10 ⑪ 12 13 14 15 16 17 18 19 20

13.1 Addition by counting on

2 Count on in ones.

Draw and label **one** jump for each calculation. Then write the missing total.

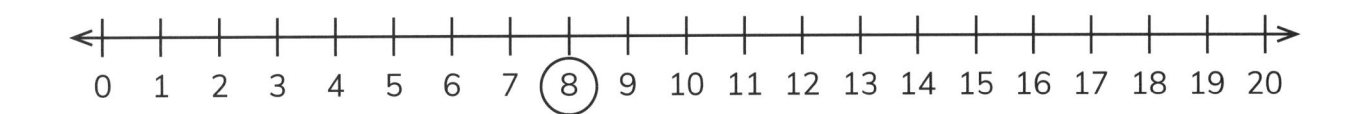

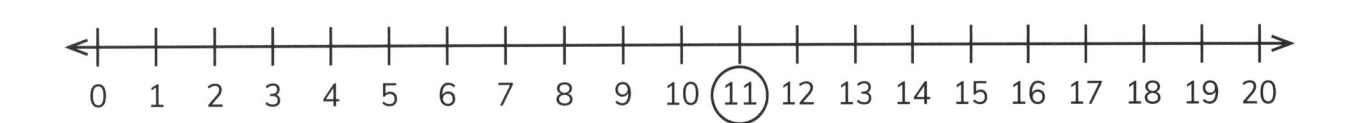

8 + 5 = ☐

```
← | | | | | | | | ⊙ | | | | | | | | | | | | →
  0 1 2 3 4 5 6 7 8 9 10 11 12 13 14 15 16 17 18 19 20
```

11 + 3 = ☐

```
← | | | | | | | | | | | ⊙ | | | | | | | | →
  0 1 2 3 4 5 6 7 8 9 10 11 12 13 14 15 16 17 18 19 20
```

3 Zara regrouped 7 into 4 and 3. Find two more ways to regroup 7.

13 Working with numbers to 20

Worked example 1

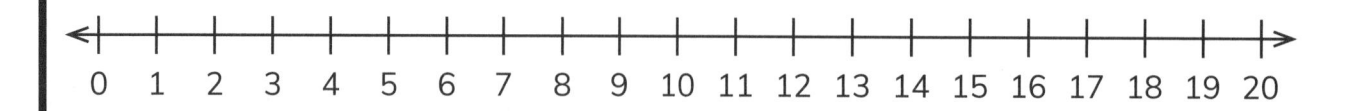

8 + 5 = ☐

0 1 2 3 4 5 6 7 8 9 10 11 12 13 14 15 16 17 18 19 20

Answer:

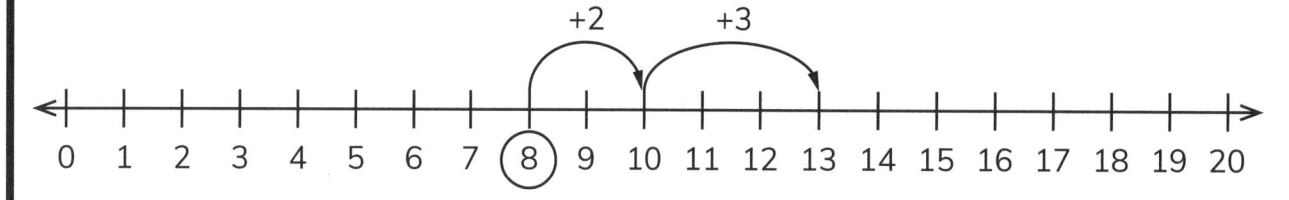

+2 +3

0 1 2 3 4 5 6 7 ⑧ 9 10 11 12 13 14 15 16 17 18 19 20

> Draw a ring around 8. I know that 8 + 2 = 10. I can draw a jump of 2 from 8 to 10.

> I have added 2. I need to add 3 more. That's another jump of 3 from 10 to 13. 8 + 5 = 13.

8 + 5 = 13

13.1 Addition by counting on

4   Show how to use complements to 10 to help you add on the number line. Then write the missing total.

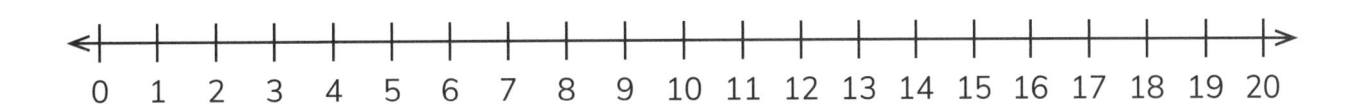

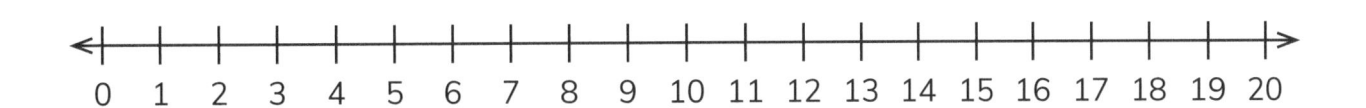

7 + 4 = ☐

0 1 2 3 4 5 6 7 8 9 10 11 12 13 14 15 16 17 18 19 20

9 + 3 = ☐

0 1 2 3 4 5 6 7 8 9 10 11 12 13 14 15 16 17 18 19 20

5   Choose which method to use to add 5 and 6 on the number line.

Write your number sentence. _____

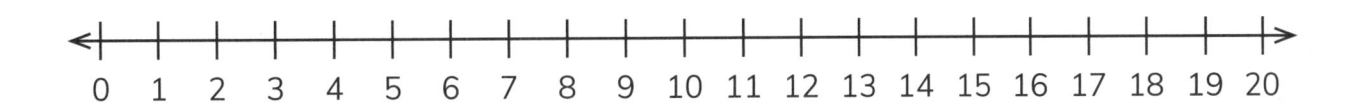

0 1 2 3 4 5 6 7 8 9 10 11 12 13 14 15 16 17 18 19 20

6   Worked example 1 showed that 8 + 5 = 8 + 2 + 3.
Write the missing numbers.

7 + 4 = ☐ + ☐ + ☐

11 + 3 = ☐ + ☐ + ☐

Tip

You don't have to use all of the answer boxes.

13 Working with numbers to 20

Practice

7   Count on in ones.

Draw and label **one** jump. Then write the missing total.

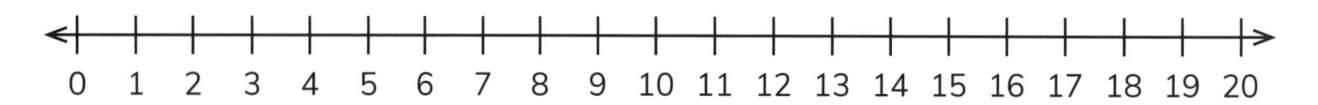

11 + 5 = ☐

←—+—→
 0 1 2 3 4 5 6 7 8 9 10 11 12 13 14 15 16 17 18 19 20

8   Regroup 6 in two different ways.

Regroup 13 in two different ways.

9   Use complements to 10 to help you add.
Then write the missing total.

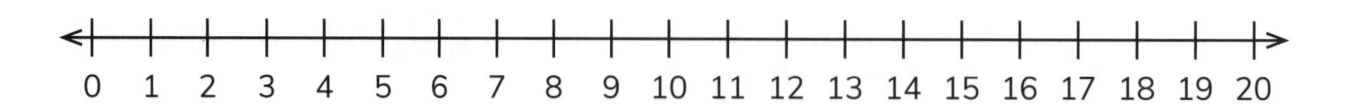

6 + 7 = ☐

←—+—→
 0 1 2 3 4 5 6 7 8 9 10 11 12 13 14 15 16 17 18 19 20

13.1 Addition by counting on

10 If question 6 was written as 7 + 6 = ☐ would you still use the same jumps?

Show your method below.

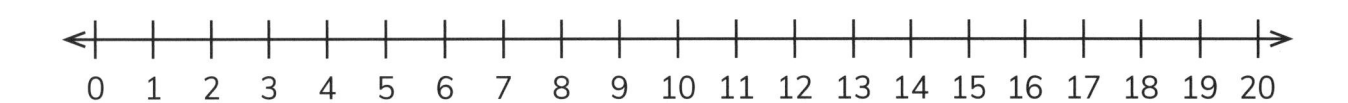

⟵|—|—|—|—|—|—|—|—|—|—|—|—|—|—|—|—|—|—|—|—|⟶
0 1 2 3 4 5 6 7 8 9 10 11 12 13 14 15 16 17 18 19 20

11 Each side of the equals sign has the same value.

Write the missing numbers.

6 + 7 = ☐ + ☐

☐ + ☐ = 11 + 5

12 Tomas drew a jump of 7 on the number line.

His total was 20.

What calculation was he solving? _____

Challenge

13 Choose two numbers to add using a complement to 10 and another jump.

Write the number sentence. _____

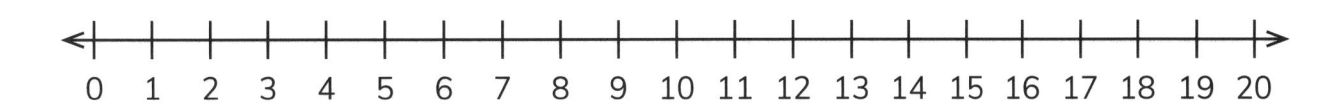

⟵|—|—|—|—|—|—|—|—|—|—|—|—|—|—|—|—|—|—|—|—|⟶
0 1 2 3 4 5 6 7 8 9 10 11 12 13 14 15 16 17 18 19 20

> **13** Working with numbers to 20

14 Milo used two jumps of 4 to add 8.

Then he decided it would be more efficient to use a jump of 2 and a jump of 6.

What could Milo's calculation have been? _____

15 Use Milo's number sentences to show that both sides of the equals sign have the same value.

☐ + ☐ + ☐ = ☐ + ☐ + ☐

> 13.2 Subtraction by counting back

Exercise 13.2

compose   decompose

Focus

1 Count back.

Draw your jumps. Then write the missing answers.

17 − 6 = ☐

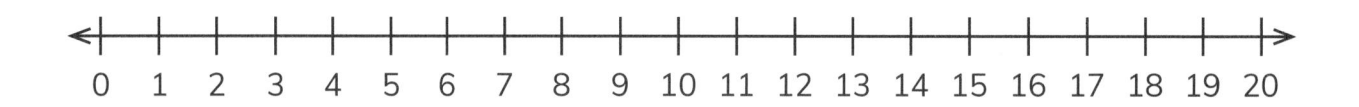

0 1 2 3 4 5 6 7 8 9 10 11 12 13 14 15 16 17 18 19 20

13 − 8 = ☐

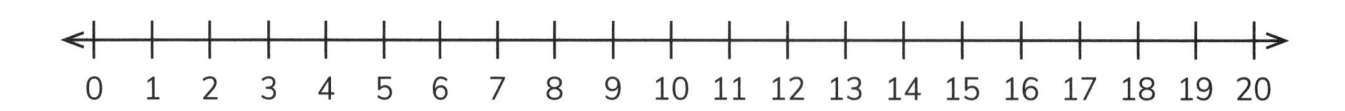

0 1 2 3 4 5 6 7 8 9 10 11 12 13 14 15 16 17 18 19 20

13.2 Subtraction by counting back

2 Draw your jumps. Then write the missing answers.

Remember to split (decompose) the number you are subtracting into a ten and some ones.

19 − 11 = ☐

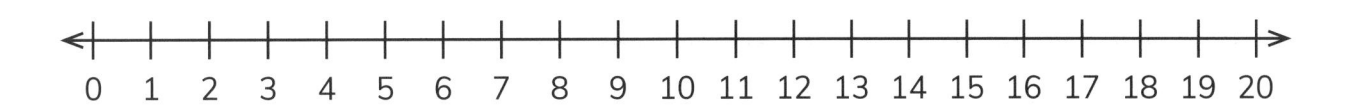

⬅|—|—|—|—|—|—|—|—|—|—|—|—|—|—|—|—|—|—|—|—|➡
0 1 2 3 4 5 6 7 8 9 10 11 12 13 14 15 16 17 18 19 20

17 − 13 = ☐

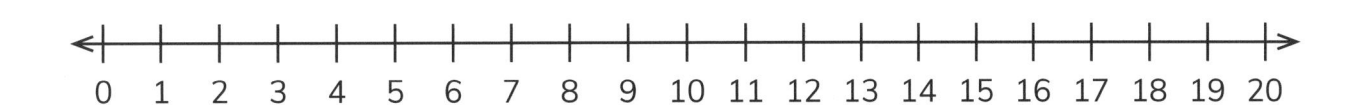

⬅|—|—|—|—|—|—|—|—|—|—|—|—|—|—|—|—|—|—|—|—|➡
0 1 2 3 4 5 6 7 8 9 10 11 12 13 14 15 16 17 18 19 20

3 Count back to 10 for your first jump.

Draw your jumps. Then write the missing answers.

14 − 6 = ☐

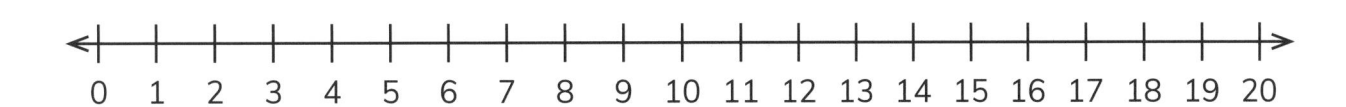

⬅|—|—|—|—|—|—|—|—|—|—|—|—|—|—|—|—|—|—|—|—|➡
0 1 2 3 4 5 6 7 8 9 10 11 12 13 14 15 16 17 18 19 20

12 − 7 = ☐

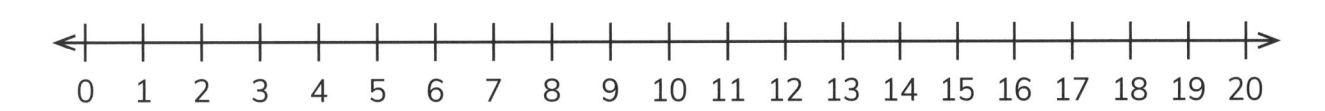

⬅|—|—|—|—|—|—|—|—|—|—|—|—|—|—|—|—|—|—|—|—|➡
0 1 2 3 4 5 6 7 8 9 10 11 12 13 14 15 16 17 18 19 20

13 Working with numbers to 20

4   Find the difference.

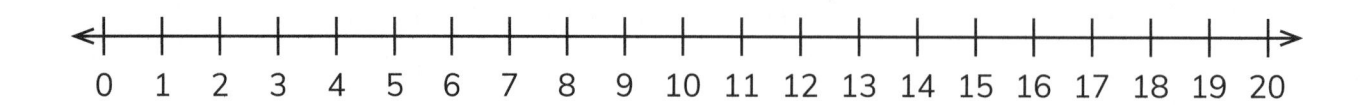

    0 1 2 3 4 5 6 7 8 9 10 11 12 13 14 15 16 17 18 19 20

    The difference between 4 and 8 is _____.

    The difference between 12 and 17 is _____.

Practice

5   Here is Arun's number line.

    What calculation was he solving?

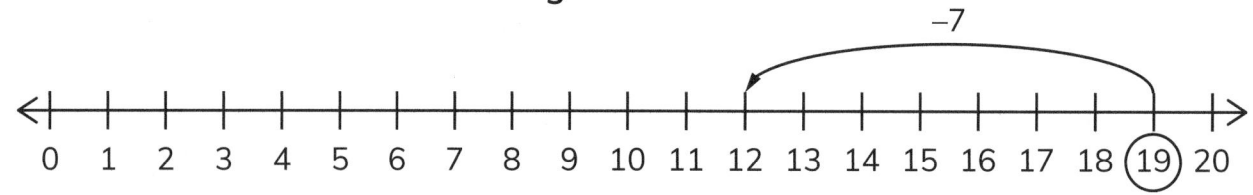

    −7

    0 1 2 3 4 5 6 7 8 9 10 11 12 13 14 15 16 17 18 (19) 20

    _____

6   Decompose 12 into a ten and some ones.

    Which number will you subtract first?

    Draw your jumps. Then write the missing answer.

    17 − 12 = ☐

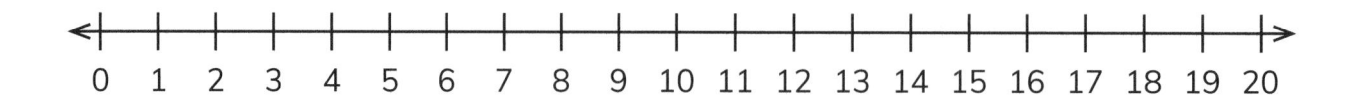

    0 1 2 3 4 5 6 7 8 9 10 11 12 13 14 15 16 17 18 19 20

13.2 Subtraction by counting back

7   Find the difference.

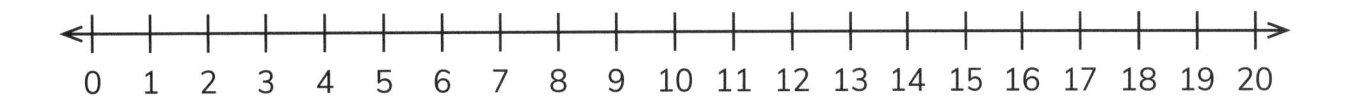

0 1 2 3 4 5 6 7 8 9 10 11 12 13 14 15 16 17 18 19 20

8 − 5 = ☐   14 − 9 = ☐   18 − 14 = ☐

Challenge

8   Choose a number from each circle.

Use your numbers to show that you know how to decompose a number greater than 10 to subtract.

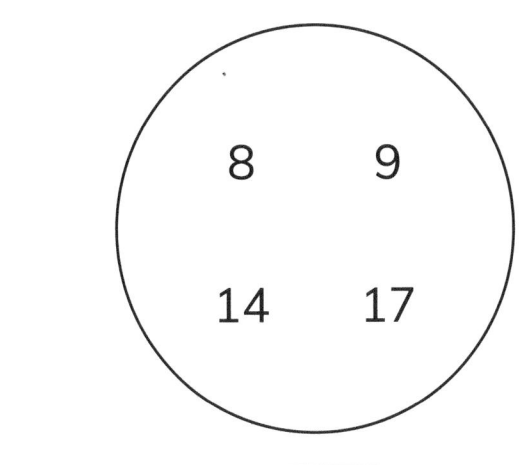

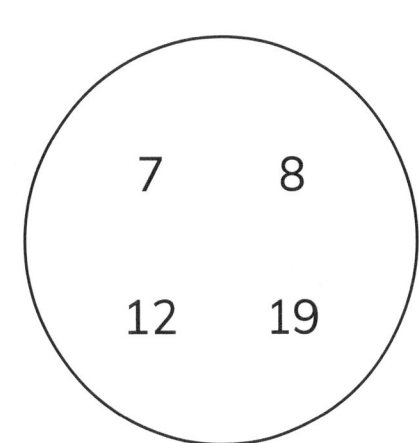

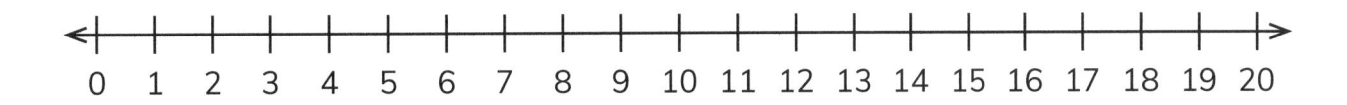

(8   9   14   17)   (7   8   12   19)

☐ − ☐ = ☐

0 1 2 3 4 5 6 7 8 9 10 11 12 13 14 15 16 17 18 19 20

13 Working with numbers to 20

9 Choose two more numbers.

Use your numbers to show that you can regroup a number fewer than 10 to subtract.

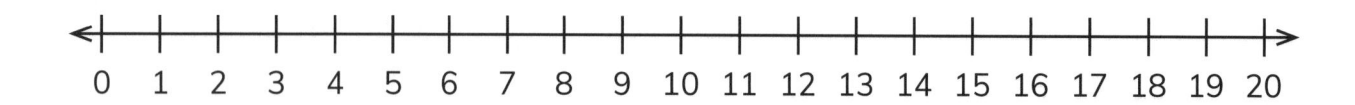

☐ – ☐ = ☐

<--+-->
0 1 2 3 4 5 6 7 8 9 10 11 12 13 14 15 16 17 18 19 20

Compose the number you subtracted to check your regrouping was correct.

10 Start at 20.

Spin the spinner to choose how many to count back.

You need to get to 0.

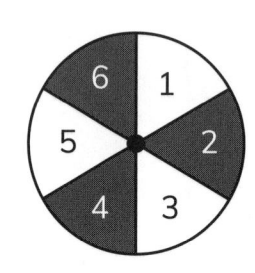

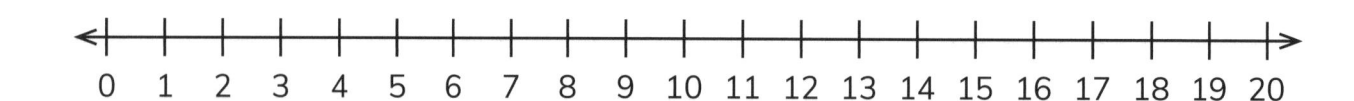

<--+-->
0 1 2 3 4 5 6 7 8 9 10 11 12 13 14 15 16 17 18 19 20

As you get closer to 0, spin again if your number is too many to land on 0.

Record your journey in number sentences.

For example, if you counted back 5 then 3, then 6, then 3, then 3, your number sentences would be:

20 – 5 = 15   15 – 3 = 12   12 – 6 = 6   6 – 3 = 3   3 – 3 = 0

> 13.3 Using the number line

Exercise 13.3

> double   word problem

Focus

1   Solve these calculations.

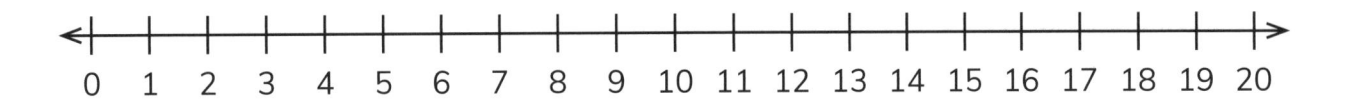

0 1 2 3 4 5 6 7 8 9 10 11 12 13 14 15 16 17 18 19 20

5 + 0 = ☐   10 + 0 = ☐   15 + 0 = ☐

5 − 0 = ☐   10 − 0 = ☐   15 − 0 = ☐

2   Your target is 12.

Record your own way to get to 12.

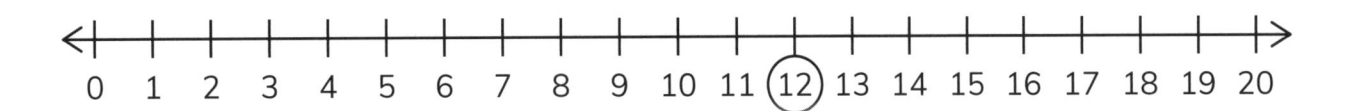

0 1 2 3 4 5 6 7 8 9 10 11 (12) 13 14 15 16 17 18 19 20

13 Working with numbers to 20

Worked example 2

There are 9 books on the shelf.

Sofia put 4 more books on the shelf.

How many books are on the shelf now?

Answer:

First there were 9, then 4 more. I need to add.

I know 9 + 1 = 10, so 9 + 4 is a bit more than that.

9 + 4 = 13. I used the number line.

+1 +3

0 1 2 3 4 5 6 7 8 9 10 11 12 13 14 15 16 17 18 19 20

9 + 4 = 13

182

13.3 Using the number line

3   Write the number sentence for each word problem.

Estimate the answer.

Then solve your number sentence.

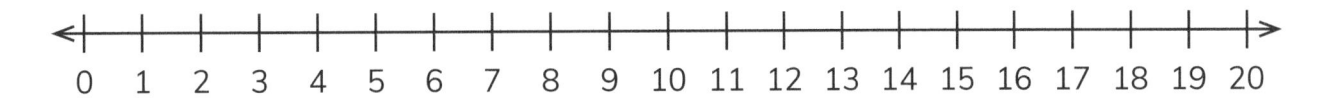

0 1 2 3 4 5 6 7 8 9 10 11 12 13 14 15 16 17 18 19 20

There were 13 books on the shelf.

Arun put 6 more books on the shelf.

How many books are on the shelf now?

There were 12 sweets in the bag.

Zara ate 4 sweets.

How many sweets are left?

4   A double is two lots of something. A double two domino has 2 + 2 spots, so 4 spots altogether.

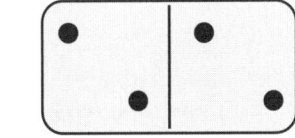

Complete the doubles table.

Number	0	1	2		4		6	7	8	9	
Double				6		10					20

13 Working with numbers to 20

Practice

5   Start at 18.

Record your own way to reach 0.

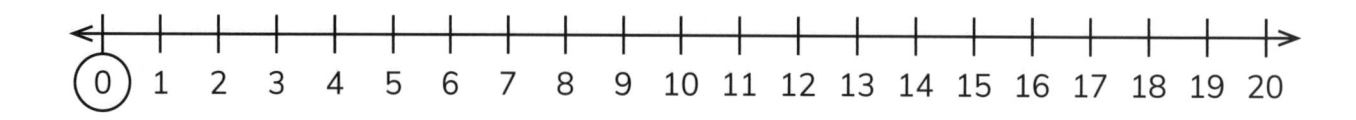

<------|---|---|---|---|---|---|---|---|---|---|---|---|---|---|---|---|---|---|---|------>
  (0) 1   2   3   4   5   6   7   8   9 10 11 12 13 14 15 16 17 18 19 20

6   Write the number sentence for each word problem.

Estimate the answer.

Then solve your number sentence.

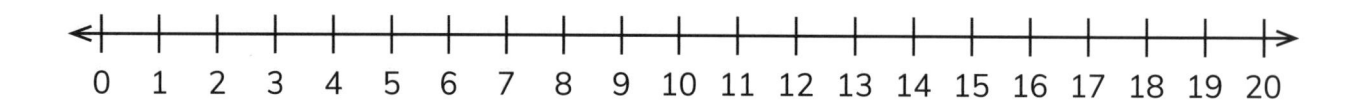

<------|---|---|---|---|---|---|---|---|---|---|---|---|---|---|---|---|---|---|---|------>
   0   1   2   3   4   5   6   7   8   9 10 11 12 13 14 15 16 17 18 19 20

There were 15 sheep in the field.

9 of them went into the barn.

How many sheep were left in the field?

There were 7 birds on a branch.

5 more birds arrived.

How many birds are on the branch now?

13.3 Using the number line

7 Find the missing numbers.

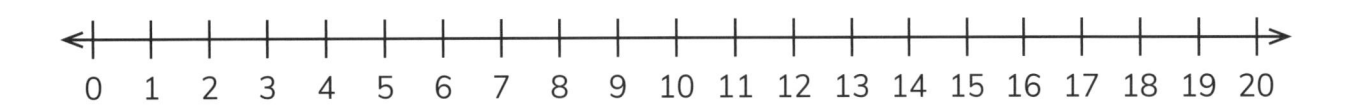

3 + 3 = ☐   Double 6 = ☐   Double 9 = ☐

Double 4 = ☐   Double ☐ = 14   Double ☐ = 18

Challenge

8 Marcus had 0 sweets.

He ate 0.

How many sweets did Marcus have left?

Write your number sentence.

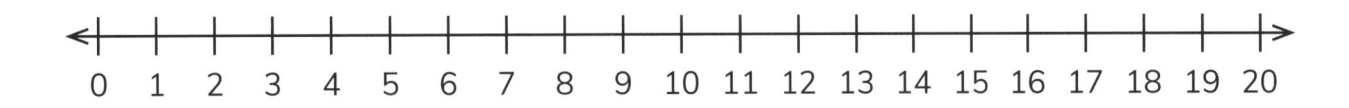

9 Record your own way to make 19.

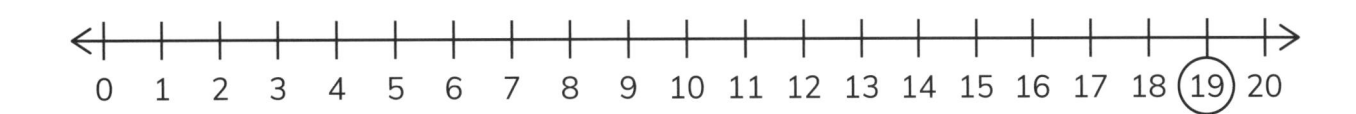

Can you reverse your jumps to get back to 0?

Record those number sentences.

How are they the same?

How are they different?

13 Working with numbers to 20

10 Sofia wrote 17 − 9 = 8 when she solved a word problem.

Write a word problem for Sofia's number sentence.

_____

_____

> 13.4 Money

Exercise 13.4

banknote   coin   money
price   value

Focus

1 Draw a line to show where each of these coins belongs.

Fewer than 10		10 or greater
	One	
	Two	
	Five	
	Ten	
	Twenty	

13.4 Money

Practice

2. Tomas made a pattern with some coins.

   1, 10, 1, 10, 1, 10

   Make a pattern with some coins or banknotes.

   Record your pattern here.

   Draw each coin or banknote. Or you could do a rubbing of each coin.

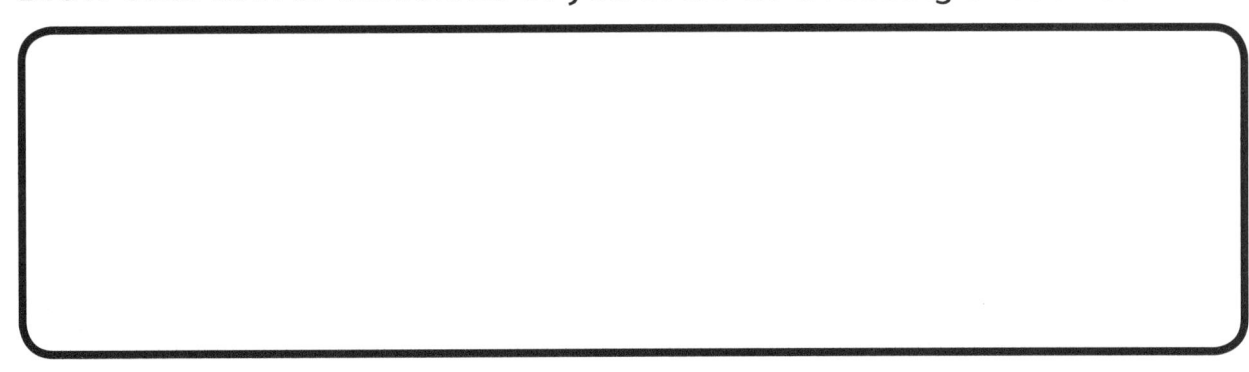

3. Are you saving money to buy something?

   Draw any money you have collected.

13 Working with numbers to 20

Challenge

4. Look at the coins you have.

   Use only 1 of each coin.

   Sort the coins into the circles.

   You will need some coins.

   odd   even

   Do you have more odd or more even coins?

   Why do you think this might be?

5. Look at this row of coins.

   Design a coin worth the same as all of these coins together.

   You can choose the size, shape, colour and design of your coin.

   2 2 2 2 2 2 2 2 2 2

14 Statistics (2)

> 14.1 Venn diagrams, Carroll diagrams and pictograms

Exercise 14.1

> **Worked example 1**
>
> Farmer Jon has some animals.
>
> There are 4 goats.
>
> There are 5 chickens.
>
> Are there more chickens or ducks?
>
> How many animals are there altogether?

1 picture = 1 animal

Answer:

There are 5 chickens and 3 ducks.

5 is more than 3.

There are more chickens than ducks.

There are 13 animals altogether.

To find out how many animals there are altogether, I counted all the animals in the pictogram.

Carroll diagram   label   pictogram   title

14 Statistics (2)

Focus

1. Sofia went to visit the zoo. These are the animals she saw.

   Use the pictogram to answer the questions.

tigers	penguins	elephants	monkeys

   1 picture = 1 animal

   Sofia saw _____ tigers.

   Sofia saw _____ elephants.

   Sofia saw _____ penguins.

   Sofia saw _____ monkeys.

   How many animals did Sofia see altogether? _____

2. Look at the numbers.

   Put them into the correct place in the Carroll diagram.

   Numbers: 5, 11, 4, 15, 12, 14, 2, 7, 16

less than 10	not less than 10

14.1 Venn diagrams, Carroll diagrams and pictograms

Practice

3   Learners in class 1 got stars ☆ when they did good work.

Gulmira got these stars this week:

Monday	Tuesday	Wednesday	Thursday	Friday
3	1	4	0	2

Draw the stars that Gulmira got each day.

Monday	Tuesday	Wednesday	Thursday	Friday

On which day did Gulmira get the most stars?   _____

On which day did Gulmira get the fewest stars?   _____

On Monday Gulmira got 3 stars.

Which other 2 days would make the same total of stars as Monday?

_____

How many more stars did she get on Wednesday than on Thursday? ☐

How many fewer stars did she get on Friday than on Wednesday? ☐

14 Statistics (2)

4   Draw lines to sort the animals into this Venn diagram.

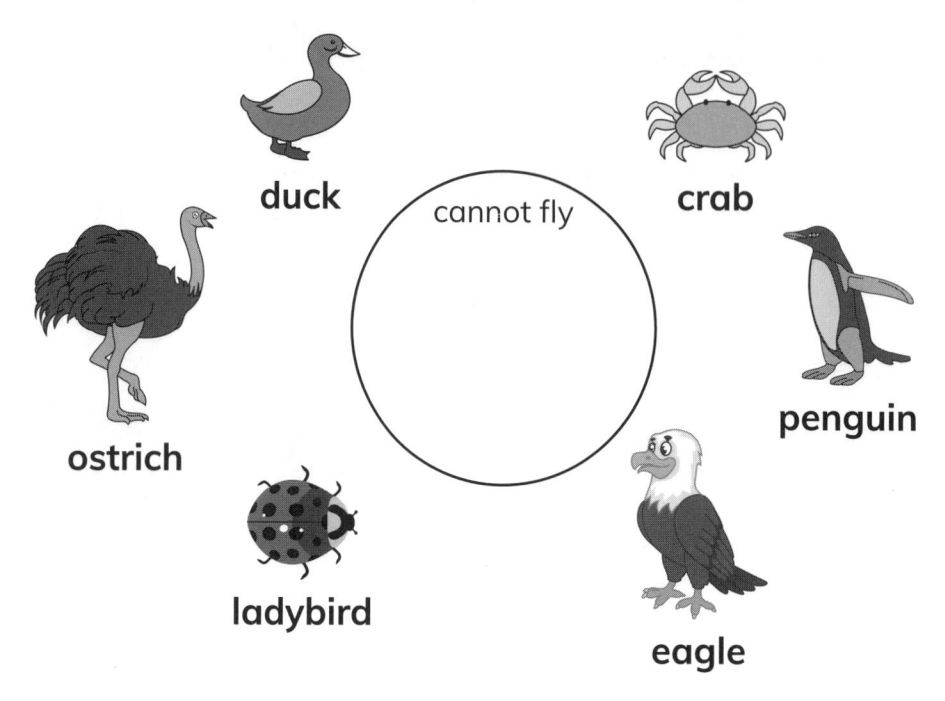

duck, **crab**, **penguin**, **eagle**, **ladybird**, **ostrich**

cannot fly

5   Sort the bugs into the Carroll diagram.
    You can draw them or write their names.

| spider | mosquito | ant | dragonfly | grasshopper | centipede | bee |

can fly	cannot fly

Tip

You might need to ask an adult to help you find out which bugs can fly.

14.1 Venn diagrams, Carroll diagrams and pictograms

Challenge

6   This pictogram shows the number of birds seen by 4 different children.

Name	Number of birds seen
Lola	🐦🐦🐦🐦🐦🐦🐦
Chan	🐦🐦
Beverly	🐦🐦🐦🐦🐦🐦
Jim	🐦🐦🐦🐦

🐦 = 1 bird

How many birds were seen by each child?

Lola ☐   Chan ☐   Beverly ☐   Jim ☐

How many more birds did Beverly see than Chan? ☐

Did Lola see an odd or even number of birds? _____

Who saw the most birds? _____

Add the birds from 2 children to make an odd total.
Which children did you choose and what is the total?

_____

_____

What is the highest odd total of birds? ☐

193

14 Statistics (2)

Make your own pictogram of birds.
Then write 4 questions for someone else to answer.

Name	Number of birds seen

☐ = 1 bird

_____

_____

_____

_____

14.1 Venn diagrams, Carroll diagrams and pictograms

7   A teacher asks Class A to pick their favourite mealtime.

breakfast   lunch   dinner

These are the data the teacher collects.

Choose your own way to present the data.

Choose from a Venn diagram, a pictogram or a Carroll diagram.

14 Statistics (2)

> 14.2 Lists, tables and block graphs

Exercise 14.2

block graph   list   table

Worked example 2

In the pictures, some mice are looking to the right.

Some mice are looking to the left.

Some mice are smiling.

Some mice are holding their arms out.

How can we find out how many there are of each type of mouse?

14.2 Lists, tables and block graphs

> **Continued**

Answer:

We can look in all the shapes for mice that are the same and count them.

Or we can look for one type of mouse and see how many are in each field.

Then we can add the numbers together.

🐭	5
🐭	4
🐭	6
🐭	4

197

14 Statistics (2)

Focus

1. Count how many there are of each type of object.

   Complete the table to show the same amount.

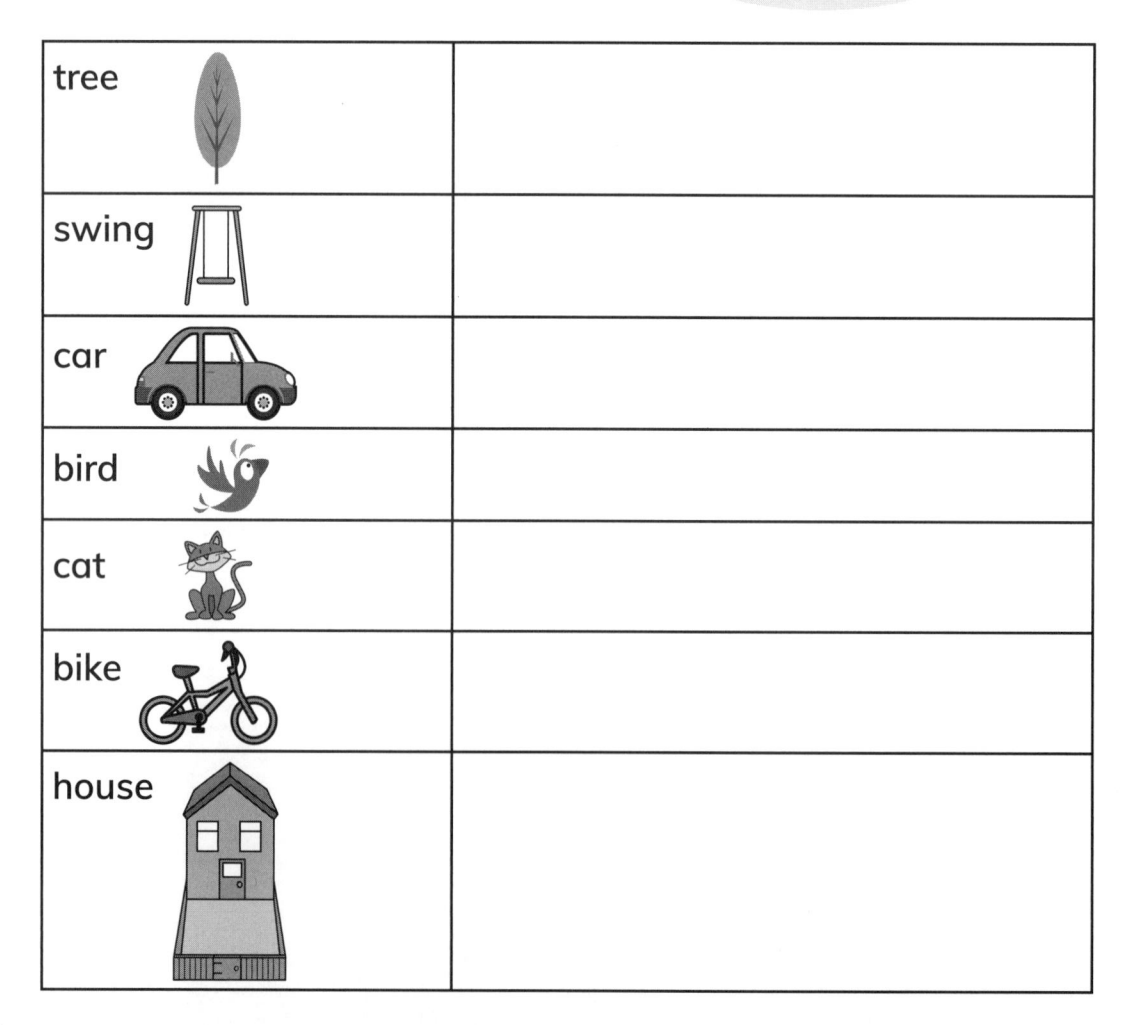

tree	
swing	
car	
bird	
cat	
bike	
house	

14.2 Lists, tables and block graphs

2 This pictogram shows different flavours of ice cream.
   How many people like each flavour of ice cream?

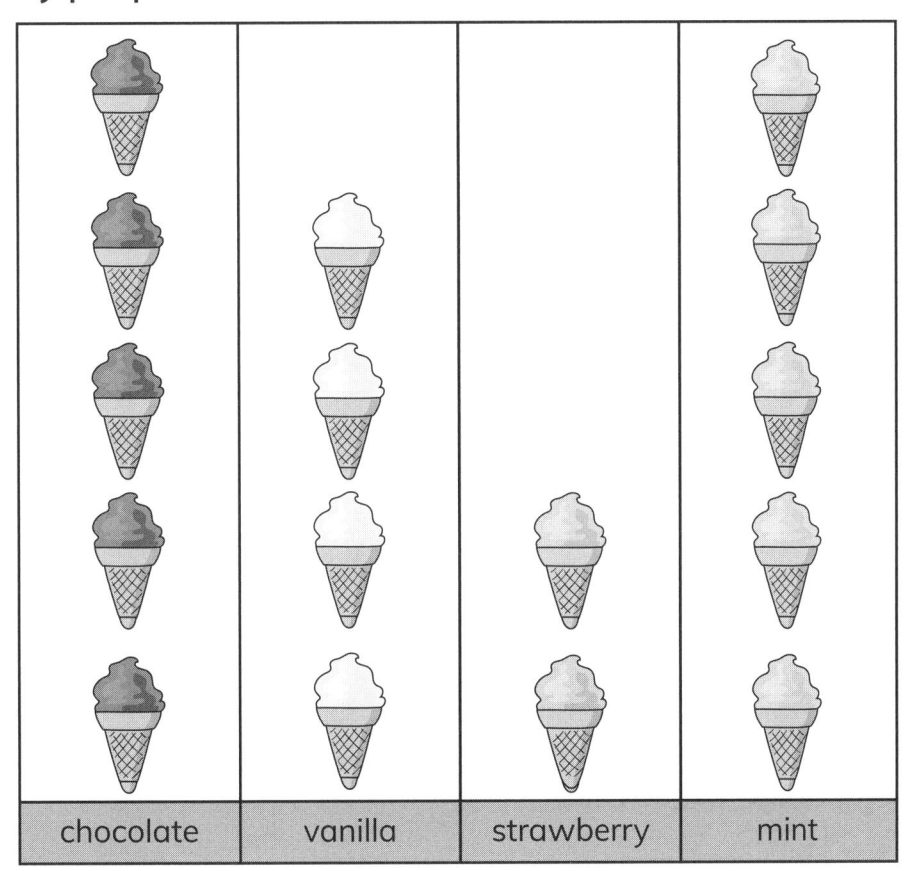

| chocolate | vanilla | strawberry | mint |

= 1 ice cream

How many people like chocolate ice cream? ☐

How many people like vanilla ice cream? ☐

How many people like strawberry ice cream? ☐

How many people like mint ice cream? ☐

Which ice cream do you like best?

14 Statistics (2)

3   **Favourite mealtime**

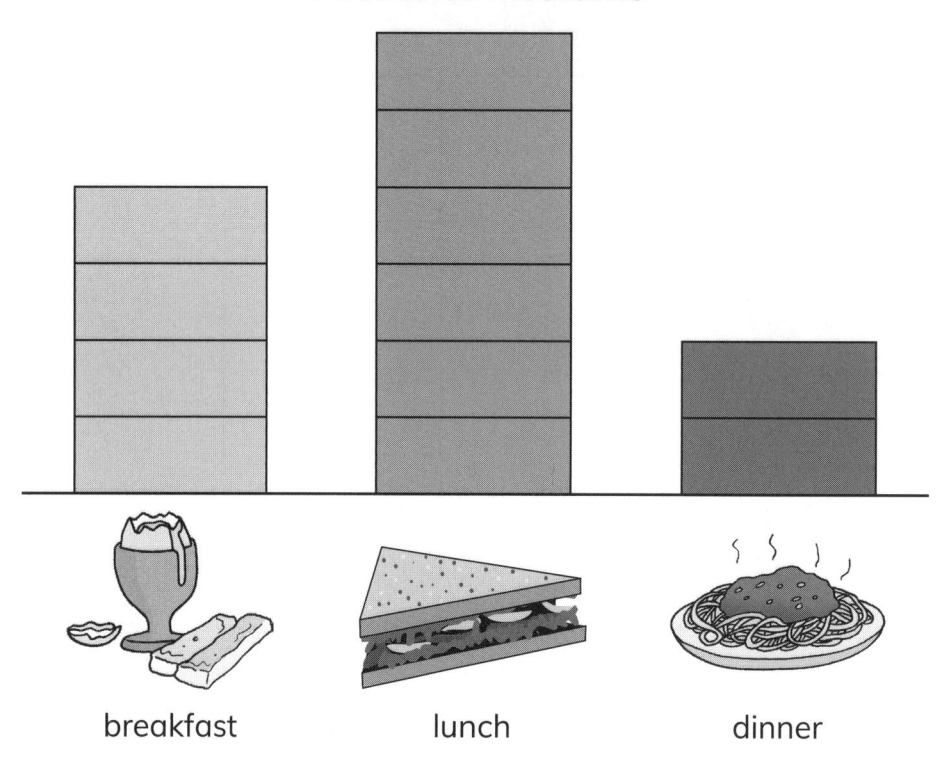

breakfast   lunch   dinner

How many people like breakfast ? ☐

How many people like lunch ? ☐

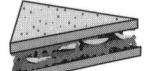

How many people like dinner ? ☐

14.2 Lists, tables and block graphs

Practice

4 Use this pictogram to complete the table.

Favourite animals	
fish	😀😀😀😀😀
dog	😀😀😀😀😀😀😀
penguin	😀😀😀😀😀
rabbit	😀😀😀😀😀😀😀😀
horse	😀😀😀😀😀😀
cat	😀😀😀😀

😀 = 1 animal

Favourite animals	
fish	5
dog	
penguin	
rabbit	
horse	
cat	

14 Statistics (2)

5 Label and colour the block graph.

Use the clues to help you. The first one has been done for you.

- 2 children like yellow.
- 5 children like red.
- 6 children like blue.
- 3 children like green.

yellow			

14.2 Lists, tables and block graphs

6 Label and colour in the block graph.

Use the clues to help you.

2 more children like bananas than apples.

1 fewer child likes apples than pineapples.

5 children like bananas.

The same number of children like kiwis and mangoes.

8 children like kiwis.

Which fruit do the fewest children like? _____

14 Statistics (2)

Challenge

7 Which block diagram matches the pictogram?

Animals at the zoo	
🦒	✓ ✓ ✓
🦁	✓ ✓ ✓ ✓
🦏	✓ ✓
🐘	✓ ✓ ✓
🐵	✓ ✓ ✓ ✓ ✓ ✓

✓ = 1 animal

a

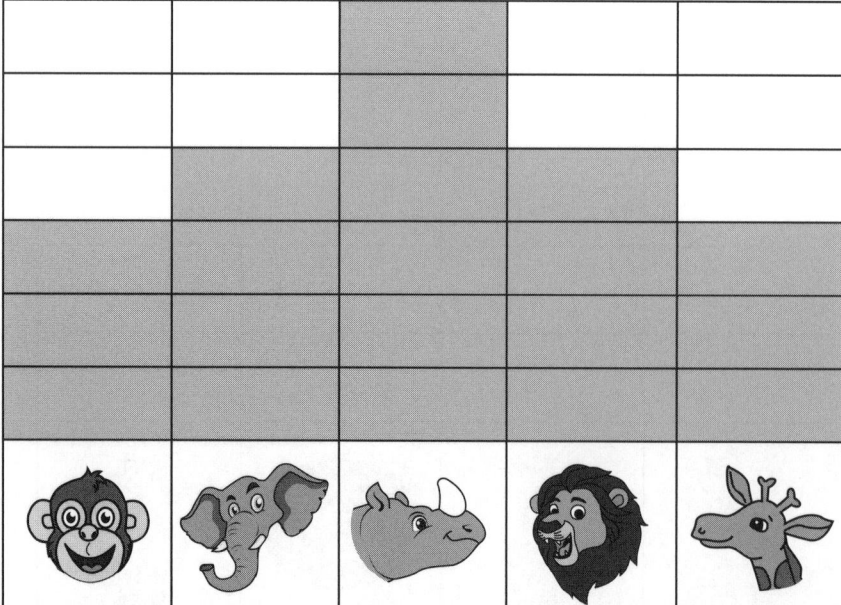

204

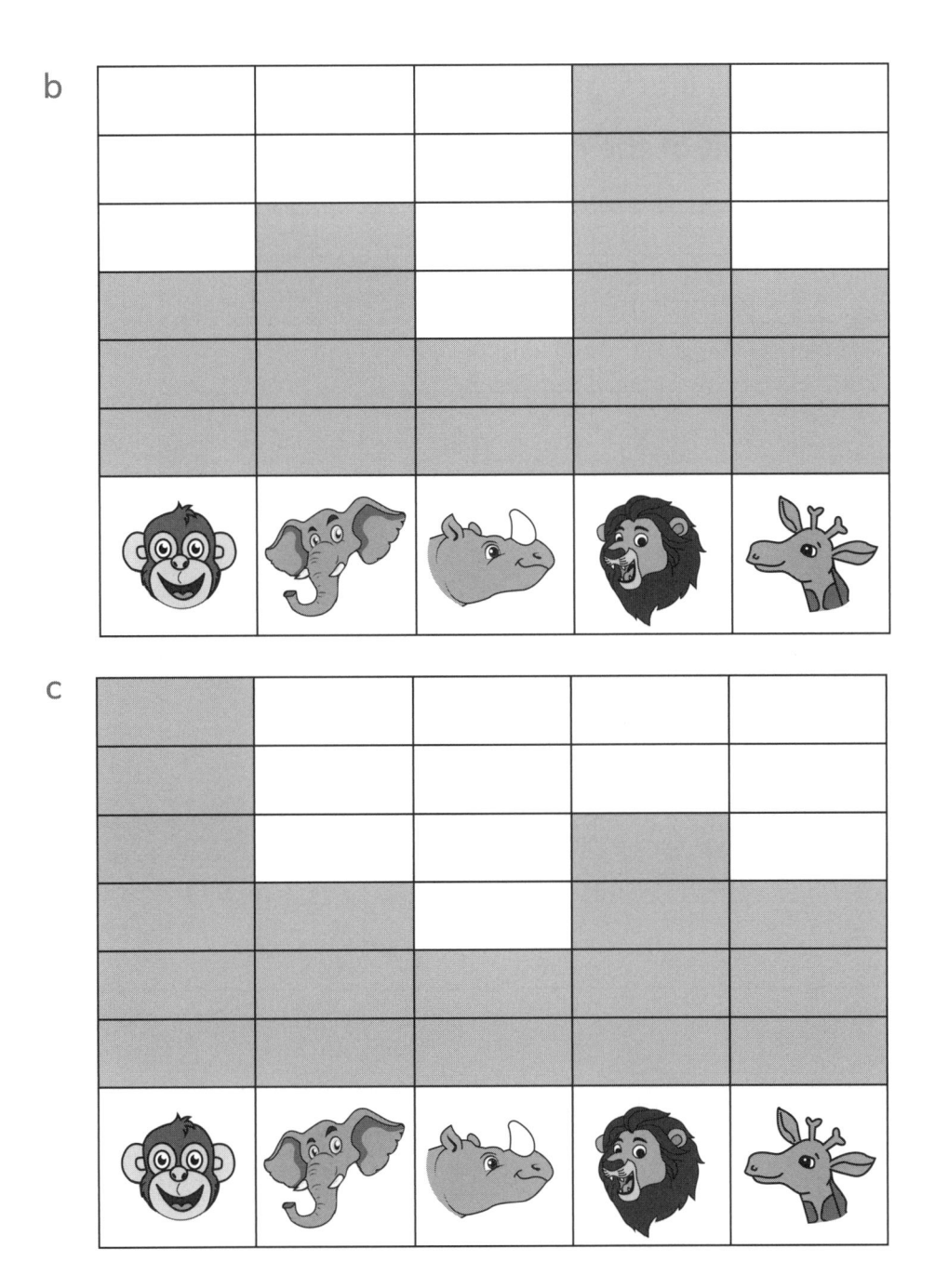

14.2 Lists, tables and block graphs

14 Statistics (2)

8 Use the data shown in this block graph to complete the table.

Favourite fruit of the children in Abduhl's class

Favourite fruit of the children in Abduhl's class	
🍎	5
🍍	4
🍇	3
🍌	6
🍊	7

14.2 Lists, tables and block graphs

9 Count the vehicles.

Choose your own way to present the data.

Choose from a list, a table or a block graph.

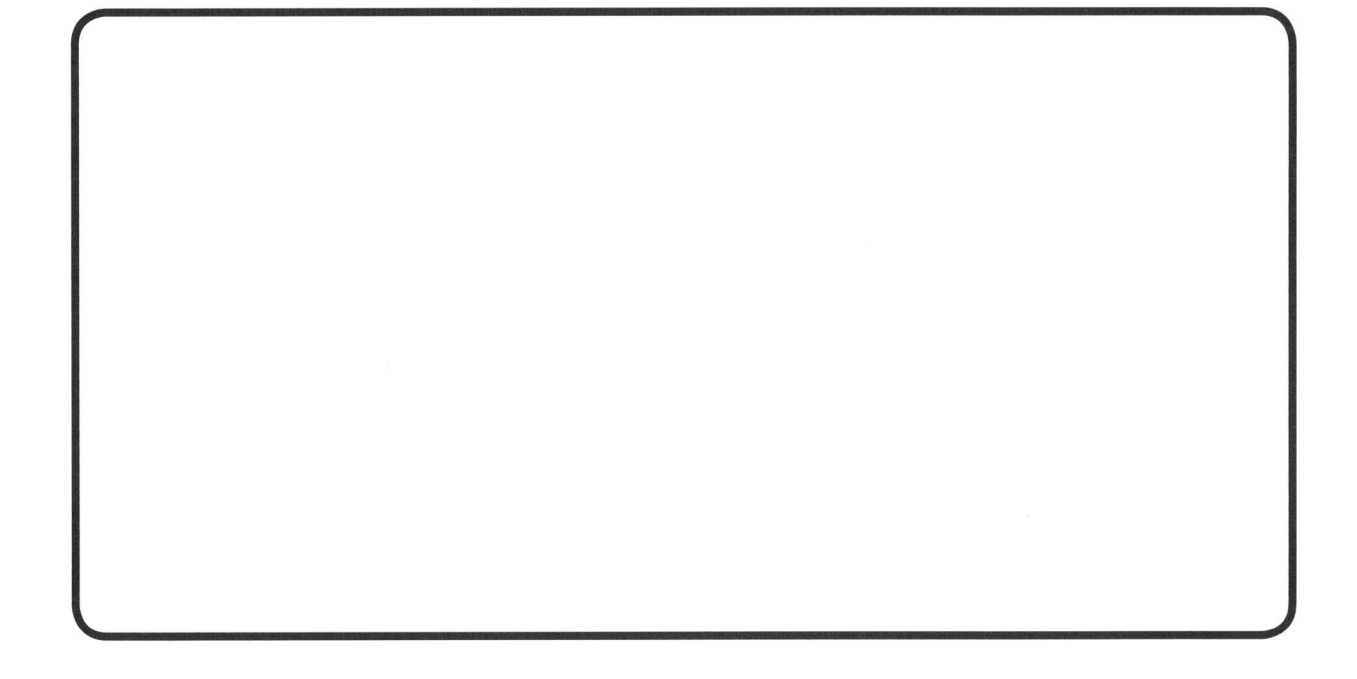

15 Time (2)

> 15.1 Time

Exercise 15.1

Focus

month   year

1   What time is it?

_____   _____   _____

> **Worked example 1**
>
> What time is it?

15.1 Time

Continued

Answer:

half past 7

When there is only one hand, it is an hour hand.

The hand is halfway between the 7 and the 8.

2 What time is it?

15 Time (2)

3 Join the clocks that show the same time.

Clocks with 2 hands   **Clocks with 1 hand**

4 Write yesterday and tomorrow in the correct places.

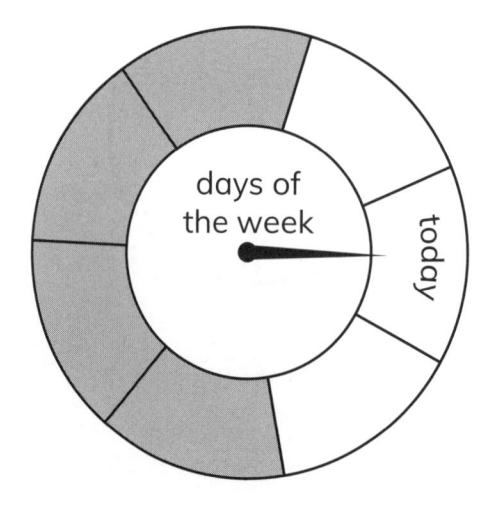

days of the week

today

5   What day is it today?   _____

   What day was it yesterday?   _____

   What day will it be tomorrow?   _____

6   The day after Wednesday is _____.

   The day before Tuesday is _____.

   Only one day begins with F. It is _____.

> **Worked example 2**
>
> It is June.
> What **month** will it be next?

Answer:

"It is June now."

"Move the pointer one space clockwise to find the next month. A month later is July."

15 Time (2)

7   What month is it now? _____

What month was it last month? _____

What month will it be next month? _____

Practice

8   Join the clocks that show the same time.

Clocks with 2 hands   **Clocks with 1 hand**

15.1 Time

9 Today is Thursday.

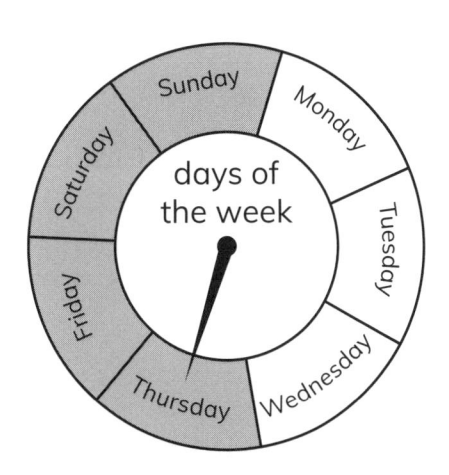

What day will it be tomorrow? _____

What day will it be in 2 days' time? _____

What day was it 2 days ago? _____

What day was it yesterday? _____

10 It is June.

What month will it be next month? _____

What month will it be in 2 months' time? _____

What month was it 3 months ago? _____

What month will it be in 13 months' time? _____

Challenge

11 Today is Thursday.

How many days until it is Thursday again? _____

Milo goes on holiday in 9 days' time.

What day of the week does Milo go on holiday? _____

15 Time (2)

12 Complete these sentences.

Two days of the week begin with T.

They are _____ and _____ .

Only one day of the week has an o in its name.

It is _____ .

Two months of the year begin with M.

They are _____ and _____ .

Two months of the year end with –**ary**.

They are _____ and _____ .

Four months of the year end with –**ber**.

They are _____ , _____ , _____ and

_____ .

15.1 Time

13 Tick ✓ the speech bubble that is correct.

Tip

When there is only one hand on the clock, it is an hour hand.

The hand is pointing to the 6, so it must be half past 6.

The hand is pointing to the 6, so it must be 6 o'clock.

14 Rakesh says that this clock is broken.

Do you agree with him?

Explain why.

_____

_____

16 Position, direction and patterns

> 16.1 Position, direction and patterns

Exercise 16.1

Focus

left right sequence

1 Write the missing words.

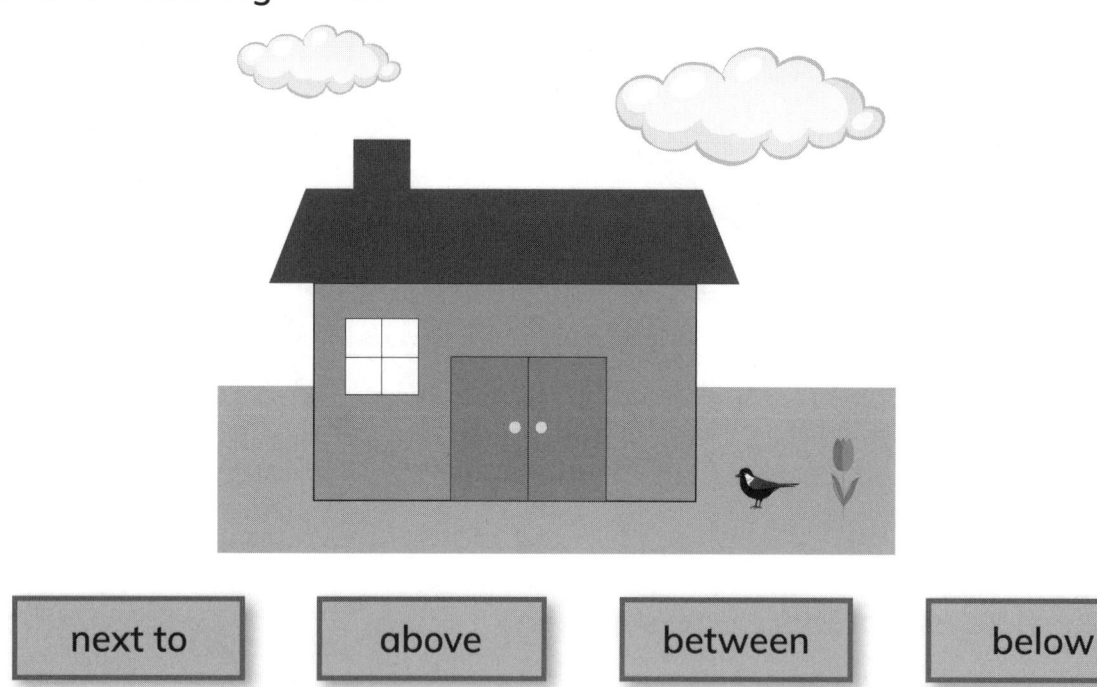

next to   above   between   below

The bird is _____ the flower and the house.

The window is _____ the door.

The clouds are _____ the house.

The house is _____ the clouds.

216

16.1 Position, direction and patterns

2   Draw the objects in the correct places.

Draw 3 birds above the boat.

Draw 2 ducks on the water.

Draw 4 fish below the boat.

The boat is _____ the clouds.

16 Position, direction and patterns

3   Move and draw the pictures. Draw the answers in the empty grid below.

- Move the chicken 2 squares to the right.
- Move the horse 1 square to the left.
- Move the farmer 3 squares down.
- Move the sheep 1 square up.

Then draw a cat 2 squares down from the chicken.

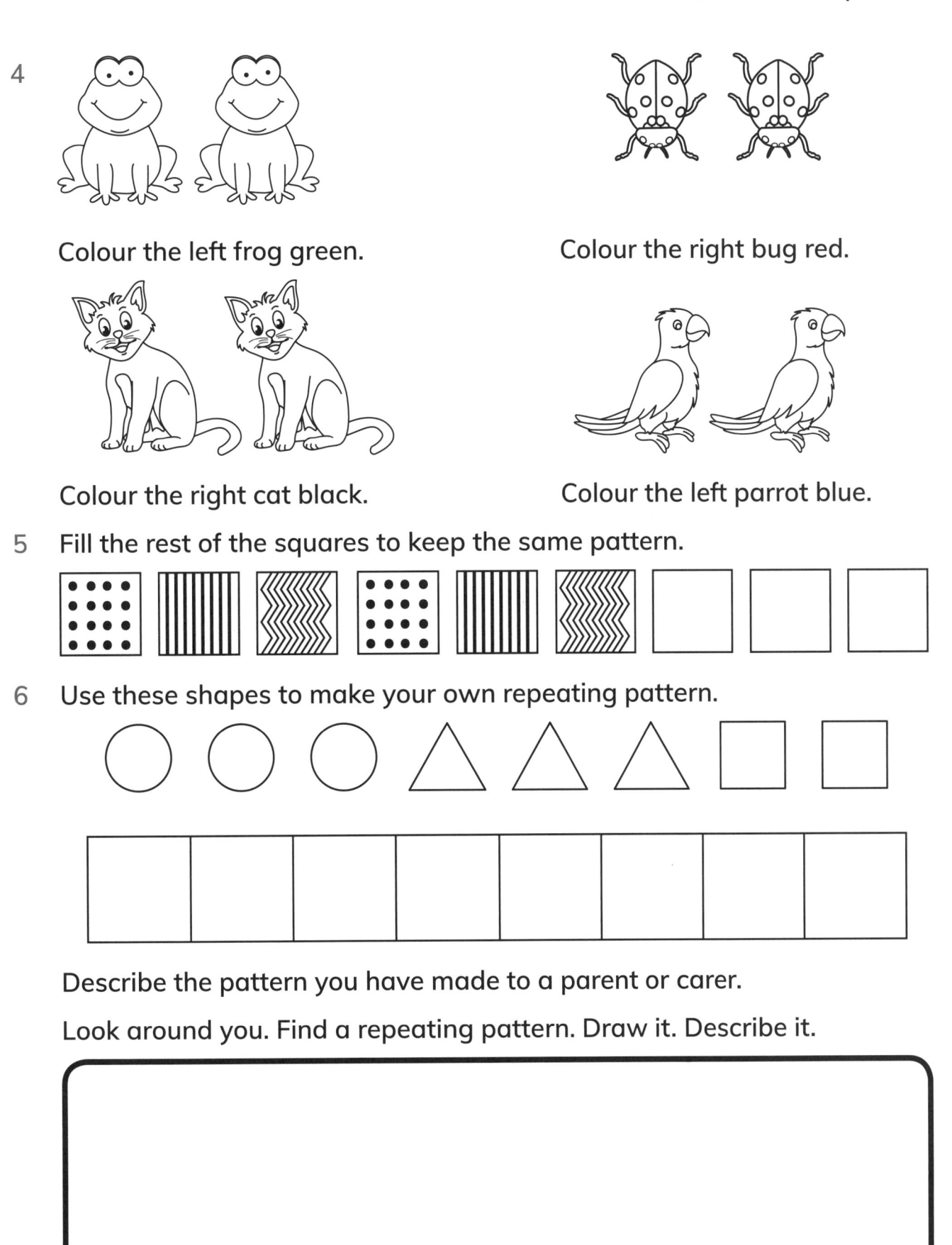

16.1 Position, direction and patterns

4   Colour the left frog green.

Colour the right bug red.

Colour the right cat black.

Colour the left parrot blue.

5   Fill the rest of the squares to keep the same pattern.

6   Use these shapes to make your own repeating pattern.

Describe the pattern you have made to a parent or carer.

Look around you. Find a repeating pattern. Draw it. Describe it.

219

16 Position, direction and patterns

Practice

7 Move and draw the pictures.
   Draw the answers in the empty grid.

   - Move the chicken 1 square up.
   - Move the goat 4 squares to the right.
   - Move the horse 3 squares to the left.

   Tip

   If you don't want to try drawing the animals, write the first letter of the animal in the square instead.

   Now write instructions to move the sheep, duck and the farmer.

   Use the words **up**, **down**, **left** and **right**.

   Draw their new positions on the grid.

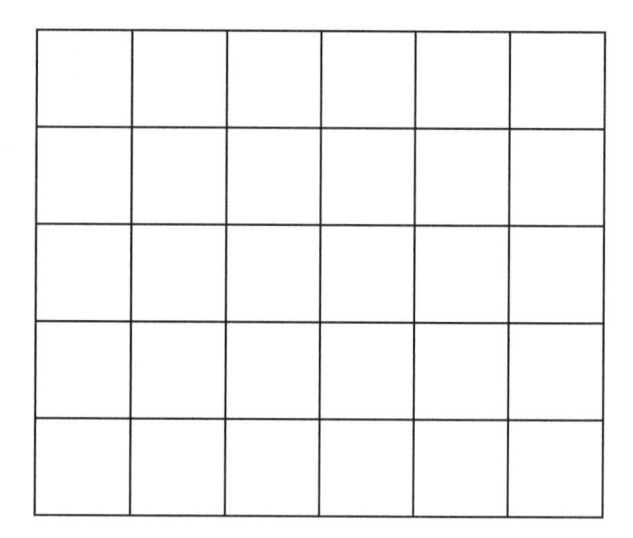

   - Move the sheep _____
   - Move the duck _____
   - Move the farmer _____

16.1 Position, direction and patterns

8   Colour the shape:

   between the triangle and the circle green

   below the triangle blue

   above the blue shape red

   below the circle grey

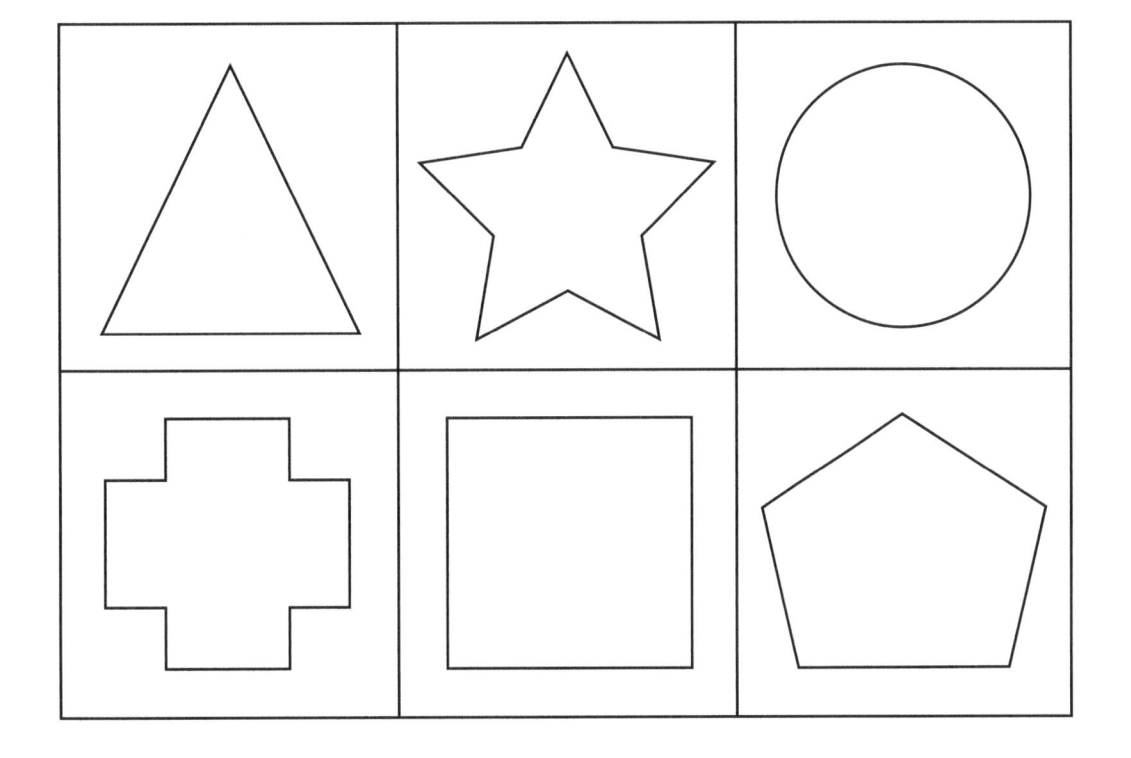

9   Colour the snails that are facing left.

   Colour the birds that are facing right.

16 Position, direction and patterns

10 Follow the directions.

Always face the way you are going.

Do not walk backwards.

Colour the squares you use.

The first instruction is done for you.

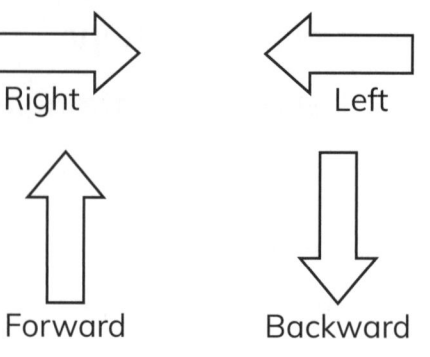

Right | Left
Forward | Backward

Walk forward 2 squares.
Turn left.
Walk forward 3 squares.
Turn right.
Walk forward 1 square.
Turn right.
Walk forward 2 squares.
Tick ✓ what is in your square.

11 Collect some objects from inside or outside.

Use them to make a repeating pattern.
Draw and describe the pattern you made.

16.1 Position, direction and patterns

Challenge

12 Using **left**, **right**, **up** and **down**, write instructions to move each object to make a single full column.

Draw what you have done in the empty grid.

Tip

If you don't want to try drawing the animals, write the first letter of the animal in the square instead.

- Move the goat _____
- Move the farmer _____
- Move the horse _____
- Move the chicken _____
- Move the sheep _____
- Move the barn _____

223

16 Position, direction and patterns

13 Follow the directions.

a Turn right.

   Walk forward 3 squares.

   Draw the object.

b Go back to start.

   Walk forward 3 squares.

   Draw the object.

c Go back to start.
Turn to the right.
Walk forward 1 square.
Turn to the left.
Walk forward 2 squares.
Draw the object.

14

Bill

Henry

Jol

Aisha

Thomas

Adaku

Lucy

Jack

Start counting from here

Who lives at the 2nd house on the **left**? _____

Who lives at the 1st house on the **right**? _____

Who lives at the 4th house on the **left**? _____

Who lives at the 3rd house on the **right**? _____

Where does Bill live? _____

16 Position, direction and patterns

15 Colour the birds that **are not** facing **right**.

Colour the ladybirds that **are not** facing **left**.

16 Follow the rules to colour all of the squares.

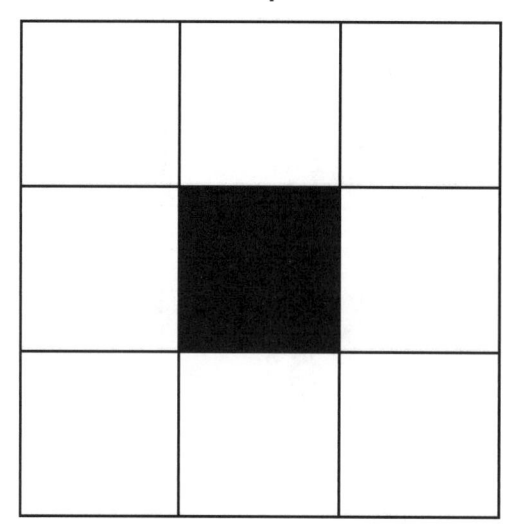

Below black is green.

Left of green is red.

Above red is yellow.

Right of green is blue.

Above black is white.

Above yellow is grey.

Right of white is red.

Between blue and red is yellow.

16.1 Position, direction and patterns

17 Collect some objects from inside or outside.

Use them to make a repeating pattern.

Draw and describe the pattern you made.

Look for a pattern around you.

Draw it.

Is it a repeating pattern?

Write how you know.

_____

_____

Acknowledgements

It takes an extraordinary number of people to put together a new series of resources and their comments, support and encouragement have been really important to us. We would like to thank the following people: Philip Rees and Veronica Wastell for the support they have given the authors; Lynne McClure for her feedback and comments on early sections of the manuscript; Thomas Carter, Caroline Walton, Laura Collins, Charlotte Griggs, Gabby Martin, Emma McCrea and Eddie Rippeth as part of the team at Cambridge preparing the resources. We would also like to particularly thank all of the anonymous reviewers for their time and comments on the manuscript and as part of the endorsement process.

The authors and publishers acknowledge the following sources of copyright material and are grateful for the permissions granted. While every effort has been made, it has not always been possible to identify the sources of all the material used, or to trace all copyright holders. If any omissions are brought to our notice, we will be happy to include the appropriate acknowledgements on reprinting.

Thanks to the following for permission to reproduce images:

Cover illustration: Omar Aranda (Beehive Illustration)

Isabel Pavia/Getty Images; MirageC/Getty Images; Steve Hix/Getty Images; Westend61/Getty Images; CHBD/Getty Images; Grant Faint/Getty Images; Andrea Donetti / EyeEm/Getty Images; YvanDube/Getty Images; Eskay Lim / EyeEm/Getty Images; Emilija Manevska/Getty Images; FrankRamspott/Getty Images; Catherine Falls Commercial/Getty Images; anilakkus/Getty Images; Surachet99/Getty Images; © Jackie Bale/Getty Images; Malcolm P Chapman/Getty Images; Robert Scherbarth / EyeEm/Getty Images; Utamaru Kido/Getty Images